continent. Year 1
A selection of
issues 1.1–1.4

continent. year 1
© continent., 2012.

This work is licensed under the Creative Commons Attribution-NonCommercial-NoDerivs 3.0 Unported License.
To view a copy of this license, visit: http:// creativecommons.org/licenses/by-nc-nd/3.0, or send a letter to Creative Commons, 444 Castro Street, Suite 900, Mountain View, California, 94041, USA.

This work is Open Access, which means that you are free to copy, distribute, display, and perform the work as long as you clearly attribute the work to the authors, that you do not use this work for commercial gain in any form whatsoever, and that you in no way alter, transform, or build upon the work outside of its normal use in academic scholarship without express permission of the author and the publisher of this volume.
For any reuse or distribution, you must make clear to others the license terms of this work.

First published in 2012 by
punctum books and continent.

ISBN-10: 06-157368-9-0
ISBN-13: 978-06-157368-9-1

Design by
Vincent W.J. van Gerven Oei
and Nina Jäger

punctum books ✳ brooklyn, ny

continent.

Year 1
A selection of
issues 1.1–1.4

edited by:
Jamie Allen
Paul Boshears
Bernhard Garnicnig
Vincent W.J. van Gerven Oei
A. Staley Groves
Nico Jenkins

with contributions by:
Jamie Allen
Alain Badiou
Vincent W.J. van Gerven Oei
A. Staley Groves
Graham Harman
Nikos Karouzos
Evan Lavender-Smith
Renata Lemos-Morais
Feliz Lucia Molina
Timothy Morton
Gregory Kirk Murray
Maggie Nelson
Michael O'Rourke
Gilson Schwartz
Ben Segal
Nick Skiadopoulos
Karen Spaceinvaders
Phillip Stearns
John Van Houdt
Ben Woodard

contents

13　Graham Harman
　　Meillassoux's
　　Virtual Future

33　Nick Skiadopoulos
　　Greek Returns
　　The Poetry of
　　Nikos Karouzos

41　Nikos Karouzos
　　Selected Poems

51　Jamie Allen
　　Phillip Stearns:
　　DCP Series

59　John Van Houdt
　　The Crisis
　　of Negation:
　　An Interview with
　　Alain Badiou

67　A. Staley Groves
　　The Return of
　　Benjamin's Storyteller:
　　Ronald Reagan as
　　the Incorruptible Saint
　　of Political Media

- 81 Vincent W.J. van Gerven Oei
  Anders Breivik: On Copying the Obscure

- 99 Feliz Lucia Molina
  A Playful Reading of the Double Quotation in *The Descent of Alette* by Alice Notley

- 105 Timothy Morton
  Objects as Temporary Autonomous Zones

- 117 Renata Lemos-Morais
  Money as Media: Gilson Schwartz on the Semiotics of Digital Currency

- 125 Michael O'Rourke
  The Afterlives of Queer Theory

- 147 Karen Spaceinvaders
  Please Mind the Gap: How to Podcast Your Brain

- 151 Ben Segal
  The Fragment as a Unit of Prose Composition: An Introduction

- 171 Ben Woodard
  Mad Speculation and Absolute Inhumanism: Lovecraft, Ligotti, and the Weirding of Philosophy

- 187 Gregory Kirk Murray
  Covering Giorgio Agamben's *Nudities*

```
┌─────────────────┐
│ Until 15th Century │
│   Monopolized   │
└─────────────────┘
         ↓
┌─────────────────┐
│ After 15th Century │
│  Democratization │
└─────────────────┘
         ↓
┌─────────────────┐
│  21st Century   │
│     Doomed      │
└─────────────────┘
```

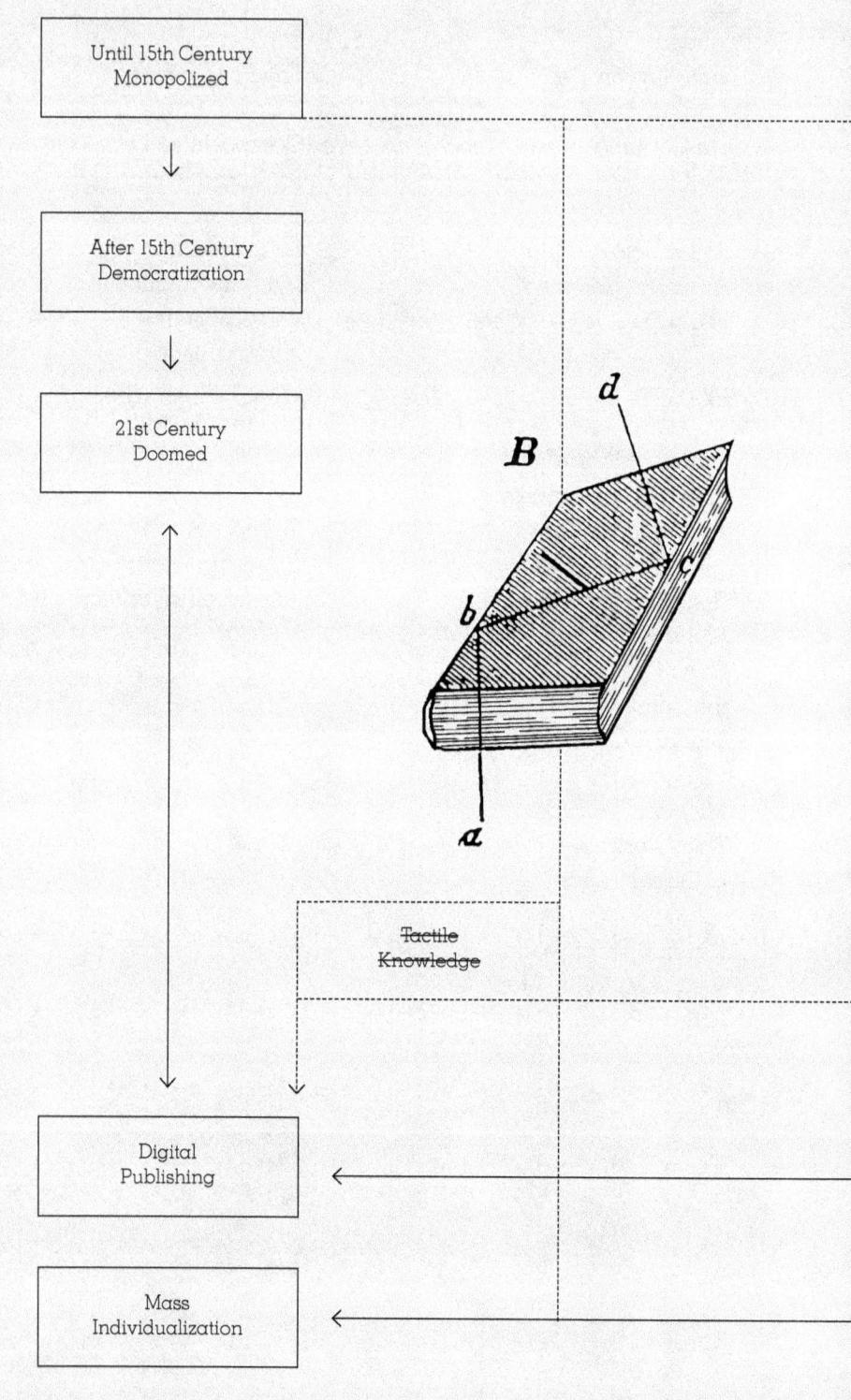

~~Tactile Knowledge~~

```
┌─────────────────┐
│     Digital     │  ←
│   Publishing    │
└─────────────────┘

┌─────────────────┐
│      Mass       │  ←
│ Individualization │
└─────────────────┘
```

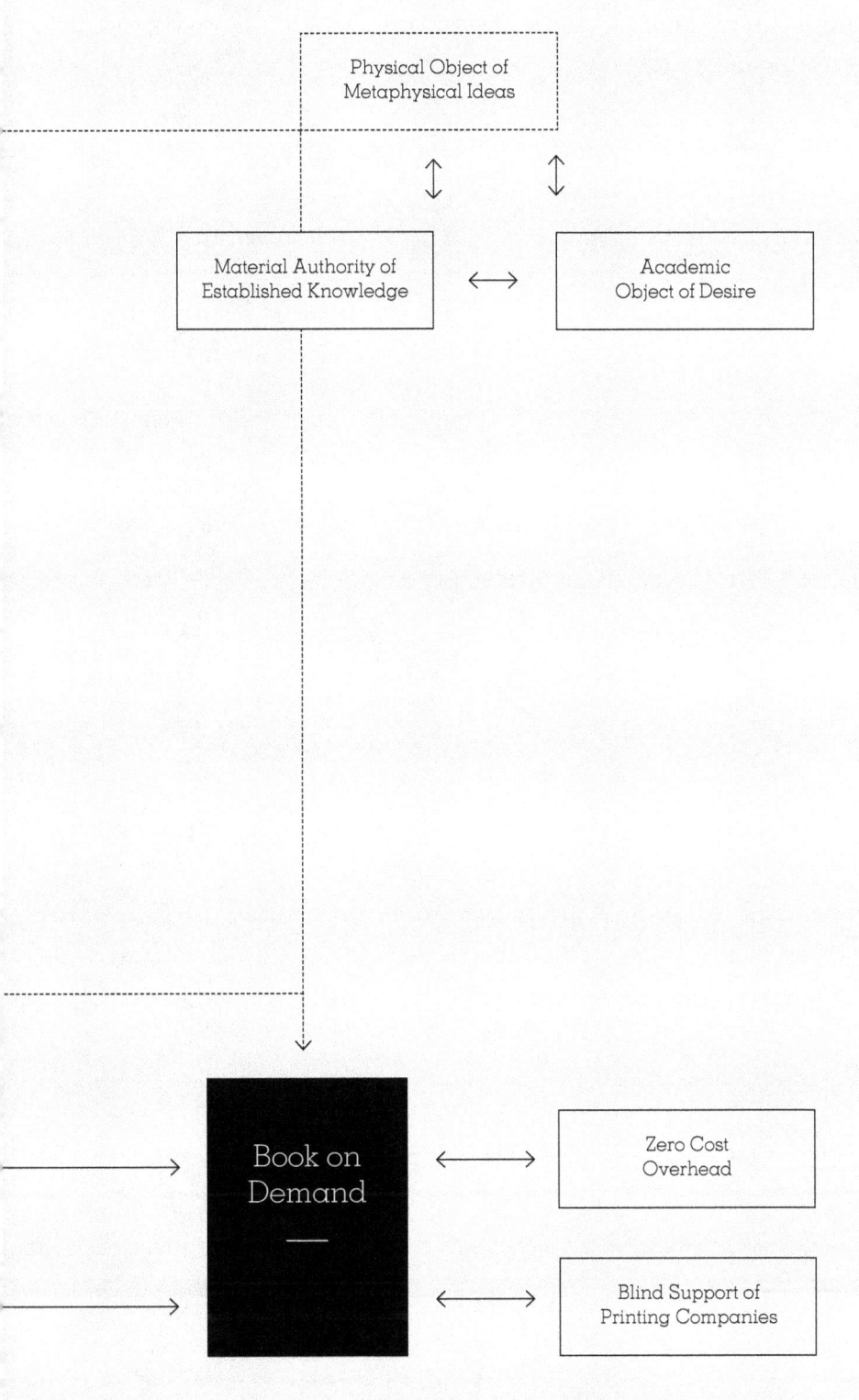

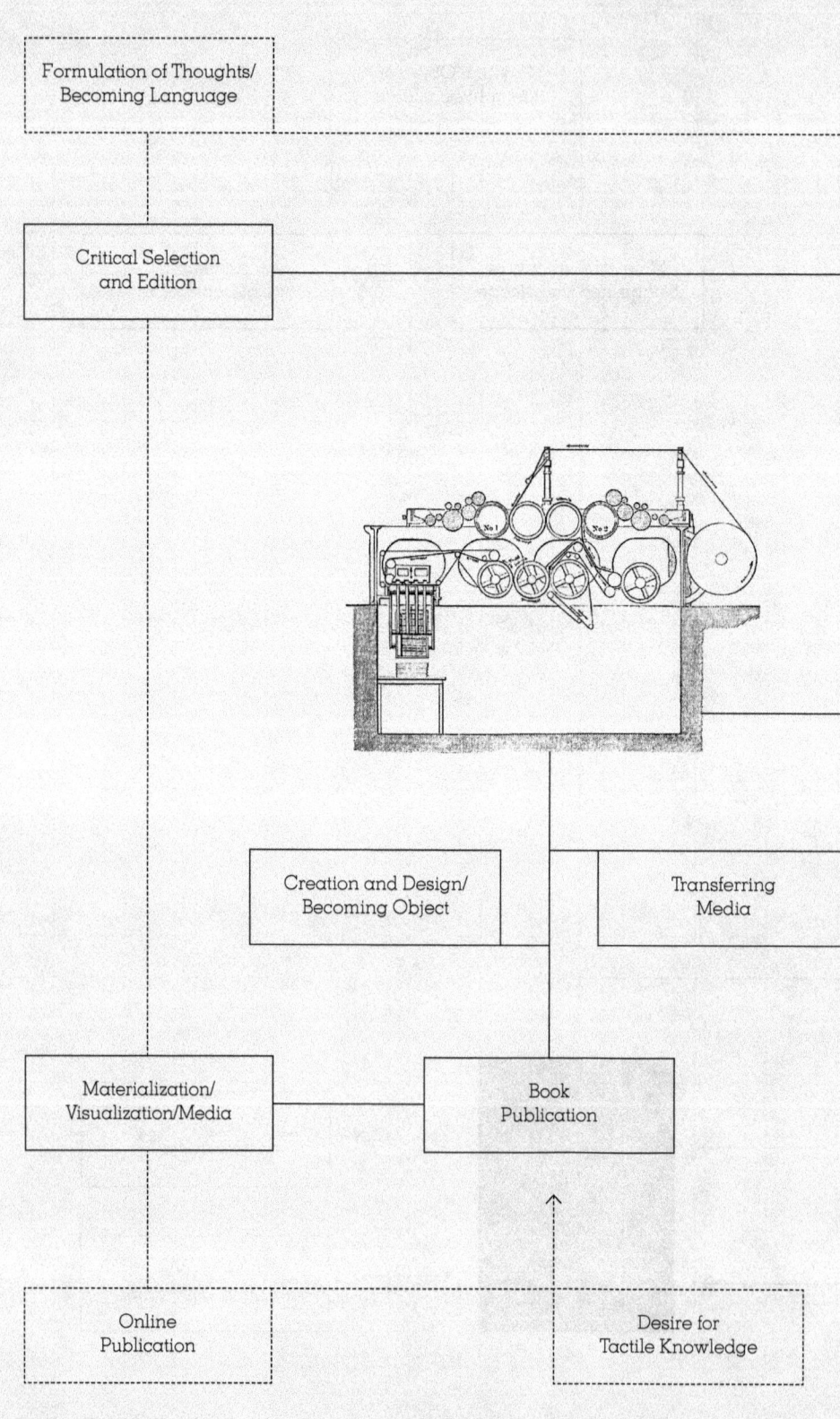

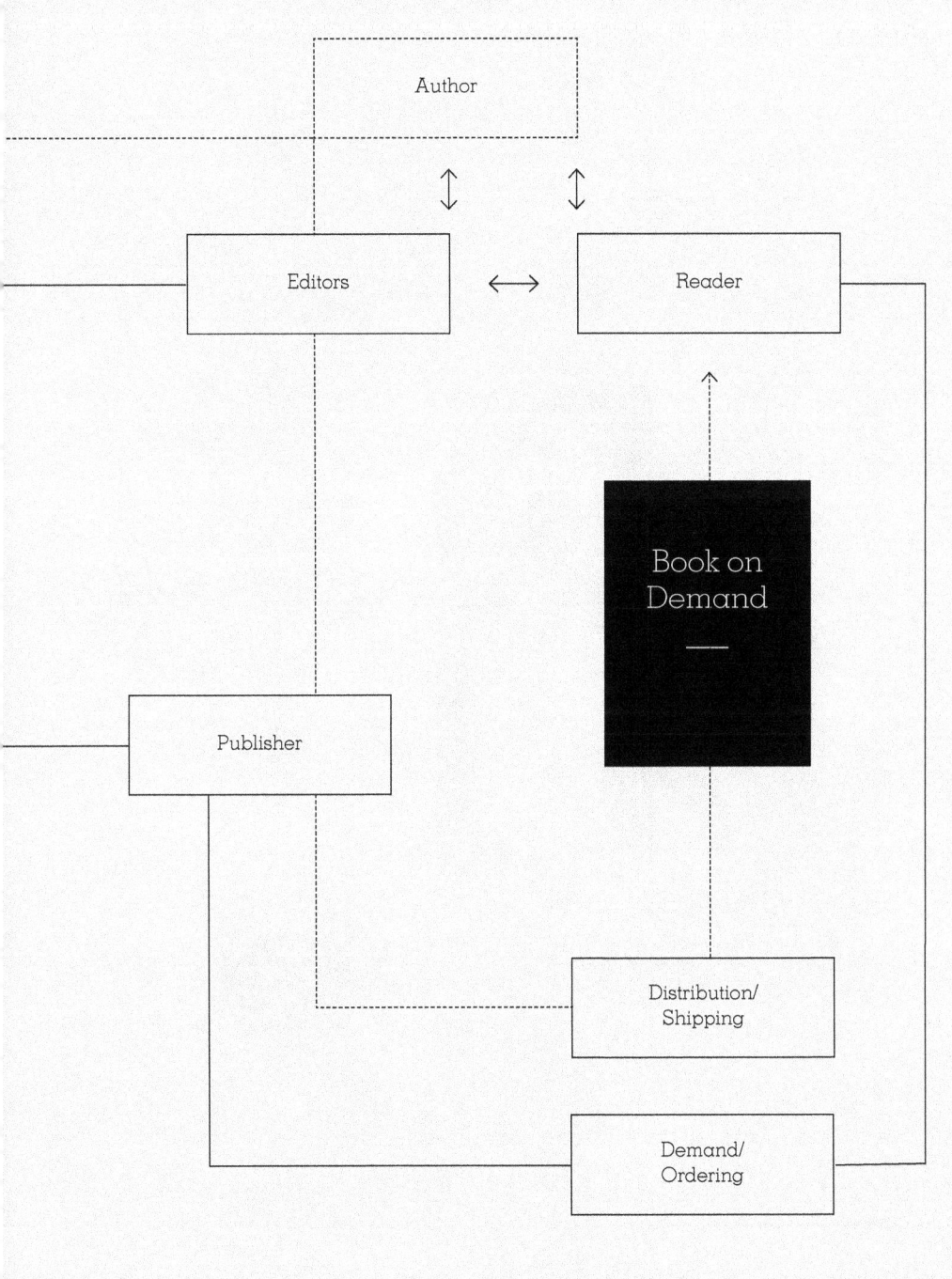

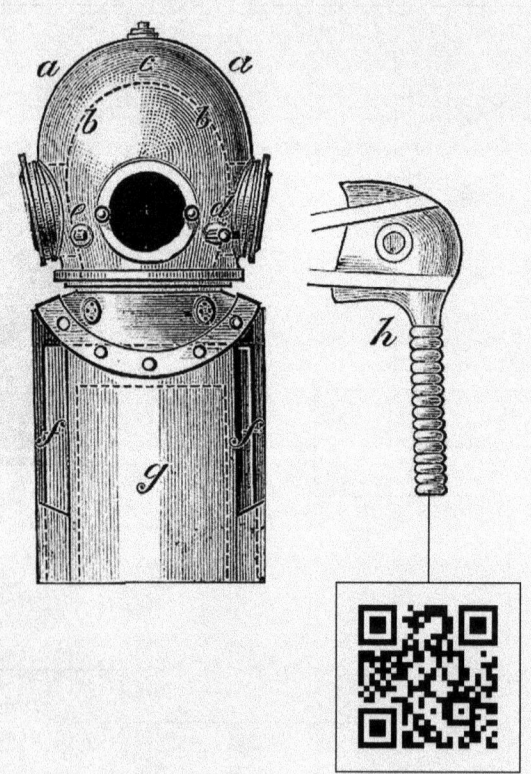

Meillassoux's Virtual Future[1]

Graham Harman

This article consists of three parts. First, I will review the major themes of Quentin Meillassoux's *After Finitude*. Since some of my readers will have read this book and others not, I will try to strike a balance between clear summary and fresh critique. Second, I discuss an unpublished book by Meillassoux only partly familiar to the reading public, except those scant few that may have gone digging in the microfilm archives of the École normale supérieure. The book in question is Meillassoux's revised doctoral dissertation *L'Inexistence divine* (*The Divine Inexistence*), with its seemingly bizarre vision of a God who does not yet exist but might exist in the future. Without literally accepting this view, I will claim that it is philosophically interesting in ways that even a hardened sceptic might be able to appreciate. Third and finally, I will speculate on the possible future of Meillassoux's speculative materialism itself. And here I mean its future development not by Meillassoux, but by those readers who might be inspired by his book. Plato could never have predicted the emergence of Aristotle's philosophy, despite the obvious debt of the latter to the former. Nor could Descartes have predicted Spinoza and Leibniz, nor Kant the German Idealists, and neither could Husserl in 1901 have foreseen the later emergence of Heidegger. How are the works of interesting philosophers transformed by later thinkers of comparable importance? While it may seem that there are countless ways to do this, I think there are only two basic ways in which this happens: you can *radicalize* your predecessors, or you can *reverse* them. I will close this article with a few words about these two methods, and try to imagine how Meillassoux might be radicalized or reversed by some future admirer. My view is that the more important thinkers are, the *easier* they are to radicalize or reverse. This helps explain why the great philosophers of the West have so often appeared in clusters, succeeding one another at relatively brief intervals during periods of especial ferment.

---

1   An earlier version of this article was presented as a lecture at SPUI25 Academic–Cultural Center in Amsterdam on March 11, 2011.

After Finitude

After Finitude is unusually short for such an influential book of philosophy: running to just 178 pages in the original French, and an even more compact 128 pages in the English version, despite the introduction of roughly eight pages of new material for the English edition. Rather than summarizing Meillassoux's book in the order he intended, I will focus on six points that strike me as the pillars of his debut book. Along the way, I will offer a few criticisms as well.

The first pillar of the book is Meillassoux's own term "correlationism."[2] Although he introduces this term as the name for an enemy, it is striking that Meillassoux remains *impressed* by correlationism much more than his fellow speculative realists are. This continued appreciation for his great enemy influences the shape of his own ontology. Is there a world outside our thinking of it, or does the world consist entirely in being thought? Traditionally, this dispute between realism and idealism has been dismissed in continental philosophy as a "pseudo-problem," in a strategy pioneered by Husserl and extended by Heidegger. We cannot be realists, since following Kant we have no direct access to things-in-themselves. But neither are we idealists, since the human being is always already outside itself, aiming at objects in intentional experience, deeply engaged with practical implements, or stationed in some particular world-disclosing mood. The centuries-old dispute between realism and idealism is dissolved by saying that we cannot think either real or ideal in isolation from the other. There is neither human without world nor world without human, but only a primordial correlation or rapport between the two. This is what "correlationism" means: philosophy trapped in a permanent meditation on the human–world correlate, trying to find the best model of the correlate: is it language, intentionality, embodiment, or some other form of correlation between human and world? Among other problems, this generates some friction between philosophy and the literal meaning of science. When cosmologists say that the universe originated 13.5 billion years ago, they do not mean "13.5 billion years ago *for us*," but *literally* 13.5 billion years ago, well before conscious life existed, and thus at a time when there was no such thing as a correlate. Meillassoux also coins the term "ancestrality" (10) for the reality that predated the correlate, and later expands this term to "dia-chronicity" (112), to refer to events occurring after the extinction of human beings no less than to those occurring before we existed.

Up to this point, Meillassoux's focus on ancestral entities existing prior to consciousness might make him seem like a straightforward realist who wants to unmask correlationism as just another form of idealism. Yet Meillassoux also admires the correlationist maneuver, which can obviously be

---

[2] Quentin Meillassoux, *After Finitude*, trans. Ray Brassier. (London: Continuum, 2008), 5. Subsequent references between parentheses. The word "correlationism" does not appear in his doctoral thesis. As Meillassoux informed me in an email of February 8, 2011, he first coined this term in 2003 or 2004, while editing for publication a lecture he had given at the École normale supérieure on a day devoted to the theme of "Philosophy and Mathematics," an event including Alain Badiou as one of the participants.

traced back to Kant. Unlike a thinker such as Whitehead, Meillassoux feels no nostalgia for the pre-critical realism that came before Kant: "we cannot but be heirs of Kantianism" (29), he says. What impresses Meillassoux about correlationism is something both simple and familiar. If we attempt to think a tree outside thought, *this is itself a thought.* Any form of realism which thinks it can simply and directly address the world the way it is fails to escape the correlational circle, since the attempt to think something outside of thought is itself nothing other than a thought, and thereby collapses back into the very human–world correlate that it pretends to escape. For Meillassoux this step, suggested by Kant but first refined by the ensuing figures of German Idealism, marks decisive forward progress in the history of philosophy that must not be abolished. Any attempt to break free from the correlate must first acknowledge its mighty intellectual power. Realist though he may seem, Meillassoux's works are filled with praise of such figures as Fichte and Hegel, not of so-called "naïve realists."

It is also the case that for Meillassoux, not all correlationisms are the same. The second pillar of his book is a distinction between various positions that I have termed "Meillassoux's Spectrum," though of course he is never so immodest as to name it after himself. He distinguishes between at least six different possible positions, and perhaps we could add even subtler variations if we wished. But in its simplest form, Meillassoux's Spectrum allows for just four basic outlooks on the question of realism vs. anti-realism. Three of these are easy to understand, since we have already been discussing them. At one extreme is so-called "naïve realism," which holds that a world exists outside the mind, *and* that we can know this world. Meillassoux rejects this naïve realism as having been overthrown by Kant's critical philosophy. At the other extreme is subjective idealism, in which nothing exists outside the mind. For to think a dog outside thought immediately turns it into a thought, and therefore there cannot be anything outside; the very notion is meaningless. In between these two is what we have called correlationism. And here comes a crucial moment for Meillassoux, since he distinguishes between the two forms of "weak" and "strong" correlationism, and chooses the strong form as the launching pad for his own philosophy.

Weak correlationism is easy to explain, since we all know it from the philosophy of Kant. The things-in-themselves can be thought but not known. They certainly must exist, since there cannot be appearances without something that appears. And we *can* think about them (which idealism holds to be impossible). They are simply unknowable due to the finitude of human thought.

Strong correlationism is the new position introduced by Meillassoux (though he sees it at work in numerous twentieth century thinkers), midway between weak correlationism and subjective idealism. The major difference between the three positions is as follows. Weak correlationism says: "The things-in-themselves exist, but we cannot know them." The subjective idealist says: "This is a contradiction in terms, since when we think the things-in-themselves, we already turn them into thoughts." But the strong correlationist says: "Just because 'things-in-themselves' is a meaningless notion does not mean that they cannot exist. No one has ever traveled to the world-in-itself and come back to make a report on it. Thus, the fact that we cannot think things-in-themselves without contradiction does not prove that they do not exist anyway. There may be things-in-themselves, we simply are not capable of thinking them without contradiction form within the correlational circle." This step is crucial for Meillassoux, since strong correlationism is the position he attempts to radicalize into his own new standpoint: speculative materialism.

As I see it, this step of the argument fails. Strong correlationism cannot avoid collapsing into subjective idealism, since the statements of the strong correlationist are rendered meaningless from within. All three of the other positions in the Spectrum make perfectly good sense even for those who disagree with them. The naïve realist says that things-in-themselves exist and we can know them; the meaning of this statement is clear. The weak correlationist can say that things-in-themselves exist but lie forever beyond our grasp; this too makes perfect sense, even though the German Idealists try to show a contradiction at work here. We can also understand the claim of the subjective idealist that to think anything outside thought turns it into a thought, and that for this reason we cannot think the unthought. The strong correlationist, alone among the four, speaks nonsense. This person says "I cannot think the unthought without turning it into a thought, and yet the unthought might exist anyway." But notice that the final phrase "the unthought might exist anyway" is fruitless for this purpose. For we have already heard that to think any unthought turns it into a thought. But now the strong correlationist wants to do two incompatible things simultaneously with this unthought. On the one hand, he neutralizes the unthought by showing that it instantly changes into just another thought. But on the other hand, he wants to appeal to the unthought as a haunting residue that *might* exist outside thought, thereby undercutting the absolute status of the human–world correlate found in idealism. But this is impossible. If you accept the argument that thinking the unthought turns it into a thought, you cannot also add "but maybe there is something outside that prevents this conversion from being absolutely true," because this "something outside" is immediately converted into nothing but a thought for us. In short, Meillassoux here seems to be offering a kind of Zen koan: his "strong correlationism" is reminiscent of the gateless gate, or the sound of one hand clapping, or the command to punch Hegel in the jaw when meeting him on the road. We cannot at the same time *both* destroy the realist challenge of the things-in-themselves in order to undercut realism *and* reintroduce that very realist sense in order to undercut idealism. In a world where everything is instantly converted into thought, we cannot claim that there might be something extra-mental anyway, because this "might be something" is itself converted into a thought by the same rules that condemned dogs, trees, and houses to the idealist prison.

This brings us to the third pillar of Meillassoux's argument, which is the key to all the rest: the necessity of contingency. His strategy is to transform our supposed ignorance of things-in-themselves into an absolute *knowledge* that they exist without reason, and that the laws of nature can change at any time for no reason at all. In this way the cautious agnosticism of Kantian philosophies is avoided, but so is the collapse of reality into thought as found in German Idealism. Meillassoux does try to prove the existence of things-in-themselves existing outside thought; he simply holds that they must be proven after passing through the rigors of the correlationist challenge, not just arbitrarily decreed to exist in the manner of naïve realism. As he puts it, "Everything could actually collapse: from trees to stars, from stars to laws, from physical laws to logical laws; and this not by virtue of some superior law whereby everything is destined to perish, but by virtue of the absence of any superior law capable of preserving anything, no matter what, from perishing" (53).

If idealism thinks that the human–world correlate is absolute, for Meillassoux it is the *facticity* of the correlate that is absolute. He tries to show this with a nice brief dialogue between five separate characters (55–9) which I covered in detail elsewhere,[3] but which I will simplify here for reasons of time. In this simplified version, we first imagine a dogmatic realist arguing with a dogmatic idealist. The realist says that we can know the truth about the things-in-themselves; the idealist counters that we can only the truth about thought, since all statements about reality must be turned into statements concerning our *thoughts* about reality. Here the correlationist enters and proclaims that both of these positions are equally dogmatic. For although we have access to nothing but thoughts, we cannot be sure that these thoughts are all that exist; there *could be* a reality outside thought, there is simply no way to know for sure. And this latter position is the one that Meillassoux attempts to transform from an agnostic, skeptical point into an ontological claim about the contingency of everything. Consider it this way. How does the correlationist defeat the idealist? The idealist holds that the existence of anything outside thought is impossible. The correlationist, by contrast, holds that something might exist outside the human–world correlate. But this "something might" has to be an absolute possibility. It cannot mean that "something outside thought might exist *for thought*," because that is what the idealist already says. No, the correlationist must mean that something might exist outside thought *quite independently* of thought. In other words, the correlationist says that idealism might be wrong, and this means it is *absolutely* true that idealism might be wrong. Thus, correlationism is no longer just a skeptical position. It holds that all the possibilities of the world are absolute possibilities. We have *absolute knowledge* that any of the possibilities about the existence or non-existence

---

3 See Graham Harman, *Quentin Meillassoux: Philosophy in the Making* (Edinburgh: Edinburgh University Press, 2011.)

of things-in-themselves might be true, and this means that correlationism flips into Meillassoux's own position: speculative materialism.

As Meillassoux sees it, there are only two options here. Option A is to absolutize the human–world correlate, which is what the idealist does: there absolutely cannot be anything outside thought. Option B, by contrast, is to absolutize the *facticity* of the correlate: its character of simply being given to us, without any inherent necessity. The correlationist cannot have it both ways by saying: "there absolutely might be something outside thought, yet maybe this is absolutely impossible." In other words, once we escape dogmatism we can only be idealists or speculative materialists, not correlationists. The human–world correlate is merely a fact, not an absolute necessity. But this facticity itself cannot be merely factical: it must be absolute. Here Meillassoux coins the French neologism *factualité*, which has been suitably translated into the English neologism "factiality" (79).[4] Factiality means that for everything that exists, it is absolutely possible that it might be otherwise, not just that we cannot *know* whether or not it might be otherwise. Just as Kant transformed philosophy into a meditation on the categories governing human finitude, Meillassoux wishes to turn philosophy into a meditation on the necessary conditions of factiality, which he calls "figures" (a new technical term for him) (80). One such figure is that the law of non-contradiction must be true, and for an unusual reason. Since everything is proven to be contingent, nothing that exists can be contradictory, for whatever is contradictory has no opposite into which it might be transformed, and thus contingency would be impossible.[5] Another such figure is that there must be something rather than nothing: for since contingency exists, something must exist in order to be contingent. It is a daring act, one that sacrifices realism to the correlational circle in order to rebuild it from out of its own ashes.

Some might conclude that the lack of reason in things is a byproduct of the ignorance of finite humans, Meillassoux is making precisely the opposite point. For in fact, the doctrine of finitude usually leads directly to belief in a hidden reason. The fact that it lies beyond human comprehension merely increases our belief in this arbitrarily chosen concealed ground. By defending anew the concept of absolute knowledge Meillassoux evacuates the world of everything hidden. The reason for things having no reason is not that the reason is hidden, but that no reason exists. Thus, even while insisting on the necessity of non-contradiction, he rejects the other Leibnizian principle: sufficient reason. Everything simply is what it is, in purely immanent form, without deeply hidden causes. Or as Meillassoux puts it: "There is nothing beneath or beyond the manifest gratuitousness of the given – nothing but the limitless and lawless power of its destruction, emergence, or persistence" (63). The world is a "hyper-chaos" (64). But this is not the same thing

---

4   See also the translator's explanation on 122–3, fn. 6.
5   In an email of December 6, 2010, Meillassoux clarifies that in *After Finitude* he only deduces the impossibility of a "universal contradiction," not of a determinate contradiction. In the same email he suggests that he can also prove the latter, though the proof is somewhat lengthier than the one found in *After Finitude*.

as flux. For the chaos of the world is such that stability might occur just as easily as constant, turbulent change.

Let's now digress a bit, and return to the question of ancestrality, which Meillassoux transforms later in the book into "dia-chronicity." Correlationism holds that all talk of a world outside the correlate is immediately recuperated by the correlate. The phrase "13.5 billion years ago" becomes "13.5 billion years ago *for us*," and the phrase "the universe following the extinction of humans" becomes "the universe following the extinction of humans *for humans*." But notice that whether we talk about the world before or after humans, in both cases it is *time* that is used to challenge the correlate. Meillassoux has no interest in challenges that might be posed by space. For example, what about a vase in a lonely country house that topples to the floor and smashes when no one is there to watch it? Isn't this also a challenge to correlationism, no less than the Big Bang or the heat death of the universe long after humans have vanished? In an eight-page supplement to the English translation of *After Finitude*,[6] possibly in response to my own 2007 review of the French original,[7] Meillassoux bluntly denies that space is of any relevance to the question. Spatial distance is a merely harmless challenge to the human–world correlate. After all, even though no one is there in the lonely country house to witness the shattering of the vase, we can say that *had there been an observer*, that observer would have witnessed the toppling and destruction of the vase. For this event still occurs in a world in which the human–world correlate already exists, whereas the diachronicity of events both before and after the existence of humans makes it impossible to say that *had there been an observer* they would have witnessed the Big Bang occurring in such and such a fashion. However, it seems to me that Meillassoux merely *asserts* that the temporal simultaneity of our existence with that of the vase in the lonely country house is enough to render it harmless. It is true that the house does not exist prior to the correlate, but nonetheless it exists *outside* the correlate, and that is enough to make the same challenge. It is difficult to see why the "had there been an observer" maneuver succeeds in the case of a vase in the countryside in April 2011 but fails in the case of the Big Bang.

This is not just a matter of nitpicking Meillassoux's argumentative style: the fact that he bases his argument on time has at least two important consequences for his position. For in the first place, even though Meillassoux insists that the laws of nature are absolutely contingent, this turns out to be true only in a temporal sense. That is to say, it is a paradoxical feature of Meillassoux's philosophy that he does allow for the existence of laws of nature, and simply believes that they can change at any moment without

---

6 Meillassoux, *After Finitude*, 18–26, in the passage falling between the two sets of triple asterisks. These pages were sent by Meillassoux to translator Ray Brassier (in French) during the translation process, and do not appear in the original French version of the book.

7 Graham Harman, "Quentin Meillassoux: A New French Philosopher," *Philosophy Today* 51.1 (Spring 2007): 104–17. The passage where I raise the question of space can be found in the first column of 107.

reason. Within any given moment, laws of nature do exist. He never suggests that different parts of the universe can have different laws at the same time, nor does he show any interest in the laws of part–whole composition that take place within any given instant. Could it be the case that rather than being made of gold atoms, a small chunk of gold could be made of silver atoms, cotton, horses, or that this same small piece of gold could be made of gigantic vaults filled with even more gold? These are not topics that draw Meillassoux's attention, since he is focused solely on how the laws of nature might change or endure *from one moment to the next.*

Another implication for Meillassoux's system is that his concept of things-in-themselves turns out to be to be inadequate. For when he proves that things-in-themselves can exist without humans, this turns out to be true only in a temporal sense as well. Namely, things-in-themselves existed ten billion years ago, and they will continue to exist after all humans have succeeded in exterminating themselves. However, being able to exist before our births and after our deaths is just one small part of what it means to be a thing-in-itself. The more important part is that even if a thing is sitting on a table right now in front of me, even if I stroke it lovingly or press my face up against it directly, I am still dealing only with a phenomenal version of the thing; the thing-in-itself continues to withdraw from all access. Yet no such thing is acknowledged by Meillassoux. For him finitude is a disaster, and absolute knowledge is in fact possible. Meillassoux's thing-in-itself exists in independence only of the human *lifespan*, not of human knowledge.

The fifth pillar of Meillassoux's argument is his use of Cantor's transfinite mathematics to show that even if the laws of nature are contingent, they need not be unstable, and thus we cannot use the apparent stability of nature to disprove his metaphysics of absolute contingency. What Cantor showed is that there are different sizes of infinity, and that all these infinities cannot be totalized in a single infinite number of infinities. Meillassoux sees this as crucial, since it allows him to discredit any "probabilistic" argument against his theory. The probabilistic argument (as defended quite clearly by Jean-René Vernes[8]) would say this: given that the laws of nature seem so stable, it is *extremely improbable* that there is no hidden reason for their remaining so stable. As Meillassoux sees it, probability is of value only when we can index an accessible total of cases. These can even be infinite: for example, there are an infinite number of points where a rope can break when stretched tight, but this does not stop us from calculating probabilities for various sections of the rope to break. By contrast, there is no way to sum up the number of possible laws of nature. For here there is no way to totalize; we cannot stand outside of nature and calculate the possible number of laws so as to determine the probabilities that any one of them might change. Therefore, although we can speak of probability when dealing with intraworldly events such as elections, horse races, and coin-flips, we cannot

---

8   Vernes is first cited on *After Finitude*, 95. See Jean-René Vernes, *Critique de la raison aléatoire, ou Descartes contra Kant* (Paris: Aubier, 1982).

use the words "probable" or "improbable" when describing alterations at the level of nature as a whole. Rather than commenting on the validity of this argument and its use of Cantor, let me simply note that it once again creates a dualistic ontology. We already saw that Meillassoux treats time differently from space. In analogous fashion, he now treats the level of world differently from that of intraworldly events. The emergence of worlds is purely contingent and virtual and governed by no probability at all, while events within the world necessarily follow laws (even if these laws can change at any moment without reason), and thus their probabilities can be calculated. It is a strategy deeply reminiscent of Badiou's own dualism between the normal "state of the situation" and the rare and intermittent "event."[9]

The sixth and final pillar of Meillassoux's book can be dealt with briefly, since we have already touched on it elsewhere. It comes at the very beginning of the book, when Meillassoux says that we must revive the distinction between primary and secondary qualities, and that the primary qualities are the ones that can be mathematized. He admits that he has not yet published a proof of this idea, though in fact it is already known as one of his primary doctrines. And here we encounter the familiar problem with Meillassoux's inadequate conception of things-in-themselves. "Primary qualities" refers to those qualities that a thing has independently of its relations with us or anything else. But if the primary qualities can be mathematized, this means that they are not entirely independent of us, since our knowledge can get right to the bottom of them. The mathematized qualities of things are independent of us only in Meillassoux's sense that they will still have those qualities even when all humans are dead. But to repeat, autonomy from the human lifespan is not the same as autonomy from human access. Here once more Meillassoux is concerned only with independence from the human–world correlate *across time*, not in any given instant.

L'Inexistence divine
In 1997, the same year in which he turned thirty years old, Meillassoux earned his doctorate at the École normale supérieure with a brazen dissertation entitled *L'Inexistence divine* (*The Divine Inexistence*). The work was substantially revised in 2003. But even then, with typical fastidiousness, Meillassoux decided that the work was not yet ready for press. It has now been scrapped in favor of some future, multi-volume work bearing the same title. While writing my book on Meillassoux for Edinburgh University Press, I was kindly permitted to translate excerpts from this unpublished work for use as an appendix in my own book; in total, the appendix contains approximately twenty percent of Meillassoux's 2003 manuscript, the first time any of it will be published in any language.

---
9   Alain Badiou, *Being and Event*, trans. Oliver Feltham (London: Continuum, 2005).

Nonetheless, a portion of the argument was already tested in the article "Spectral Dilemma," published in English in the journal *Collapse*.[10] There the philosophical motives for the virtual God are already made clear. What troubles us most are early deaths, brutal deaths, deaths of especial injustice – the sorts of deaths in which the twentieth century was so abundant. And here, neither the atheist nor the believer can help us. The atheist can offer nothing but sad and cynical resignation when reflecting on the victims of these terrible crimes. The believer does little better, being unable to explain how God could have allowed such things to happen, due to the famous intractability of the problem of evil. The solution offered to this dilemma by Meillassoux is bold, and all the more so given that he emerges from such a deeply Leftist, materialist, and unreligious background. His solution is that God does not yet exist, and therefore is not blameworthy for these catastrophes. Given that everything is contingent in Meillassoux's philosophy, this God and divine justice might never exist, but they can at least exist as an object of hope.

Let's begin by jumping to the end of *L'Inexistence divine*, where the alternatives are laid out so nicely. There are four basic attitudes that humans can have towards God, Meillassoux says. First, we can believe in God because he exists. This is the classical theist attitude, rejected for the simple reason that it would be amoral and blasphemous to believe in a God who allows children to be eaten by dogs, to use Dostoevsky's example. Second, we can disbelieve in God because he does not exist: the classical atheist attitude. But this leads to sadness, cynicism, and a sneering contempt for the greatness of human potential. The third option, rather more complex, is to *disbelieve* in God because he *does* exist: in other words, to exist in rebellion against God as the one who must be blamed for the evils of the earth. The examples here might range from Lucifer himself, to the more human figure of Captain Ahab in Melville's *Moby-Dick*, to Werner Herzog's even more recent catchphrase: "Every man for himself, and God against all." That leaves only the fourth option: *believing* in God because he *does not* exist. Meillassoux closes his book by saying that the fourth option has now been tried (namely, in the course of his own book), and that now that all four have been specified, we must choose.

The first reaction to this theory of the inexistent God will be laughter. Few readers will ever be literally convinced by it, and probably none will *immediately* be convinced by it. But if we ask ourselves why we laugh, the answer is because it sounds so *improbable* that an inexistent God might suddenly emerge and resurrect the dead. It obviously sounds more like a gullible theology than a rigorous piece of philosophical work. Yet two things need to be kept in mind. First, Meillassoux's theories are hardly more unlikely than those of great philosophers of the past such as Plato, Plotinus, Avicenna, Malebranche, Spinoza, Leibniz, Nietzsche, or Whitehead. We read the great

---

10 Quentin Meillassoux, "Spectral Dilemma," *Collapse* IV (2008): 261–75.

philosophers not because their systems are plausible in commonsense terms that can be measured by the laws of probability. Instead, we read them precisely because they shatter the existing framework of common sense and open up new windows on the universe. Second, and even more importantly, Meillassoux has already rejected probability as a valid measuring stick in philosophy. Or rather, he accepts probability in the intra-worldly realm (where it is linked with potentiality), and rejects it at the level of the world itself (where potentiality is replaced with what he calls virtuality). The virtual God can appear at any moment for no reason at all, just as any other new configuration of laws of nature can appear: in a manner that the laws of probability cannot calculate. Responding to those who might ridicule the idea of a sudden emergence of God and a resurrection of the dead, Meillassoux cites Pascal, who asserts that the resurrection of the dead would be far less incredible than the fact that we were born in the first place.

This shifts philosophy onto new ground. Rather than concerning ourselves with what is *likely* to happen in the world as we know it, we focus instead on the most important things that *could* happen. For this reason, the expected objection that a virtual God is no more likely to appear than a virtual unicorn or a virtual flying spaghetti monster misses the point. Unicorns and spaghetti monsters could also appear, just like any other non-contradictory thing. But these would just be novel bizarre entities among others, not the heralds of completely new worlds. For Meillassoux, the emergence of matter, life, and thought have been the three truly amazing advents of the world so far, each of them dependent on the advent(s) preceding them. As he sees it, there can be no greater intraworldly entity than the human beings who already exist, since nothing in the world is better than the absolute knowledge of which humans alone are capable. This means that the next great advent must be something that perfects human beings rather than superseding them. And this can only be the world of justice, in which the dead are resurrected and their horrible deaths partially cancelled (Meillassoux never considers the possibility of a God who would literally erase the pre-divine past so that it never happened at all). The only immortality worth having is an immortality of this life, not an existence in some ill-defined afterworld.

Human existence, he holds, must always be governed by a "symbol" that gives us the "immanent and comprehensible inscription of values in a world." And just as cosmic history made the three great contingent leaps of matter, life, and thought, with a leap to justice as the only one still to come, a similar structure occurs within human culture and its symbols, which consist so far of the cosmological, naturalistic, and historical symbols, with a "factial" symbol still to come. We can review each of these symbols briefly. The cosmological symbol refers to the ancient dualism between the terrestrial and celestial spheres. Here below everything is conflict, corruption, and decay; but in the heavens nothing is perishable, all movement is circular, and everything is arranged in mutual harmony. This symbol is ended by modern physics when Galileo discovers such blemishes as sunspots and craters on the moon, and when Newton integrates both celestial and terrestrial movement into a single gravitational law. Next comes the naturalistic or romantic symbol, in which perfection comes not from the sky but from nature itself. The world is filled with pretty flowers (Meillassoux claims that the ancients never discussed the beauty of flowers until Plotinus in the third century) and with living creatures naturally moved by pity, at least until society corrupts them. This symbol collapses in the face of reality as we know it, since pity is no more common than war, corruption, and violence. This brings us to the historical symbol, which only now is passing away. Bad things may happen, but history has an inner logic of its own, such that everything works out in the end. The ultimate form of the historical symbol is the economic symbol, whether in a Marxist or neo-liberal form. Just as the Marxist holds that the inner economic logic of the capitalists will inexorably lead them to self-destruction, the neo-liberal assumes that the sum total of individual selfish actions will lead, in the long run, to the greatest possible good. We worship the economy and let it guide history for us, just as the ancients worshipped celestial bodies and held them to be free from blemish. The final remaining symbol is the factial symbol, which Meillassoux hopes will now emerge. Factiality, we recall, is his term for the absolute contingency of everything that exists. Once we have grasped this absolute contingency, we are free to expect the dramatic advent of the coming fourth World: the world of justice, inaugurated by a virtual God and even mediated by a messianic human figure. There is the added feature, however, that this messiah must abandon all claims to special status once the messianic realm of justice is achieved. The messianic figure will then be no more special than any person on the street, since a reign of human equality will have arisen.

Although this focus on human being might seem like a return to standard humanism, Meillassoux holds that human pre-eminence has never truly been maintained. Previously, humans have been treated as special only because they contemplate the Good, because they resemble their omnipotent creator, or because they happen to be the temporary victors in a cruel Darwinian death-match between millions of living species. For Meillassoux, by contrast, humans have value because they know the eternal. But it is not the eternal that is important, since this merely represents the blind, anonymous contingency of each thing. What is important is not knowledge *of the eternal*, but *knowledge* of the eternal. We should not admire Prometheus for stealing fire from the gods; Prometheus is simply as bad as all the gods, no matter how much he increased our power. Feuerbach and Marx were wrong to say that God is a projection of the human essence, since for Meillassoux the usual concept of God represents the *degradation* of the human essence. If the traditional God was allowed to inflict plagues and tsunamis on the human race, the Promethean human of the twentieth century simply assumes the right to inflict death camps and atomic fireballs instead. In this respect, we have simply begun to imitate the degradation of humanity that was formerly invested in an omnipotent and arbitrary God.

In response to charges that absolute contingency might lead to political quietism, Meillassoux counters that the World of justice would mean nothing unless we had already hoped for it beforehand. A World of justice that came along at random would merely be an improved third World of thought: indeed, a perfect one. But it would have satisfied no craving, and would therefore have no redemptive power. For this reason, we must actively hope for the fourth World of justice for such a fourth World ever to arise. Not only justice, but *beauty* is dependent on such hope: for Meillassoux, who is here somewhat dependent on Kant, beauty means an accord between our human symbolization and the actual world, which could never be present in a World of the blessed any more than justice could. And just as a messianic figure is needed to incarnate our hope and then abandon power once the World of justice is realized, it is the figure of *the child* whose fragile contingency shows us a dignity and a demand for justice beyond all power.

Meillassoux Radicalized or Reversed

Given the promising reception of Meillassoux's first book, it would not be groundless to engage in early speculation about what it might take to earn him a place in the history of philosophy. Maybe this will never happen – who knows? – but quite possibly it will: his lucid argumentative methods and sheer philosophical imagination at least make him a good candidate to be read well into the future, especially following further elaboration in print of his mature system.

Philosophy is often practiced as though it were nothing more than the amassing of "knockdown arguments." But this is no more insightful than saying that good architecture is the amassing of steal beams. It is true that poorly constructed building cannot stand for long, but sound construction is merely the first, indispensable step in building. In fact, I am inclined to say that what really makes a philosopher important is not being right, but being wrong. I mean this in a very specific sense. I once heard the interesting remark about twentieth century culture that "you have to remember that the sixties really happened in the seventies." That is to say, it was in the 1970s rather than the more honored 1960s that civil rights, free love, long hair, and the rock and roll drug culture really took root. With respect to the history of philosophy, we might just as easily say: "you have to remember that Plato really happened in Aristotle," that "Kant really happened in Hegel" or "Hume really happened in Kant," or that "Husserl's phenomenology first achieved its truth in Heidegger." One becomes an important philosopher not by being right, but by attracting rebellious admirers who tell you that you are *wrong*, even as their own careers silently orbit around your own. To recruit faithful disciples may be comforting and flattering, but the greatest thinkers have generally had to experience refutation at the hands of their most talented heirs. For this reason, I would propose that we size up the magnitude of living thinkers not by deciding how many times they are right and wrong, but by asking instead: who would take the trouble to *refute* this author? For this reason I do not ask: "Is Meillassoux right?" since I do not believe in the virtual God myself, nor am I convinced by any important aspect of Meillassoux's philosophy. Instead, I ask if there are interesting ways to overturn him. Only by being overturned, by no longer remaining a contemporary, does one become a classic.

Let's begin with a simple model of refutation, which can be refined further at a later date once the basic point is established. One kind of refutation simply consists in saying: "This author is a complete idiot." The refuter now walks away in celebration, and no link between the present and the future is built; all is reduced to rubble. But this sort of mediocre triumphalism is generally practiced by those who achieve little of their own, and is not especially interesting. Much more interesting is the sort of refutation that *does not* take its target to be a complete idiot. I would like to suggest that there are just two basic ways in which this can be done: *radicalization* and *reversal*. It has not escaped my notice that this is a fairly good match for the Deleuzian distinction between irony and humor. Whereas irony critiques and adopts the opposite principle of what it attacks, humor accepts what it confronts but pushes it into highly exaggerated form. The ironist is like the worker who sows chaos by rebelling and contradicting the boss, while the humorist is like the worker who follows orders to an absurdly literal degree, with equally chaotic results.

Let's start with a few examples. In Aristotle's treatment of Plato, and Heidegger's of Husserl, we find reversal. Plato's *eidē* are transformed by Aristotle into mere secondary substances, and the individual worldly things despised by Plato become what is primary. For Husserl what is primary is whatever is present to consciousness, while for Heidegger this is precisely what is secondary, since the primary stuff of the world withdraws from any form of presence at all. As for radicalization, it is most easily found in the transformation of Kant by German Idealism: "Kant was right to wall off the things-in-themselves from human access, and simply should have realized that the thought of the *Ding an sich* is also a thought, and thereby the noumena are just special cases of the phenomena," with much following from this discovery. It would also be easy to read Spinoza as a radicalizer of Descartes, and Berkeley and Hume as radicalized versions of Locke. Perhaps the distinction is now sufficiently clear. Admiring refutations are not those that say "Professor X is an idiot," which is merely the flip side of the eager disciple's fruitless "Professor X got everything right." Instead, it will be some variant of one of the following two options: "Professor X is important, but got it backwards," or "Professor X is important, but didn't push things far enough." In the history of philosophy these two latter cases have often been painful in purely human terms: Aristotle expresses sadness at refuting Plato, Kant is openly annoyed at Fichte, and Husserl feels betrayed and used by

Heidegger. Rude handling from later figures almost seems to be the *sine qua non* of being a great philosopher.

Now, it has already been claimed that Meillassoux is an emerging philosopher of the first importance, and by no less a figure than Alain Badiou: "It would be no exaggeration to say that Quentin Meillassoux has opened up a new path in the history of philosophy..." (vii). But rather than taking Badiou's word for it, or rejecting his word, we might experiment by asking how Meillassoux could be radicalized or reversed. Are there interesting ways of doing this that might launch whole new schools of philosophy, unexpected or even condemned by Meillassoux himself? While no one can see the future, the present is poor when it is not riddled with virtual futures.

The relation between philosophers and their predecessors and successors is always somewhat complicated, of course. But generally there is one *central* divergence at stake, which might be taken as the key to all the others. On this basis we could say that new thinkers *primarily* radicalize or *primarily* reverse the main ideas of their chief philosophical forerunner. There may be specific historical conditions and perhaps even personality traits connected with these two types, but this question can be left aside for now. More important for us is that radicalizers will generally be followed by reversers, and vice versa. Consider the textbook example of a reversal in the history of philosophy: Kant's Copernican Revolution, which inverts the so-called dogmatic tradition that addresses the world itself, and makes the world revolve instead around the conditions by which it is known. While it is not completely impossible that Kant's successors might have re-reversed this principle back into a new and stronger dogmatic realism, conditions were premature for such a move. Anyone doing this too early would likely have been an angry anti-Kantian reactionary rather than an original thinker in command of a genuinely new realist principle. The far more likely outcome is the one that actually happened: Kant's reversal of his predecessors was viewed as incomplete, or as retaining lamentable bits of the traditional view, which despite his admirable breakthrough he was unable to shake off. This was the view of German Idealism, anyway. In similar fashion, Spinoza could also be viewed as a radicalizer of Descartes, who is equally accused of preserving various Scholastic dogmas in an otherwise radical project of philosophical reversal. The point is this: reversals in the history of thought tend to be followed soon thereafter by radicalizations of those reversals.

The same may hold true in reverse: radicalizations might generally be followed by reversals, given that it is not always possible to be more radical than the radicals have already been. Consider the case of Husserl, who radicalizes Brentano's early vagueness about what lies beyond immanent objectivity, and Twardowski's assertion that there must be an external object lying outside the intentional content, by collapsing *everything* into the intentional sphere: there is no difference between the Berlin in my consciousness and the actual Berlin that is home to millions of people. It is difficult to see how one could be even more radical than Husserl's idealist turn here. And thus the road is paved to Heidegger's reversal of classical phenomenology, in which the key point is what lies *deeper* than any presence to consciousness: the *Sein* whose power and obscurity cannot be made exhaustively present, but only sends itself in historical epochs. In similar fashion we might also read Leibniz as a reverser of Spinoza's radicalization of Descartes, retrieving a strong sense of individual substance and a certain validity of what the Scholastics had said.

Returning to Meillassoux, we might ask which kind of philosopher he is: a radicalizer or a reverser? At present, Meillassoux looks to me like a radicalizer (though for now his future remains shrouded in mist). He takes the correlationist tradition, which allows us to speak only of the relation between human and world, and tries to raise it into an even more extreme claim about the absolute contingency of everything. But whereas German Idealism did this by trying to collapse the distinction between thought and world entirely into the "thought" side, Meillassoux does it by trying to shift the non-absolute contingency of the thought–world correlate from epistemology to ontology. It is no longer a question of the inability of human knowledge to *know* what lies outside the correlate, but the inability of *reality itself* to be rooted in any definite laws.

Furthermore, if we look at the six basic features of Meillassoux's philosophy identified earlier in this article, all but one are already so radical that there is no obvious way to push them further. The one exception would be his claim that the world as a whole can change for no reason at any moment, coupled with the inconsistent claim that *within* a given world there are laws of nature that everything must follow. If gravitational attraction between all masses is a current law in our world, then for Meillassoux there can be no exceptions to this law for as long as it remains in force. A toppled vase will fall to the floor every time for sure, *unless* there is a cosmic change by which the laws of nature as a whole have altered. (This is reminiscent of the late medieval distinction between the absolute and ordained power of God, according to which God has the power to set or change the laws of nature, but not to contravene those laws locally once they are set.) On this point, to radicalize Meillassoux would simply be to say: there are no laws of nature even in the local sense. Everything that happens, even in the world here and now, is purely contingent and not governed by even a trace of law. And while this would be a more consistent development of Meillassoux's thoughts on contingency, it is difficult to see how it could lead to a new philosophy.

Instead, the admiring successors of Meillassoux are more likely to reverse one of his already sufficiently radical points. At least four candidates come to mind:

First, we have seen that Meillassoux thinks correlationism is challenged by a time before or after consciousness, but not by a space lying outside it. Perhaps this could be reversed into saying that spatial exteriority is the really crucial point. The arguments on this point are perhaps the least convincing in *After Finitude* (and do not even occur in the original French edition), and therefore it might be a candidate for the "blind spot" of which no philosopher is ever free.

Second, Meillassoux uses Cantor to claim that the contingency of laws of nature would not entail that they are unstable. A successor of Meillassoux might claim that it *does* make them unstable, and celebrate this fact. This person would then have to explain why common sense *seems* to encounter a relatively stable world despite its truly rampant instability. Whereas Meillassoux's problem is to show how stability might exist despite contingency, this successor's problem would be slightly different: to show why actual, full-blown instability might have the *appearance* of stability.

Third, Meillassoux claims that the primary qualities of things are those that can be mathematized. He might be reversed by a successor who says the opposite: the mathematizable qualities are the secondary ones, and the primary ones are those that elude symbolic formulation. While this is a perfectly valid possible objection to Meillassoux, it is one that is made in advance by some of his predecessors and is still made by some of his peers, making it less interesting for futurology than some of his other points.

Fourth and finally, whereas Meillassoux claims that God does not exist but might exist in the future, a successor might argue even more bizarrely that God has always existed but might vanish in the future.

Let's arbitrarily select the first of these possibilities, and imagine briefly where it might lead, if pursued in the future by admiring detractors. Meillassoux comes from the circle of Badiou, and some of Badiou's most ardent admirers are found in Latin America. So, let's imagine that towards mid-century some ingenious reversers of Meillassoux emerge in that portion of the Spanish-speaking world. Just for fun, let's call them Castro and Chávez. And in order to avoid any confusion with the present-day politicians of those names, we will stipulate that Meillassoux's great successors are both women.

The philosopher Castro (we will suppose she comes from Peru) reverses Meillassoux's argument that the ancestral or diachronic are what most threaten the human–world correlate. Instead, she claims that the diachronic does not threaten the correlate at all, and that we must instead look at space as what ruins the correlate and demands a strange new realism. What would such a philosophy look like? In order to determine this, we might ask what price Meillassoux pays for doing it the opposite way. As I see it, he pays in two separate ways. One is that laws of nature for him are contingent *over time*. The laws of nature apply to the universe as a whole at any given moment, and would be changed globally if they are ever changed at all. The second price he pays is that Meillassoux has no *mereology*, or theory of parts and wholes. Everything for him is on the level of the given, or immanent in experience, with the sole proviso that the laws governing this immanence might change without notice at any given moment. In reversing Meillassoux, Castro makes the following claims in the preface to her stunning debut book of 2045, *The Cosmos and its Neighborhoods*, rapidly translated from Spanish into all the languages of the world:

> Despite his brilliant analysis of the contingency of laws of nature over time, Meillassoux gets two important assumptions wrong. First, he allows for only one set of contingent laws to govern nature as a whole. Second, he allows laws to govern only the world that is immanent in experience, and thereby fails to explore the contingency among part–whole relations. In this book I will argue, first, that the laws of nature vary in any given instant between one region of the universe and the next; and second, that the world is made up of layers of parts and wholes that are also contingent with respect to one another.

Those are the words of Castro. This may sound like a hopeless free-for-all of chaos, yet the book somehow succeeds in drawing some compelling deductions about how laws must vary from one place or level in the world to the next. Trapped in the limited horizon of 2011, and not yet inspired by the heavily balkanized political and technological situation of 2050 that somehow lends additional credence to Castro's vision, we can only vaguely grasp what such a philosophy might look like.

After this reversal of Meillassoux by Castro, the usual pattern leads us to expect a radicalization by Chávez, a young Argentine student of Castro. How could the already strange theories of Castro be radicalized? Perhaps as follows, in a disturbing new book entitled *The Implosion of the Neighborhoods*, which argues as follows:

> Castro was right to shift the Meillassouxian framework of contingency from time to space. However, in this respect she retained a surprisingly traditional opposition between the two. In this book I will show that time and space collapse into one another. This may sound too much like the discredited four-dimensional block universe of twentieth century physics and philosophy. However, the four-dimensional universe is a model biased in favor of space, merely adding an extra dimension to the commonsense spatial continuum while stipulating that the serial passage of time is an illusion. In this book I will argue instead for a one-dimensional space-time modeled after our experience of time, in which there is no simultaneous co-existence at all between different parts of the universe, or 'neighborhoods' as my esteemed teacher Castro has called them. Instead, the various portions of the universe link to one another by succession rather than by coexistence. Buenos Aires, New York, and Amsterdam do not exist simultaneously in the same landscape, but one after the other in the mind of some observer, and this observer can only be an observer much larger than any human. Against Meillassoux's notion of a virtual God that does not exist now but might exist in the future, I will argue for an actual God that surveys the universe in sequence, thereby generating the illusion of spatial diversity and even the illusion of individual minds located within that diversity. Once this divine observer dies, the universe as a whole must perish.

Again, these ideas are so bizarre that we of 2011 can barely comprehend them, just as Aristotle would have had a difficult time grasping the theories of Descartes. We could then perhaps imagine a further reversal of this theory, emanating from the intellectually resurgent Philippines of the twenty-second century. The Filipino School might argue that the universe is *already* dead, given the collapse of its spatial richness into the serial observations of a flimsy and mortal God. The virtual universe does not yet exist, but might exist in fully spatial form in the future, and this would require the death of God and the resulting liberation of God's succession of images as independent, spatially situated realities.

With a bit of sharpening, we might be able to make all of these imaginary thinkers more intuitively clear. Along with the history of philosophy, there might arise a new discipline generating imaginary futures for philosophy. The richness of Meillassoux's system comes not from the fact that he is plausibly right about so many things, but because his philosophy offers such a treasury of bold statements ripe for being radicalized or reversed. He is a rich target for many still-unborn intellectual heirs, and this is what gives him the chance to be an important figure.

Greek Returns:
The Poetry of Nikos Karouzos

Nick Skiadopoulos

> "*Poetry is experience, linked to a vital approach, to a movement which is accomplished in the serious, purposeful course of life. In order to write a single line, one must have exhausted life.*" – Maurice Blanchot[1]

Nikos Karouzos had a communist teacher for a father and an orthodox priest for a grandfather. From his four years up to his high school graduation he was incessantly educated, reading the entire private library of his granddad, comprising mainly the Orthodox Church Fathers and the ancient classics. Later on in his life he sold the library for money, only to buy a little more time before he went broke again. Selling his only remaining capital for a few thousand drachmas, Karouzos traded not simply life, but language for poetry. What twisted type of economy upholds this very decision? Can we speak of a certain investment, with specific returns? "I am talking about the fate of Lazarus: at once pauper and saved."[2]

Nowadays – and ridiculously recently – we are more than apt to speak of a certain insouciance pertaining to the Greek form of expenditure: expenditure without any type of investment. This imprudent stance still conjures a "capital punishment": each time, at each act of excess what is at stake is a caput, a head – the haunting dead metaphor for capital.[3] Decapitation, as a road of no return, implies that capital is the condition for the possibility of

---

1 Maurice Blanchot, *The Space of Literature*, trans. Ann Smock (Lincoln and London: University of Nebraska Press, 1989), 89.
2 Nikos Karouzos, Συνεντεύξεις [*Interviews*] (Athens: Ikaros, 2002), 95. Henceforth, I.
3 "*Capitale* (a Late Latin word based on *caput* "head") emerged in the twelfth to thirteenth centuries in the sense of funds, stock of merchandise, sum of money or money carrying interest. […] The word and the reality it stood for appear in the sermons of St. Bernardino of Siena (1380-1444) '… *quamdam seminalem rationem lucrosi quam communiter capitale vocamus*', 'that prolific cause of wealth that we commonly call capital'" (Fernand Braudel, *The Wheels of Commerce*, trans. Siân Reynolds [Los Angeles and Berkeley: University of California Press, 1992], 232–3).

returns – at least in this life. In that sense, the argument against imprudent economic conduct is not itself economic, but ethical if not ontological – Max Weber being our witness.

We had to wait for Nietzsche for the question to be overturned: life has an intrinsic value, and as such it is fully lived only when exhausted. And no one knew how to exhaust it better than the Greeks: "Oh, those Greeks! They knew how to *live*: what is needed for that is to stop bravely at the surface, the fold, the skin; to worship appearance, to believe in shapes, tones, words – in the whole Olympus of appearance! Those Greeks were superficial – *out of profundity!*"[4] However the individual is not the ultimate consumer of his life; as Blanchot points out, writing – and in particularly poetry – also exhausts life, in detriment of individual integrity. The integrity of the poet being poetry's capital must be reproduced poem after poem. The poet not only answers to the calling of writing; he must also answer the call of return – a task that poetry itself cannot possibly fulfill. Nikos Karouzos stands as a poet who continuously re-emerged from poetry's excessive consumption. By devoting himself to poetry in an unconditional manner, he became its capital, a head sacrificed at each word, verse or poem.

Reading his poetry is a way of tracing his re-emergence. But his returns are inseparable with the many faces of the Greek experience. Each time Karouzos comes back, the Greek experience returns as well, in all its maddening multiplicity: Apollonian and Dionysian, Orthodox Christian and Pagan, materialist and utterly metaphysical, dead and alive. This experience can never fit a national or even a philosophical narrative. It only survives in language; and it can only be manifested in poetry. In turns.

"*I do not guarantee a single word.*"[5]

A short account of his life, written at the back of a book clearly states the situation: "He has been living in Athens for forty years as he struggles breathlessly in a 'mysterious debauchery with words.' 'An aristocrat from God,' his life has no meaning besides poetry."[6] In one of his interviews he talked about his unconditional dedication to poetry, commenting: "Only death can deliver me from that."[7]

To speak of the Greek experience is to speak about a half-dead language (part of it "ancient" and part of it "modern") that still utters in life what is

4 Friedrich Nietzsche, *The Gay Science*, trans. Bernard Williams (Cambridge University Press, 2001), 8–9.
5 Nikos Karouzos, Τα Ποιήματα, τ. A΄ & B΄ [*Collected Works*, Vol. I & II] (Athens: Ikaros, 1993), II, 454. Henceforth, CW.
6 Nikos Karouzos, Ερυθρογράφος, [*Redwriter*] (Athens: Apopeira, 1990).
7 Abstract from a TV interview.

excluded from it, as something out of this world, as something that will never return. Still, in contrast to death as a recently revived academic fashion, the Greek experience is impossible to be revived in its totality. From antiquity to Byzantium and up to the modern age, the Greek language speaks through an incessant historical dissemination that obliterates written and spoken dialects and languages, giving birth to new ones, entombing the old ones in books. Anyone who is aware of this terrifying polymorphy and still calls himself a poet, must stand against a white sheet of paper, pen-in-hand, with a very particular duty: to be as fully inconsistent as possible. In the formally ironic uniqueness of the poem, the poet functions as "a band-aid for lesser and greater antinomies" (CW I 251). Antinomies that are far from being only linguistic: they are historical, political and, alas, existential. Yet, beyond appearances, it is language that ruthlessly encodes them through history, submitting the poet to the temptation of placing them one next to the other on a single white sheet. The closer their neighboring, the greater the scattering of the writer.

In a work where poetic license is described as a "freedom-impasse" (I 51), this task is undertaken in full conscience of its consequences: "what I am interested in is escaping individuality (envisioning the non-ego) [...] Nevertheless, my dissociations never achieve duration" (I 74–5). This failure in our attempt to escape existence (described wonderfully in Levinas's *De l'évasion*) is what keeps poetry alive. If it weren't for this lack, return as resurrection would be impossible: "Everyone resurrects himself through dying [...]. Resurrection is the switching of mortalities" (I 94). However, this very return also annihilates existence through an uncompromised living death: "I am with the killed. Hence my deepest solitude. I do not feel this tremendous macho society, beyond from the fact that it is a ruthlessly consuming one. It is me who pays all the time" (I 57). Who said that the society of the dead is not a consuming one as well? Maybe it is the consumer-society par excellence, as it derives ruthless returns from the poet's self-consumption.

"We are the sanguinary amateurs of the Real."[8]

The poet is not an ancillary of return – and in that, he is not a philosopher. The return of poetry might well be eternal[9] and its circle necessarily vicious, but the return demanded from the poet is always singular, existential, and unmasked. Though poetry is called the "deserted direction of will,"[10] the

---

8   CW II 9.
9   "Return is the being of becoming, the unity of multiplicity, the necessity of chance: the being of difference as such or the eternal return" (Gilles Deleuze, *Nietzsche and Philosophy,* trans. Hugh Tomlinson [London and New York: Continuum, 1986],189).
10 Nikos Karouzos, Πεζά Κείμενα [*Texts/Non-Fiction/Prose*] (Athens: Ikaros, 1998), 62.

stance of the poet is not that of a Nietzschean "great man."¹¹ Whereas drunkenness provides a thread between the poem and the excess it both presupposes and infuses ("Poetry always enlarges. 'Drunkenness' is nothing more than that" [I 85]), whereas language flashes in loudmouth spurts of *déraison* ("When I am alone I do something else. I utter words. For example, while having my ouzo and listening to music I am most likely capable of randomly shouting 'Electricity!'" [I 138]), the poet never gives in to the double affirmation¹² that would eventually risk the "element of pleasure in discourse" (I 80). Poetry cannot be written with the very hammer of historical process that made linguistic antinomies possible. It can neither replicate nor rationalize it.

The surprising beauty of chiming antinomies is our existential failure to transcend them. A voisinage that does not emerge from necessity of chance as an eternal return. On the contrary, the poetic practice is a return from that very return: "Let us treat Yes as a No to No and No as a Yes [...] And let us not forget that this pissed affirmation crumbled down Nietzsche's intellect in the dark paths of this world" (I 88). This return from the "vicious circle" should in no way be taken as a form of artistic prudence. It can well be seen as a game of masks, a dribble of demonic inconsistency as Dionysus transforms himself into a Christ that is in turn de-theologized: "Who can forbid that? Every man is capable of his own theology, nothing can stop him" (I 73–4). However, this is far from being a never ending game: from the very first turn to poetry, a continuous process of existential defeat counts towards the poet's expiration date: "after the defeat of the popular front I raised the question 'why do we exist?' while others were asking 'why we failed'" (I 57).¹³

Poetry comes as a question of return after a defeat that is confessed in full profanity. Though it accepts the necessity of existential defeat, it does not affirm it. And though it necessitates defeat, it demands return. Poetry is not simply born *post mortem*; it is born AD. It signals a return to Christ as "groundless religiousness in the surprise of the real as such" (I 72), which is

---

11 "A great man – a man whom nature has constructed and invented in the grand style – what is he? First: there is a long logic in all of his activity, hard to survey because of its length, and consequently misleading; he has the ability to extend his will across great stretches of his life and to despise and reject everything petty about him, including even the fairest, 'divinest' things in the world" (Friedrich Nietzsche, *The Will to Power*, trans. Walter Kaufmann and R. J. Hollingdale [New York: Vintage Books, 1968], 505 [§962]).

12 Cf. Deleuze, *Nietzsche and Philosophy*, 186–9.

13 In this 1982 interview Karouzos refers to the end of the communist movement in Greece after the civil war of 1946–1949 between the Governmental Army and the Democratic Army of Greece, the military division of the Greek communist party. Karouzos's father was a member of the communist National Liberation front (EAM) members of which formed the mainly resistance movement (ELAS) in Greece during WWII. The poet was a member of the United Panhellenic Ogranization of Youth (EPON), which was a youth division of EAM. After the end of the war, ELAS was called to disarmament in view of the formation of a National Army. The members of EAM resigned from the government of national unity and a series of protests led to a 3 year civil war between ELAS and the Government Army. After the defeat of ELAS the Communist party was outlawed and many communists were exiled in deserted Greek islands. Karouzos, who took action in the Greek resistance and was active during the Greek civil war, was exiled in Icaria on 1947 and in Makronisos on 1953 where two years earlier he was called to do his military service.

at once a return to the refuge of childhood. It is not a question of endurance towards an eternal return. Rather it is a question on the possibility of an existential return – or rather of existence as return. Returning in the world as someone who cannot enjoy any returns, exactly because he is averse to guarantees. A return without returns.

◇

> "PHOTOCOPY OF HAPPINESS
> When I was young I used to pin down cicadas
> and step on ant nests.
> I used to stand there silent for hours.
> With threads I decapitated bees.
> Now I am a dead man breathing."[14]

Karouzos's turn to poetry coincides with a young communist's return to the "paradise of childhood" (I 68), after a series of political defeats, incarcerations and exiles. In a country torn up by a civil war, the morning after World War II. Historically, all these facts resulted in the defeat of the communist movement in Greece and opened up a long turbulent road that would peak in the dictatorship of 1967. Existentially they led to a series of disillusionments: mental breakdown, divorce, abandonment of studies in law school. To the question "why do we exist" the answer was poetry. Nevertheless, the turn to poetry as a return to chidhoold is all the more dangerous when the devouring refuge of its memory becomes the synonym of adulthood. Hence the return demanded by poetry is a trap, keeping the poet busy in reconciling a past unbridgeable and insupportable.

This effort does not only concern some Greek poet, who happened to be an existentially and politically defeated individual etc. It also relates to the historical fate of a nation that after its modern constitution never stopped dreaming of the glories of its past youth, in a present that was (and is) sweepingly disappointing. Isn't this return to youth a way of *compensating* for a loss of youth, fatally resulting in a losing adulthood? Will Greeks, the eternal children of Plato and Nietzsche, ever learn? How to return without dying, how to remember without wasting time, how to grow up?

◇

> "The great illusion of the musicality of things."[15]

Beyond the historical tragedies of modern Greece and away from any personal disappointments, the relation that this land holds with language and

---
14 CW II 336.
15 CW II 297.

history is mediated through the Greek light – whose omnipresence is the very condition of its transcendence. All historical contradictions from Dionysus to Christ took place under this light; all those disseminated dialects were spoken beneath its warmth. To paraphrase Lévinas,[16] light is both the condition of the world and of our withdrawal from it – a withdrawal towards the invisibility of God, of the dead, of meta-physics, resulting from the temptation that all is still here, *behind* this light the visibility of which they once evaded: "birds, the allurement of God" (CW I 17).

Under that luminous sky, if Greeks can do anything at all, it is to envision a return that will never come. All they can do is write poetry – which is doing nothing; other than lending an ear to a disseminated language whispering a unity that cannot be promised, as an adulthood in defeat is ready to recognize. Trying "to trap the invisible in visibility" (CW II 483) they forget that they have grown up and one day they die – with the promise of return.

No, poetry does not pay. It does not signal salvation – but its broken promise. Poetry is messianic – but in announcing nothing but itself. And of course we have been fooled, all this game of returns came up to nothing. To the ears of an aged continent it means that the return to/of poetry is a losing game, a return without returns. "Europe, Europe... you are nothing more than the continuation of Barabbas" (CW I 295).

"Life is not there to verify theories."[17]

The records show that Karouzos was finally given a second-class pension from the Greek government, at the time when he was being recognized by the literary press as one of Greece's major contemporary poets. Being neither a bourgeois nor a nobelist, he proclaimed himself to be an anarcho-communist, unconditionally faithful to the utopia of a classless society. He also drank, heavily. "Capitalism made an animal out of man/Marxism made an animal out of truth/Shut up." (CW II, 369)

Perhaps one of the most scandalous divides of our times has been the one between the living and the dead: the latent prohibition that the living should not be concerned with the dead based on the mere impossibility of the dead to be concerned with the living in the first place. Adding to the scandal, this

---

16 "Existence in the world qua light, which makes desire possible, is then, in the midst of being, the possibility of detaching oneself from being. To enter into being is to link up with objects; it is in effect a bond that is already tainted with nullity. It is already to escape anonymity. In this world where everything seems to affirm our solidarity with the totality of existence, where we are caught up in the gears of a universal mechanism, our first feeling, our ineradicable illusion, is a feeling or illusion of freedom. To be in the world is this hesitation, this interval in existing, which we have seen in the analyses of fatigue and the present" (Emmanuel Lévinas, *Existence and Existents*, trans. Alphonso Lingis [Dordrecht, Boston, and London: Kluwer Academic Publishers, 1988], 43–4).

17 Abstract from a TV interview.

divide abuses anything that cannot return to us by subsuming it under the same futility. Hence death is no longer "loss" in the usual sense. It no more refers to the things we lost but to *our* "loss" (of time, money and well-being) as we insist to dwell on them. Death is a waste – of time.

It is this waste to be found in the insouciance of Greek expenditure; the waste in dealing with a language that most of its historical part is no longer spoken (a dead language); the waste in translating a poet who is *ex definitio* untranslatable; the waste of his vision, his money, his life. The waste of dealing with anything that cannot return and that cannot bring in any *returns*.

But it is also the waste of life that poetry itself presupposes, the waste of dealing with invisibility, with anything that is out of this world and thus invokes the fear of death that is in turn – and surprisingly – nowhere to be found. Instead of death, what is there, beyond the light, is the being without us (to recall the Lévinasian *il y a*), the mumble of our own nothingness, calculating the price to be paid for writing poetry under an *evergreek* light. To understand this to-and-fro, is to realize that poetry is something out of this world that nevertheless *takes place* within it. But to ridiculously equate this to-and-fro with death as non-existence, is to exile poetry along with its own possibility: "I do not believe that poetry will ever disappear from this world. […] But I am also sure that it does not have many chances of playing, as you say, a redemptive role in our vertiginous technological future. Without being endangered as a creative need, it will be placed on the side of history" (I 32).

Poetry needs to be endangered: it is exactly there that we would like to locate the poetry of Nikos Karouzos. If we are willing to include the Greek original it is because we consider that it will be both a waste of time for us to do so (since most of you cannot read Greek) and because it might induce you to the even larger waste of learning it. We would additionally be glad if this small introduction served as an equally wasteful, academically useless piece of reading, gesturing towards a taboo of investing in anything Greek – that is in anything dead among the living, in anything that will never come back and maybe was never there in the first place. This is the only way to reserve for ourselves the possibility of poetry and preserve the light of its promise.

    "To return: that is the miracle."[18]

---
18 CW I 17.

Selected Poems

Nikos Karouzos, translated by
Nick Skiadopoulos and Vincent W.J. van Gerven Oei

ΙΗΣΟΥΣ ΑΝΤΙ-ΟΙΔΙΠΟΥΣ[1]

Γιατί κρατούσαμε κάποτε ώς την πέμπτη μέρα
    το πασχαλινό πρόβατο;
Τα κείμενα λένε: μ' αυτού του θύματος το κρέας
έπρεπε να καθαρίσουμε όλες τις αισθήσεις.
Για να δώσουμε κύμα στη ζωή λευκότατο
θαυμάσιες ευωδιές στην έκταση του στήθους.
    Ιδανικά στο χάρο.
Για να βλέπουμε τα λαμπρά
χαράματα του Άψινθου και να 'ναι η ψυχή
στόλισμα βαθυχάρακτο
    της πλώρης που την είπαμε θέληση.
Τότε πολλές δορκάδες τρέχοντας
    ανάμεσα στην καταπράσινη
φύση με τους υδάτινους ύμνους,
τότε, κατεβαίνοντας οι αθέλητοι άγγελοι
με κυλινδούμενο το ύψος στην ορμή τους
χαρίζονται της αστραφτερής Περιπέτειας.
Όθεν η μιλιά γι' αυτό χρειάζεται
    και τα δεινά σκεπάζονται ωσάν
τους τιμημένους νεκρούς με σημαίες.
Ασώματο δάχτυλο δείχνει τα φλογώδη
    και μοσχοβόλα ολοκαυτώματα
στους κουρασμένους ορίζοντες
    στα εξουθενωμένα πλάτη καθώς
ανάβουν οι χαρές του νεραϊδόξυλου
και τρέμει ολόκληρη η πρασινόφυλλη αγάπη.
Κάτι θα κελαηδούσε πάλι
    αν δεν το διώχναμε –
μπορεί της προβατίνας το χορτάρι.
Κάτι θα μας καλούσε στην απέραντη ανάσταση –
    μπορεί του έαρος η χάρη.
Μα η καρδιά μας άγρια τυφλώθηκε
    πέρασε στα φαινόμενα του Άδη.
Σιγή και πάγος αδιάκοπα σκεπάζει
στους αχυρένιους καιρούς το Νήπιο Πνεύμα.
Την ώρα που ονειρεύονται οι βυσσινιές
και λάμπουν αμυδρά μες' στο απλότατο σκοτάδι
    τίποτα δε στοχάζονται οι βαβυλώνιοι
στα εργαστήρια με τ' αυτόματα χρωματιστά φώτα.
Πώς να χαρούμε πια την πέμπτη μέρα του προβάτου;
Φουρκίσαμε τ' αστέρια.

......
1   From Ερυθρογράφος [Redwriter] (Athens: Apopeira, 1990), 9–10 = CW II 463–4.

JESUS ANTI-OEDIPUS

Why were we once saving till the fifth day
    the Paschal lamb?
The scriptures say: with this victim's meat
we ought to cleanse all of our senses.
To give life to the whitest wave
miraculous odors to the extension of the chest.
    Ideals to death.
For us to witness the illustrious
dawns of Absinthe and for the soul to be
a deeply carved ornament
    on the fore we named will.
Then many deer running
    amidst the evergreen
growth with watery hymns,
then, the unintended angels descending
with heights spiraling in their momentum
indulge in the luminous Adventure.
Whence the need for speech
    and our sufferings covered with flags
like the glorified dead.
An incorporeal finger pointing at the flamboyant
    and fragrant holocausts
within the tired horizons
    and the exhausted breadths with
joys of the mistletoe on fire
and shivering all of the green-leaved love.
Something would have chirped again
    had we not driven it away –
maybe the ewe's grass.
Something would have called us to the eternal resurrection –
    maybe the grace of spring.
But now our heart is fiercely blinded,
    withdrawn to the appearances of Hades.
Silence and ice incessantly cover
the Infant Spirit in thatched times.
While the cherry trees are dreaming
faintly glowing in absolute darkness
    there's nothing the Babylonians can contemplate
in labs with automatic colored lights.
How to rejoice now in the fifth day of the lamb?
We forked the stars.

Γίναμε σιγά-σιγά δήθεν υπέροχοι
με μαδημένες χίμαιρες στα χέρια.
   Μας νέμεται σκληρά η επιστήμη.

ΔΙΑΛΕΚΤΙΚΗ ΤΟΥ ΕΑΡΟΣ[2]

Χριστός η ορθή γωνία· Χριστός το πυθαγόριο
   θεώρημα.
Χριστός ο απειροστικός λογισμός άνωθεν όλβια
   Χριστός τα Σύνολα.
Χριστός η ψηφιδογραφία στα μαζικά σωμάτια
   Χριστός η μάζα μηδέν.
Άρα ψεκάζουμε αριθμούς και πεδία λαγνείας.
Είμαστε τυφεκιοφόροι νοσούσης λογικής και κάτι --
παρατηρούμενο σημαίνει παρατηρητής και Εκάτη
σκότος το πάμφωτο και φως εν τη σκοτία η Αστάρτη
   συνδαιτημόνες δαίμονες απ' άρτι.

CREDO (ως είθισται να λέμε λατινιστί)[3]

Α
Πιστεύω εις ένα Ποιητήν εκτός ουρανού / φυγάς θεόθεν και αλήτης,
Εμπεδοκλής / και επί της γης / εξόριστος πάνω στη γη κ.λπ. του
Βωδελαίρου /.

Β
Πιστεύω εις ένα Υπολογιστήν εντός κεραυνού και δια της ύλης.

Γ
Υποφέροντας άχραντα / ουσιαστικόν / ο Ποιητής ανατείνεται
βραδυφλεγής αυτόχειρας εξυπακούοντας πολύωρους ύπνους.

Δ
Τα υποψήφια λάθη λιγοστεύοντας.

Ε
Ορατών τε πάντων και αοράτων ιερουργώντας την αποκρομμύωση.

---

2   From Ερυθρογράφος [*Redwriter*] (Athens: Apopeira, 1990), 18 = CW II 472.
3   From Λογική μεγάλου σχήματος [*Large Sized Logic*] (Athens: Erato, 1989), n.p. = CW II 521–3.

We've gradually become supposedly sublime
with plucked chimeras in our hands.
    Avenged relentlessly by science.

DIALECTICS OF SPRING

Christ the straight angle; Christ the Pythagorean
    theorem.
Christ the infinitesimal calculus from above the blessed
    Sets Christ.
Christ the tessellation of massive particles
    Christ the zero mass.
Hence we spray numbers and fields of lust.
We are carabineers of diseased logic plus something –
Observed means observer and Hekate
The darkness luminous and light in the dark Astarte
    banqueters demons from today.

CREDO (as we are used to say in Latin)

    Α
I believe in one Poet expelled from heavens/fugitive from the god and
vagabond, Empedocles/and here on earth/exile on the
earth etc. of Baudelaire/.

    Β
I believe in one Computer inside thunder and through matter.

    Γ
Suffering undefiled/substantive/the Poet uplifts himself
slow-burning suicidal implying lengthy sleeps.

    Δ
Cutting down on prospective mistakes.

    Ε
Of all things visible and invisible officiating the onion-peelings.

Ζ
Ο Ποιητής έχει τίποτα / βλέπε τους αναχωρήσαντες /.

Η
Πιστεύω εις ένα Ποιητήν που λέει: η τρέλα μ' αρέσει· γελοιοποιεί την ύπαρξη· ας ανάψω απ' τη μάνα μου.

Θ
Συνταχτικό δεν το γνοιάζεται στην προσταγή της μουσικότητας. Μαζί και μ' άλλες ακόμη λευτεριές, και τα νυ παίζονται κατά την έννοια ήχος οπουδήποτε. Π.χ. τον χειμώνα εδώ, το χειμώνα εκεί· δε θά 'ρθει – δεν θα καταλαγιάσουμε, κ. λπ. κ.λπ.

Ι
Ο Ποιητής γυμνάζει τη σκέψη σε απογύμνωση.

Κ
Κι αν είναι έλληνας οφείλει να σπουδάζει πάντοτε της Αττικής τη λεπτότητα, σε φως, βουνά, χωράφια και θάλασσα. Διδάσκει γλώσσα η λεπτότητα τούτη.

Λ
Κι αν είναι βαθιά πεπρωμένος ο Ποιητής εκφράζει το ανεξήγητο του εξηγητού· τυγχάνει νόμιμος διάδοχος του επιστήμονα και προκάτοχός του.

Μ
Στον αφρό δεν έχει διάρκεια· στο πατοκάζανο μαίνεται ο Ποιητής.

Ν
Φλογοδίαιτος και ποτέ ξελυτρωμένος.

Ξ
Ο Ποιητής κάποτε πρέπει να λέει: μεγάλη κατανάλωση παρουσίας – γενείτε και λίγο μοναξιάρηδες!

Ο
Ο Ποιητής είναι αμφίφλοξ.

Π
Επιδέχεται θανάτους και αναστάσεις.

Ρ
Ακροθωρίζει και υπάρχει σε ξαφνοκοίταγμα.

   Z
The Poet has nothing/see the departed/.

   H
I believe in one Poet that says: madness I enjoy; he ridicules existence; let me light up from my mana.

   Θ
Syntax he doesn't care about when musicality commands him. Along with still more licenses, and Ts are played according to the concept sound anywhere. E.g. the winters here, he winters there; it will not come – I will not rest, etc. etc.

   I
The Poet exercises thought until it's stripped down.

   K
And if he's Greek he must always study the fineness of Attica, in light, mountains, fields and sea. For this fineness teaches language.

   Λ
And if he's deeply destined the Poet expresses the unexplainable of the explained; he happens to be a rightful heir to the scientist and his predecessor.

   M
On the froth he does not last; the Poet blusters at the bottom of the pot.

   N
Flamebred and never redeemed.

   Ξ
The Poet must sometimes say: what a consumption of presence -- be a bit lonely for a change!

   O
The Poet is twilit.

   Π
He is susceptible of deaths and resurrections.

   P
He looks from the corner of his eye and exists in a glance.

Σ
Είναι ουραγός της μητέρας.

Τ
Ανέσπερος από ηλικία.

Υ
Πιστεύω εις ένα Ποιητήν που λέει: να συμπέσουν οι αγνότητες. Μέχρι την Κόρινθο του Σύμπαντος ή μακρύτερα.

Φ
Σε ανώτερη απελπισία.

Χ
Σε φαεινότερη πεμπτουσία.

Ψ
Σε μια αίσθηση που πτηνούται.

Ω
Συγχωρώντας τους πάντες.

Σ
He follows behind the mother.

Τ
Eveningless when it comes to age.

Υ
I believe in one Poet who says: let the purities coincide. Until the Corinth of the Universe or even farther.

Φ
In a higher despair.

Χ
In a brighter quintessence.

Ψ
In one sensation that lifts off.

Ω
Forgiving everyone.

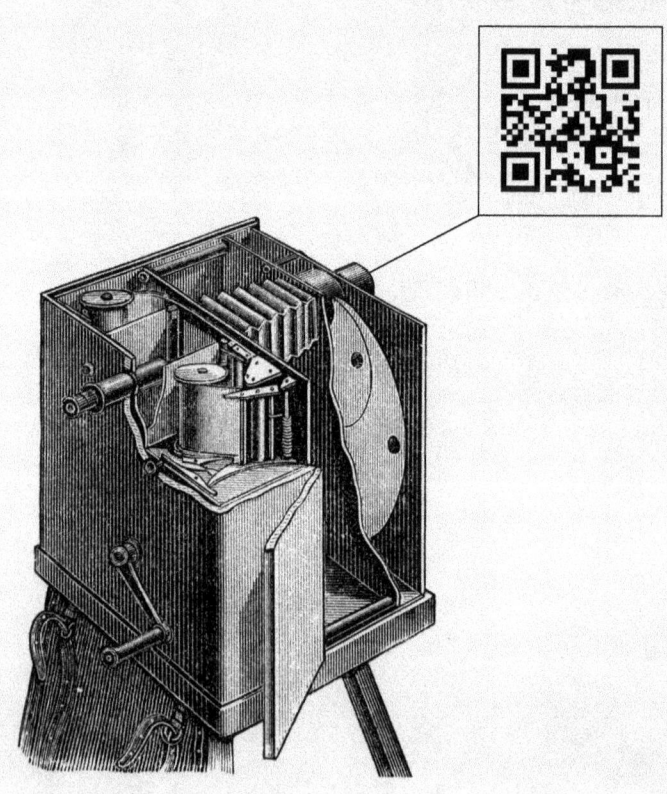

Phillip Stearns:
DCP Series

Jamie Allen

> "With the digital photo, this light, from out of the night, no longer comes entirely from the day, it doesn't come from a past day that would simply have become night (like the photons emenating from Baudelaire's face.) It comes from Hades, from the realm of the dead, from underground: it is an electric light, set free by materials from deep within the belly of the earth. And electronic, that is to say, a decomposed light. Digitization breaks the chain, it introduces manipulation even into the spectrum, and by the same token, it makes phantoms and phantasms indistinct. Photons become pixels that are in turn reduced zeroes and ones on which discrete calculations can be performed. Essentially indubitable when it was analog (whatever its accidental manipulability), the this was has become essentially doubtful when it is digital (it is nonmanipulation that becomes accidental)."
> – Bernard Stiegler[1]

A collection of Images produced by intentionally corrupting the circuitry of a Kodak DC280 2 MP digitalcamera. By rewiring the electronics of a digital camera, glitched images are produced in a manner that parallels chemically processing unexposed film or photographic paper to produce photographic images without exposure to light. The *DCP Series of Digital Image*s are direct visualizations of data generated by a digital camera as it takes a picture. Electronic processes associated with the normal operations of the camera, which are usually taken for granted, are revealed through an act of intervention. The camera is turned insideout through complexes of shortcircuits, selected by the artist, transforming the camera from a picture taking device to a data capturing device that

---

[1] Jacques Derrida and Bernard Stiegler, "The Discrete Image," in *Echographies of Television: Filmed Interviews*, trans. Jennifer Bajorek (Cambridge: Polity Press, 2002), 153.

renders raw data (electronic signals) as images. In essence, these images are snapshots of electronic signals dancing through the camera's circuits, manually rerouted, written directly to the onboard memory device. Rather than seeing images of the world through a lens, we catch a glimpse of what the camera sees when it is forced to peer inside its own mind.[2]

The DC280 was the first Kodak digital camera to be released with a 2 megapixel sensor in 1999.

There are so many ways to take something apart. Deconstruction, differentiation, dissection, dissolution. A whole slew of concepts and processes towards atomization which aim, eventually, to evoke or locate an essence of some kind, in material science as in philosophy. In picking things apart, what is it we attempt to do? To simplify? To comprehend? To confront? To disprove?

With Stearns's *DCP Series* we see that destructive scrutiny can sometimes bring about new forms. To create this series of images, Stearns applies circuit bending techniques to modern photography – his fingers and stray wires cutting across the camera's circuitry at the moment of registration. As with Moholy-Nagy's vinyl records and Nam June Paik's cathode ray TVs, Stearns deconstructs the technological inscription of his era. In so doing, the function of the digital camera is revealed, but its transduction inverted: A recorder becomes a synthesizer, the scientist an artist. In a single, simple gesture, these works example a media archeology of the present.

We resist the urge to call these photographs.

Above right: The back of a Kodak DC210 1 megapixel camera after adding circuitry to facilitate manipulation;
Below right: Detail of the CCD chip of a Kodak DC210 with wires extending signals away from the chip for further off-board manipulation.

......
2   From the project description on http://phillipstearns.wordpress.com/projects/dcp_series/

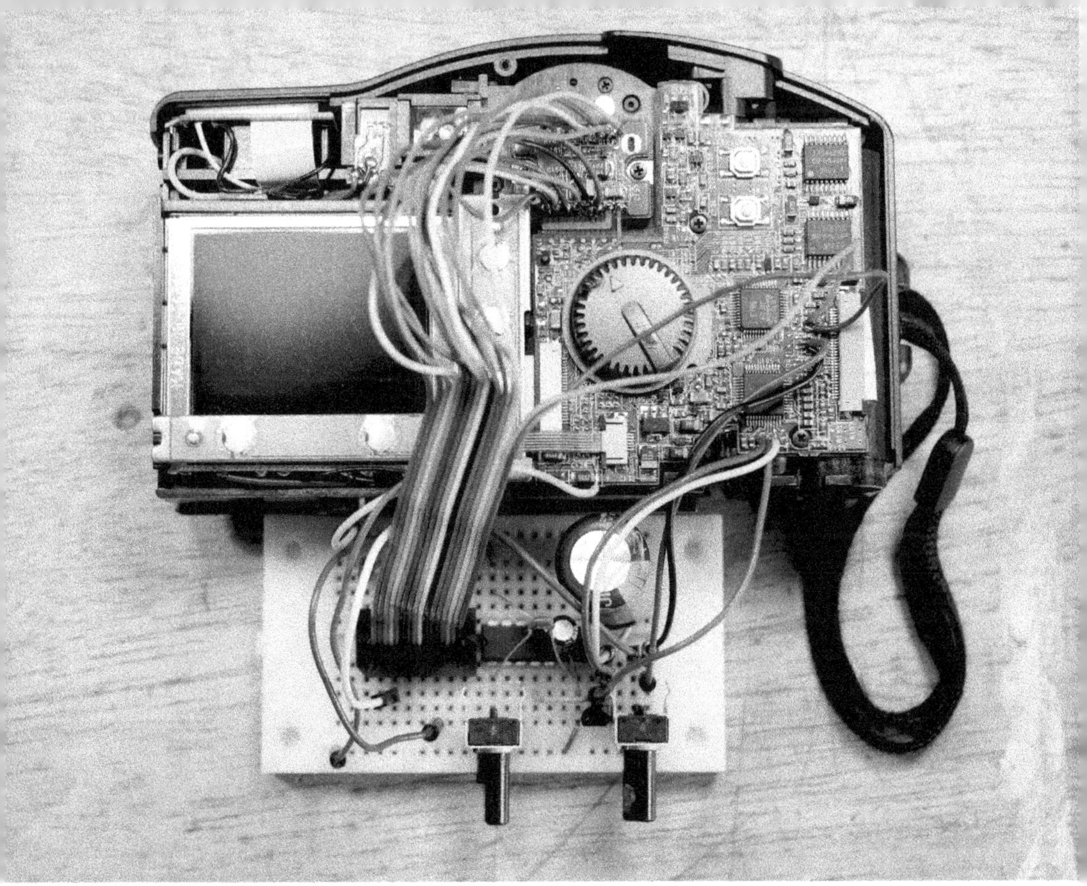

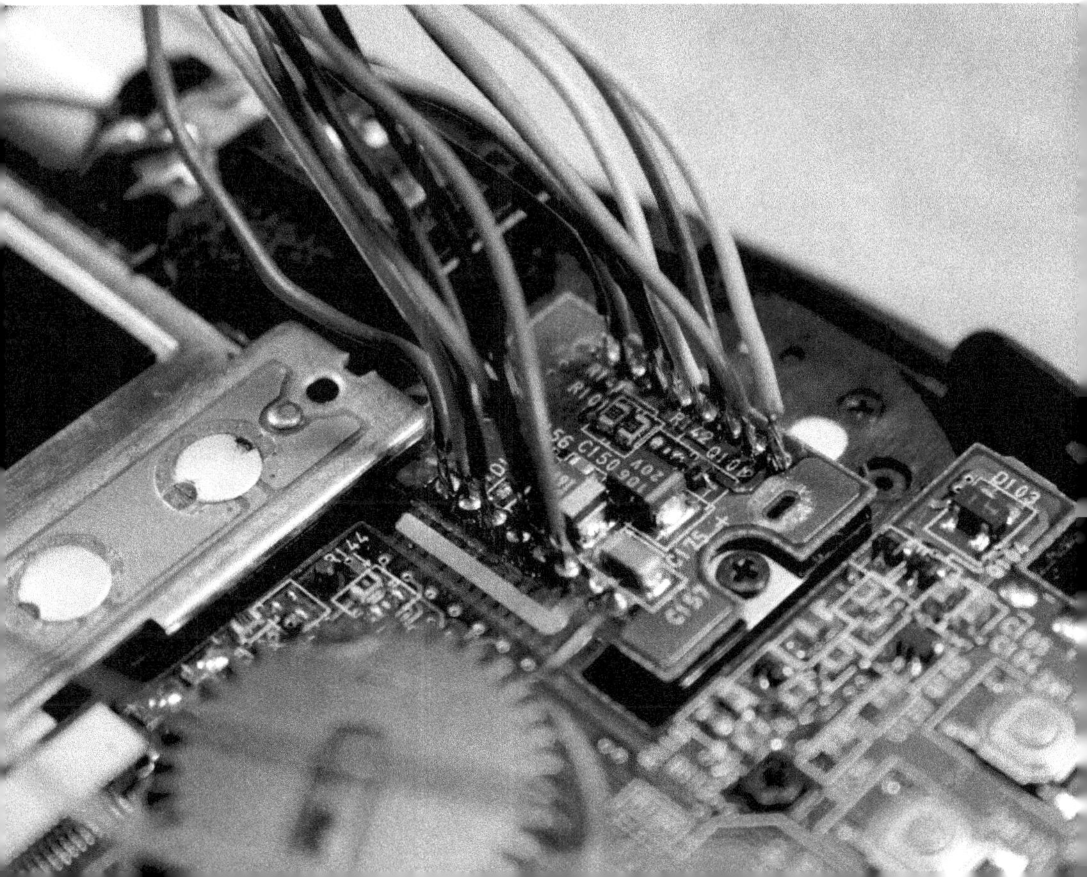

DCP_1313

Allen/Stearns · DCP_Series

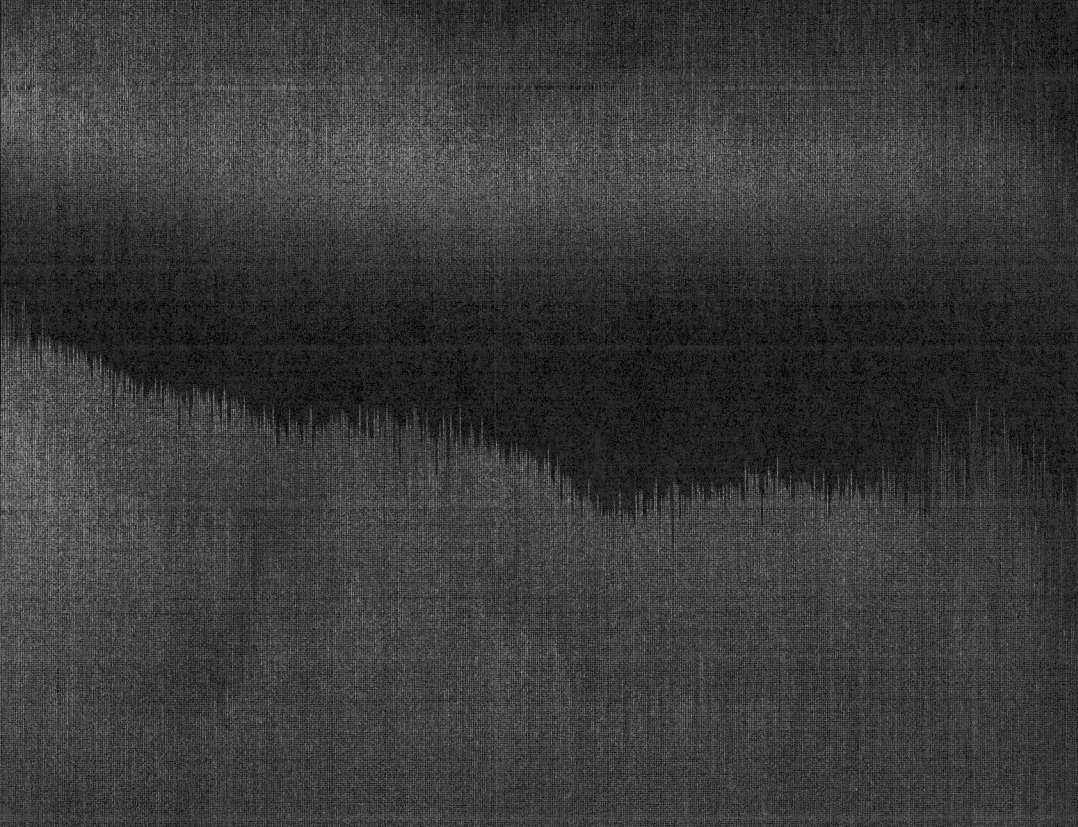

DCP_1355

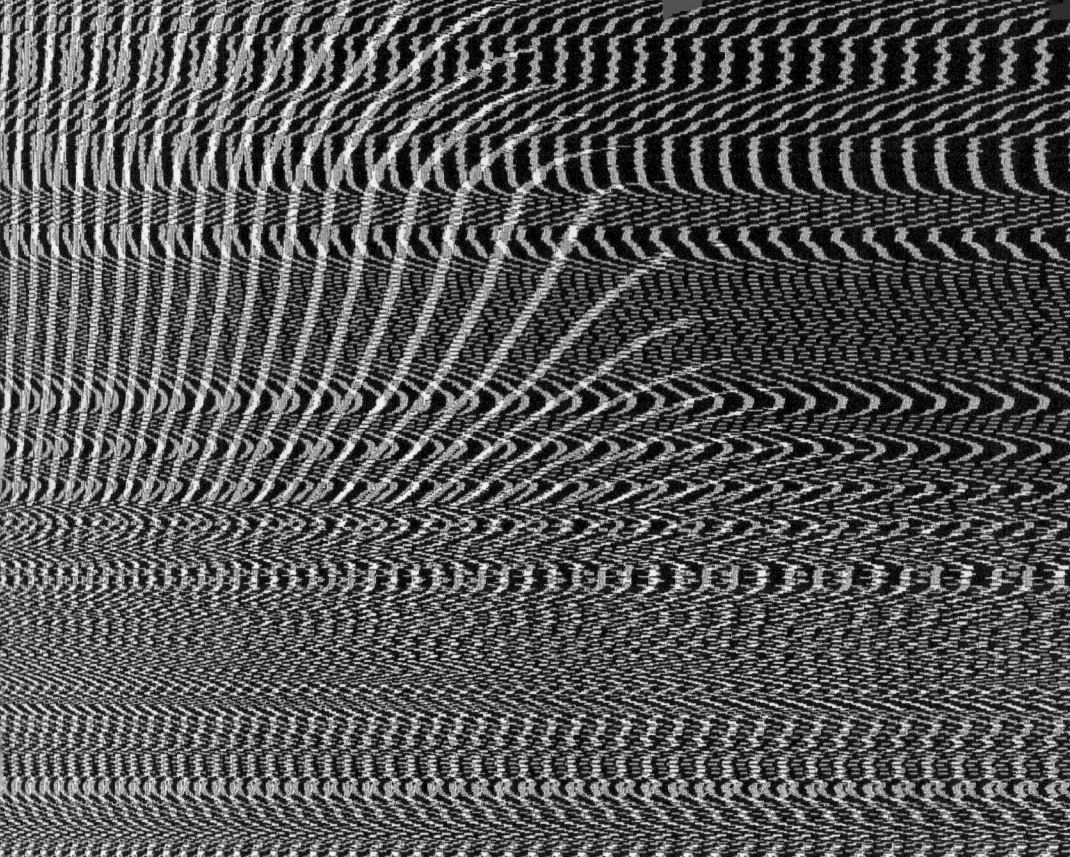

DCP02802

Allen/Stearns · DCP_Series

DCP02803

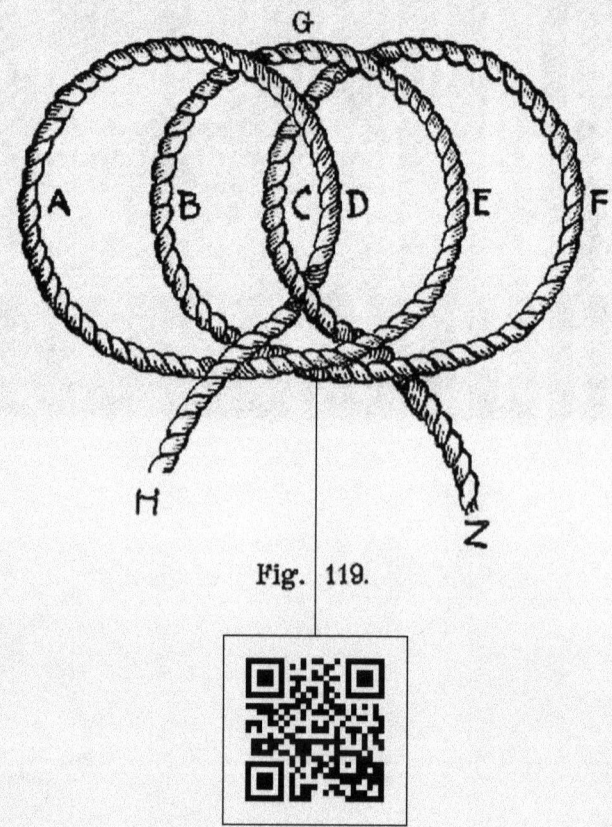

Fig. 119.

The Crisis of Negation:
An Interview with Alain Badiou

John Van Houdt

John Van Houdt (JVH): From Kant to Husserl, and now to your work, the move to transcendental philosophy has, for the most part, taken place in times of "crisis." For Kant it was the potential failure of classical accounts of rationality at the skeptical hands of David Hume, for Husserl it was the collapse of the spirit of philosophy under the joint pressure of modern science (the critiques of psychologism) and the onset of Nazism (the *Crisis*), and for you the problem is what you call "the crisis of negation." How do you define "negation" and why it is in crisis today?

Alain Badiou (AB): My answer is a simple one, in fact. The very nature of the crisis today is not, in my opinion, the crisis of capitalism, but the failure of socialism. And maybe I am the philosopher of the time where something like the "Great Hypothesis" coming from the nineteenth-century – and maybe much more, for the French Revolution – is in crisis. So it is the crisis of the idea of revolution. But behind the idea of revolution is the crisis of the idea of another world, of the possibility of, really, *another* organization of society, and so on. Not the crisis of the pure possibility, but the crisis of the historical possibility of something like that is caught in the facts themselves. And it is a crisis of negation because it is a crisis of a conception of negation which was a creative one. The idea of negation is by itself a negation of newness, and that if we have the means to really negate the established order – in the moment of that sort of negation – there is the birth of the new order. And so the affirmative part or the constructive part of the process is included in negation.

Finally, we can speak also of the "crisis of dialectics" in the Hegelian sense. In Hegel we know that the creative part of the negation was negation of negation, so the negation of negation was not a return to before, but was on the contrary, the degradation of the content, the positive content of negation. And there are so many things of the failure of this vision that so proves that very often negation is under a negation. And that is the crisis of negation. On all sides today we know that the pure views of negation are practically very often militant to negation, and to the future of negation's negations. Exactly, that the future of revolution, victorious revolution, has been finally a terrorist state. The complete discussion of all that is naturally much more complex, necessitates dates, and all that, but philosophically there is something like that.

So therefore we must pronounce that *there is a crisis of negation*, and from this problem, there are two possible consequences: first to abandon purely and simply the idea of revolution, transformation of the world, and so on, and to say that the capitalist world, with moderate democracy, and so on, is the best world after all – not so good but not so bad, and finally we have with that answer, the first vision. And so it is a vision where in some sense the relationship between philosophy and history is *separation*. Because it is my conviction that if the history of humankind has as its final figure the figure of our world, it is proof that history is of no philosophical interest, that there is only left a pragmatic position, and so the best is business. In that case, the best is not philosophy but business! So that is why if, precisely when I speak of the "crisis of negation," I name "negation" the revolutionary conception of negativity which was dominant from the French Revolution until sometime at the end of the last century; it was the 80s I think. The 80s, something like that, the time of your birth, maybe?

> JVH: Yes, indeed, it is. So if that is the case, if we are facing this situation of the crisis of negation, where do you think French philosophy fits within this situation, not just in your own work but where is French philosophy in general going? What do think is the "future" of French philosophy? For instance, in the 80s you talked a great deal of the role played by the *nouveaux philosophes* in denuding philosophy of that impact, of that possibility of negation. Do you think that there is a future for French philosophy? Is there a hope for negation?

AB: I think there is. Certainly in the actual forms of existent French philosophy there is something which is that source of direction, not only of my work, but more generally. There are, for example, the attempts which are included in "speculative realism" in England, which is not only in England but which is also in France with Quentin Meillassoux, and so on. And we don't know what is precisely the future of all that. But I can say this is a world which *searches* for new forms of negation, certainly. A new vision of the world where negation is not exactly dialectical negation, but something else. And in all the currents, all the *articles politiques et philosophie* in France today, if you discuss with young philosophers, you generally agree that the question is, in fact, the question of the failure of classical negation, if you will. Naturally, I formalize all that in my manner, but I think that there is a future of French philosophy today. There is a good chance much of it will be around this question.

And so, it is very important to say everywhere that French philosophy is not dead. *Really*. During a period of practically twenty years my hope was a limited hope because there was a sequence where many French philosophers abandoned finally the political vision, accepted the established order, allied with the analytic current, you know, Anglo-Saxon form, or in a political vision of absolutely a non-transformative nature. So during this period from the end of the 70s or so to the beginning of the 90s, the situation was not a good one. And I was practically the last negative critic (*dénoter*). Now today that is not the case. Today there is a new generation which after all of that sort of debate is not the generation of May '68, which is without personal objections to the past and is open to the idea that we must find something new, find a new way. So I think during the ten or twenty years which are coming, there will be a new order of French philosophy.

> JVH: In the Preface to the second tome of *Being and Event, Logics of Worlds,* you describe your new method as a kind of "calculated" phenomenology (*phenomenologie calculée*). Obviously phenomenology was one of the dominant forms of philosophy in the last century. In fact, in a telling passage of *Logics of Worlds,* you refer directly to your relationship to Husserl's method. Can you elaborate on your relationship to previous forms of phenomenology, especially those of Hegel, Heidegger, and Husserl?

AB: My response is a simple belief: What I accept from the phenomenological vision is that we must have to the world a sort of descriptive position which neutralizes our effect. It is a Husserlian position, mind you, *my* Husserlian vision – *epochē*, suspension of judgment and all that – and the possibility to absorb or create what I name precisely a "logic of the world." Not an esthetic description of the world, not a pure science of the laws of the world, but the possibility to propose a configuration of the world in the sort of logical framework the center of which is the idea of the consistency of the world – why the world is consistent and not a pure chaos.

And so it is really a Husserlian perspective. The point of divergence is that finally Husserl reinstitutes correlationism which is: everything is referred to consciousness and all the movement of time, and so on, is referred to consciousness. And I negate the same thing because, finally, there is properly no history of the world as such; there is a history of *Dasein,* and the history of *Dasein* is also the medium by which the world is always the horizon of subjective experience. And so this is why I speak purely of an *objective* phenomenology, a phenomenology which assumes that there is no subject at all. It is naturally paradoxical, it is a paradoxical expression, but it is my attempt. And so it is the idea that appearing and the existence of the world is not constituted by subjective experience but it is a manner in which the world exists as such and that we have to (and this is why I agree with the realism of my friends from London), we must be realists, that is, a proper or true relationship to all that, which must be free of any deference to constitutive subjectivity.

And so, I can speak of phenomenology in the sense, first, that it is not *ontology* properly (because ontology properly at the beginning of *Being and Event* is finally the formal ontology of multiplicities), and so it is not ontology, and it is something like a description of the *possible* logical structure of appearing, but without any reference to consciousness or subjectivity. And it is also my relationship with Hegel which I explain to a certain extent. I agree with Hegel that we can describe some figures of experience, but these figures of experience are not the consistent history of *Spirit*.

And finally, to conclude this point, it is why I speak of "calculated" phenomenology – because the result of objective phenomenology is always the abstract formalism of a possible figure of the world. And so, the possibility to have a rational description of the world without reference to subjectivity is, in art and science, finally, disposed in this formalism – which is not the formalism of pure multiplicities but is the formalism of relations.

> JVH: Calculated phenomenology then seems not to return to "things-in-themselves," for instance, in order to analyze the intentional stances we can take up toward an object, but instead treats general phenomenon as given and only then creates formal, that is, mathematical, models to explain that given phenomenon. These logical formations help to explain how that given phenomenon functions, the "logic" of the situation, and also helps to isolate those features of the situation which are not reducible to that situation, what you call the site of the "inexistent" in the situation. As an example, you describe Carl Schmitt's political logic of the "friend–enemy" binary as an example of "classical" logic for which the distinction is governed by the principle of "non-contradiction" (or identity) and whose separation is protected by the principle of "excluded middle." If the method of calculated phenomenology constructs formal paradigms to interpret phenomenon, is there not something arbitrary or contingent about these formal paradigms and does this not undermine the "necessity" of logical relations? Moreover, is there a general "logic" governing the application of this logic, or is this what you mean by "Greater" and "Ordinary" logics?

AB: You have to understand that the formal paradigms are not contingencies of formal paradigms if you understand formal paradigms not as a formal dimension of precise worlds but as an exploration of what are the paradigms of *possible* worlds. So we can take empirical examples, and we can engage from empirical examples some formal paradigms. But these formal paradigms are in relationship to a pure world, on the one side, and on the other side are only *possible* forms from *possible* worlds.

It is then interesting the fact that we assume there exists an infinity of different worlds. This is why it is the first thesis of all the development in the

Logics of Worlds. Because with paradigms – if you hold that there is *one* universe and if you want to propose a formal paradigm for this world – you must demonstrate that this is really the paradigm of *this* world and not to propose a paradigm by an arbitrary choice. But this is not the case with an infinity of different worlds. And I propose some paradigms which are certainly examples of possible paradigms for existing worlds. And after that, I observe that there exist only a few fundamental relations to construct these paradigms. So, all the discussions are not concerning the possible final possible paradigms. I speak of actual worlds, I speak of worlds with inexistence, and worlds without inexistence, and so on – but much more – the fundamental relations are the important ones. And for this it is the idea of a logical structure of what exists as such.

My proposition is at the beginning to formalize not what the paradigm of the world is but what the fundamental relations are which formalize, finally, the fact for a multiplicity to be the world. That is the point. After that, when you know what the transcendental is, what the discussion of the multiplicity of the transcendental, and so on is, you can propose many forms, in fact an infinite multiplicity of different forms of the paradigm of the world. And so, I cannot make an arbitrary choice, but only to say that this world seems to propose that sort of paradigm. So if someone wants to criticize the construction, it is a construction which is absolutely open for discussion, you must begin from the beginning. The structure, the nucleus structure, of appearing of a thing as an object in the world, is reasonably shown by these relations and is known by these sorts of operations. But for the moment nobody really proposes to me another type of operation. But that is not a proof.

And so, to conclude concerning the beginning of the question, there is in some sense a "return to the things themselves" because there is a return to the idea that it is really the things themselves which appear. There is this kind of idea in *Logics of Worlds* and this is why it is so difficult, in fact: that if the things themselves are pure multiplicities, if it is really a pure multiplicity which appears and nothing else, then it is *being* which appears. And so, there is not the Kantian distinction between the thing-in-itself, which we cannot know, in fact, and the organization of a thing which is a transcendental nature. In my region, the transcendental is the transcendental of the thing and we can absolutely know the thing *as thing* – by mathematics, precisely by the mathematics of multiplicity. But to know the thing not only *as thing*, a being-qua-being, but as being *as appearing in the world*, we can also know something of that. But we must only assume that there is something other than pure multiplicity in its mathematical composition, there is something which is like an indexation, like a mark, of the multiplicity which is the thing that the multiplicity appears to be within a determinate world. So it is almost a thing-itself but with the transformation of the notion of "thing." That is the point.

JVH: The classical philosophical tradition has been conventionally separated into two camps: the rationalist and the empiricist camps. Contemporary philosophy, beginning with the German romantics, attempted various ways of overcoming this opposition, for instance, in Hegel's formulation: the "Total is the True," which you criticize in *Logics of Worlds*. Nevertheless, in the two tomes of *Being and Event* you seem to build a system on the distinction described in the introduction of *Logics of Worlds* as the difference between "*onto*-logy and onto-*logy*." This distinction implies a strong distinction between the empirical and formal criteria for existence. How do understand this distinction? Is there a criterion by which to judge the existence of a new possibility, or an event?

AB: Yes, it is true that my philosophy is – concerning the opposition of rationalism and empiricism – my position is not inside this opposition, precisely. Because, in fact, if mathematics is ontology, the thinking of being-qua-being is a rational one; and if appearing is the system of the transcendental laws of a description of a determinate multiplicity of the systematic rationalism of the world, the empiricism is also rational. And if empiricism is in my phenomenology, in some sense, this empiricism is also rational. So the distinction between existing world and the experience of this existing world, and being-qua-being and rational knowledge of the empirical, this distinction is resumed finally in the opposition, in my work, between mathematics and logics. (And you know that this opposition is a very logical one, because of the way logic is mathematicized, and on the other side, there is no mathematics without logics.)

So I propose neither to abandon the opposition nor to go beyond the opposition but rather to be *in* the opposition. Thus, it is not a Kantian position, it is not an empiricist position, it is not a purely Hegelian position. Because I create a space where first we can have a rational vision of the relationship between being and appearing and where, inside all that, we can propose the addition of what is the *truth*, an event as an ontological definition and also as a phenomenological definition.

The point which is not finished in my work is the correlation between the two, concerning the two, between being and event. The theory of an event in *Being and Event* is not exactly the same as the theory of an event in *Logics of Worlds*, so we have an ontological theory of an event and a phenomenological theory of an event. But in the first case, the criterion is genericity, the set which is generic is really the ontological definition of a truth, and the second is the apparition of a new body with formal, definite features, and I don't speak at all of "genericity," in the second book. And so, I say sometimes with regard to these books, we have to discuss the relationship between genericity, on one side, and the universal body, on the other side, and it is the same thing, because it is the same truth, and so on. So it is not finished, but you see that I admit *not* the separation, *not* the fusion, and *not* the dialectical going beyond the division. We can create a space where we dispose of this division in a unique rational space.

> JVH: As a final question, I would like to ask you about your relationship to Hegel. The position of Hegel in your work is ambiguous. In *Theory of the Subject* (1982), Hegel plays a central, even positive role. And indeed, many of your formulations seem to take a Hegelian inspiration. But in the two tomes of *Being and Event* your relationship is more critical. There you criticize Hegel for being a philosopher of the One and of the Whole. While these are relatively traditional critiques, recent work on Hegel seems to make these kinds of critiques problematic (I am thinking particularly those of Bernard Bourgeois, Catherine Malabou, and of course, your friend Žižek, to name a few). How would you describe your relationship to Hegel's work?

AB: In response to the last question, you know that I love Hegel, personally. I think that my most important masters, not of today with Lacan, Althusser, but of the past, are certainly Plato, Descartes, and Hegel. Hegel I read constantly with great pleasure and I always find something new in Hegel.

Because there are two manners of reading Hegel: the global reading which is systematic, and conforms to the maxim that "the true is the whole," and there is another manner in which you read some pages in Hegel, full of new ideas, and sometimes with difficulty to place all that in the whole. I prefer the second manner because I always find something very interesting. I was always saying that I cannot admit that "the true is the whole," because there is no whole at all. So naturally, I have some difficulties with Hegel.

But my relationship to Hegel is *not* fundamentally a relationship of *critiques* of Hegel. And if a new vision of Hegel and my friendship with Žižek create new conditions to incorporate much more Hegel in my philosophy, I shall be very glad.

– August 2009, Saas-Fee, Switzerland

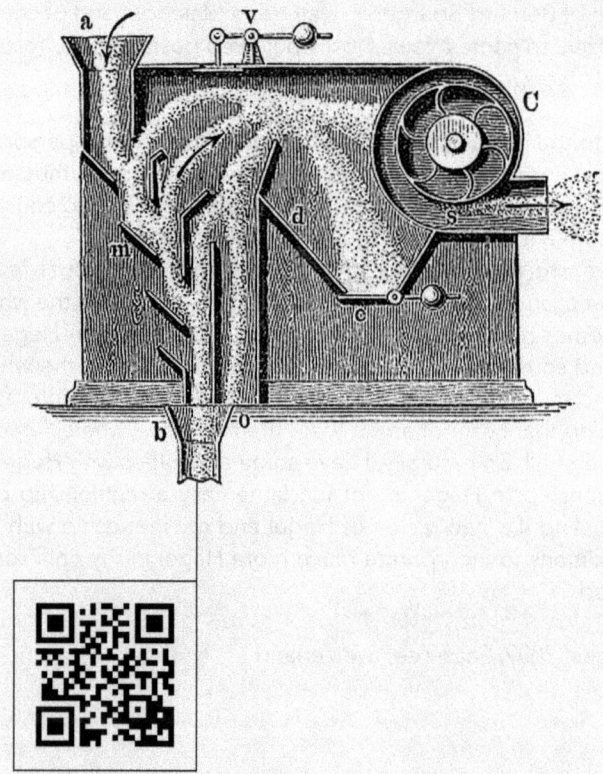

The Return of Benjamin's Storyteller: Ronald Reagan as the Incorruptible Saint of Political Media

A. Staley Groves

St. Reagan and the Return of the Storyteller

The 2004 Republican National Convention was a significant event concerning language and aesthetics in contemporary politics. The Reagan myth appeared as a stellar aura of sentimentality that churned a cultic swoon. Among the polity this spectacular mystery passed a glow upon the shoulders of gleeful followers. Engulfing George W. Bush's body, the Reagan aura of the protector, the prophet, the historian, and narrator of American destiny oft portrayed as a humble man who simply transmits "content" bequeathed upon the sitting president his missionary staff to guard that "shining city on a hill." This proverbial key to New Jerusalem follows Reagan's own mythical thinking about the sacred role of the United States. After all the organism-city was under attack by "terrorism." The "real America" had to be preserved from suitcase nukes and radical Islam, what was needed, in fact, was the wise counsel of Reagan-Bush to survive not only as a nation, but as a world.

When Bush ceremoniously accepted his spectral host, his image was woven into Reagan's, the ultimate sovereign who rode off into the screen on a white stallion. This journey scene manifested after two key elements of memorial montage: the late leader's image preceded by a surging fighter plane that merged into the image of a priest calming his flock at what appeared to be Reagan's own funeral service. With Reagan returning from heaven through media he assured the converted any crisis facing American providence was only a point of passage. Having returned a short time after ascension his "final journey to the West"[1] was an aura every conservative leader need embody and project. Reagan's channelers, the conservative

---

1 Quoted from Ronald Reagan's memorial as broadcasted by *FoxNews*: http://www.youtube.com/watch?v=By_Mann9p_I

faithful, amplified the aura of father Exceptionalism. This novelistic perpetuity endowed the faithful with an ability to overcome not only history and its seismic interruption but as much the finitude of mortality. Contemporary crises of origin have, as we attempt to theorize here, breached a certain threshold of experience through broadcast media.

This phenomenon is provisionally linked to authenticity and language, similarly articulated by Christopher Fynsk concerning the "way" one takes "in the saying of language." The way is complicated by the "fact" of language itself, and the fact of language may indeed be our devices that transmit political messages.[2] Thus how we engage what appears or inflects essentially in the experience of media persists in relation to our own speaking or saying. The first barrier is a thinking with devices we inhabit daily. It is easy to call this a type of agency, yet to target the device in hand obscures the question of the apparatus itself and its relation to language. Far more ephemeral than the Reagan myth something surpassed a key threshold related to that question.

The "funerary moment" as Jacques Derrida conceived of it examples, perhaps, the distinction Fynsk makes between Hegel and Heidegger on the fact of language in consideration of the way of its saying essence. It links to a moment of terror and war as capitalism enters into its late phase. Fynsk sets out in the introduction to *Language and Relation* intimating such advising that one must "attend to an implication of approach and object that is no less intricate than (though fundamentally different from) the one purposed by Hegel."[3] Method denotes the problematic of the death in language and the way it relates to political discourse, or, as we propound, the way death is turned against subjectivity.[4] Derrida's observation of Hegelian semiotics perhaps underscores this "fact" of language, that is, if we are concerned with recovering discourse from aesthetic manipulation, as a type of death-speaking in media devices, it is a language of a peculiar factuality:

> Hegel knew that this proper and animated body of the signifier was also a tomb. The association *sōma/sēma* is also at work in this semiology, which is in no way surprising. The tomb is the life of the body as the sign of death, the body as the other of the soul, the other of the animate psyche, of the living breath. But the tomb also shelters, maintains in reserve, capitalizes on life by marking that life continues elsewhere the family crypt: *oikēsis*. It consecrates the disappearance of life by attesting to the perseverance of life. Thus the tomb also shelters life from death.

---

2   I refer in general to Christopher Fynsk's inaugural questions concerning the "linguistic turn." See *Language and Relation ...that there is language* (Stanford: Stanford University Press, 1996).
3   Fynsk notes that verb status of essence relates to the "way-making that occurs properly in the speaking of language" whereby discerning essence and language might lead, via Heidegger to an experience with language "...namely, the relation of essence and language as it involves the human engagement of speaking its essence." See Fynsk, *Language and Relation*, 76–7.
4   I have begun a theory of such a recovery, See A. Staley Groves, "Ultima Multis: The Raising of Deathcare," *artUS* 29 (2010).

> It warns the soul of possible death, warns (of) death of the soul, turns away (from) death. This double warning function belongs to the funerary moment. The body of the sign thus becomes the monument in which the soul will be enclosed, preserved, maintained, kept in maintenance, present, signified. At the heart of this monument the soul keeps itself alive, but it needs the monument only to the extent that it is exposed – to death – in its living relation to its own body. It was indeed necessary for death to be at work […].[5]

Reagan became an incorruptible saint by a death at work, a mythical force indelibly printed through the incumbent Bush and his bio-formative constituency. Limited not to a particular ideological identity, the embodiment of American providence and its sacral mission is at stake in this transferal of aura. Sure to spring from his or her mouth are the wise maxims and proverbs. In other words Bush attained the attributes of Benjamin's storyteller as a Reaganesque narrator: speaking wise counsel from beyond the pale of broadcasting lumens. The device in hand holds a few distinctions when related to Benjamin's concept of the novel and its crystalized narrator. One such distinction is the peculiarity of a solitary reader (hence viewer of broadcast politics) reunited with their own death-speaking capacity in the faces of characters on the screen. The distinction between the novel and the device is in the withdraw from reading a novel and return to the realities of life. When does one return from a broadcast? Our devices today are increasingly attached to our mode of encountering and cracking phenomenon once demarcated by the actual pages and limited by distances that gave readers a chance to see a report for what it was. The blinking of the page is as much the turning of a channel.

Reagan's ubiquitous Americana, telegraphed through folk speak crafted by his minders, is constantly recycled by neophytes. The likes of Sarah Palin, Michelle Bachmann, and Christine O'Donnell present to the American public an evolving candidate. Each variation holds special attributes of a general storyteller narrating the myth. These acolyte test models seem to perfect a neo-romantic element of American cult. This is not limited to partisans. Barack Obama's attempt at Burkean consensus invokes Reagan.[6] Given the lack of "substance" or consensus in conservative candidates today, the ultra-synthetic reality surrounding political leaders denotes a crisis in authentic discourse. This demands a deeper meditation on the nature of essence, that is, where essence vanishes into the impossibility of nature and further, whether or not we can even think this distinction without committing an incredible fault of curiosity, that is, running the risk of "participating" in a fully synthetic discourse. Our naive animality, if not our "bare life," the ability to

---
5   Jacques Derrida, "The Pit and the Pyramid: Introduction to Hegelian Semiology," in *Margins of Philosophy*, trans. Alan Bass (Chicago: The University of Chicago Press, 1982), 82.
6   Sam Tanenhaus has observed that Obama is most likely a consensus conservative in the Burkean sense of calculation. See *The Death of Conservatism* (New York: Random House, 2009).

distinguish what was given away to the device, understands more and more of our bodily movement. We are accustomed to thinking by way of self-reflection. The experience of discovery has always lent itself to the destructive and "secret" mores of an ideology of progress. If I participate, no matter what, things might change. This matter of technological agency means language, or speech has entered an eidetic blender. Therefore beyond this tendency to call Reagan acolytes religious lunatics we have entered a time of political eschatology. Candidates and the sophisticated elements of their campaigns who gamble on the odds of our increasingly faltering capacity to grasp our own capacity for language. How are we to think the appearances of these figures in order to gain access to the displacement of a synthesis of reason, the crafting of thinking we have apparently left behind?

The content of Reagan and Obama's speeches are stabilizations of a death-lost polity. This is analogous to the emergencies of a stock market. The nature of machine-driven trading demands a more emotive check on tensing outcomes. The practice of language (questioning) is in doubt because the usurpation of discursively built community have lost access to storytellers. Communities have adopted the logic of information as the basis for their meaning: broken, without brevity and lack of context. The media device is an interesting object then, it at once rescues what was lost from community and mediation but introduces such graphically. Its capacity to subjectify or structure perception depends on our lingering from actual reality in the same way the novel and the newspaper did. We cannot however limit our thinking to the object. Appearances are linked to the fact of language. If engagement with forming language continues by way of device habitation we take part in a type of legislation or representation, which is the material rule of law. Law takes its place in the body. The body marks the limit of freedom by moving to the limits prescribed by representative law. A perpetual image crystalizing a general condition in the American polity suggests the reflections of salvation, a blindness of vanity or the narcissistic awe of our devices and networks allows essence to meet this law beyond our perceptual capacity of reflection. The law is no longer engaged by the body in formal thinking, it is engaged by whatever imagination may be, arguably the furthest extent of a thinking, human body, the difference between reality and the actual, metaphysical world. Imagination would become the essence of a new law in its relationship to its representation. Neo-romantic vision quests for the real America become the blinding element of political identity dominated by the aesthetics of an obscure authenticity. What is the authenticating body then, for whom? The American polity has hit an ideological bottom. Wandering in portable magic mirrors listening to every revelation spouting about produces a result that pushes once calculative governance by argument into endless oblivion. The craft of reason aimlessly drifts into a multi-polar voidance. The question "how do we think of the multiple?" is perhaps phrased more effectively as "how do we avoid what appears as reasonable discourse?"

Shock Values:
Masses in a Post-Electro-Mechanical Age

We think we are part of political movements every time we stroke our screens. Therefore when Reagan reappeared from death he was Benjamin's storyteller, he was a saint incorruptibly true. This is the experience of devices and the claim of their ability to channel appearances of facts. This glazed upon Obama, who, no matter how brilliant, proves unable to stabilize the destruction of civic spaces. Political strategists will continue to manipulate this factoring of language whether known to them or not. And the world beat essence of Obama once hailed as messiah can no longer keep up with the national quest for origin. "Birthers," in fact, are a nonpartisan phenomenon that lends to our theorization. Birthers' desire for authentic origin by way of mythical delusion indicates the power of appearances and a need of perceptual literacy.

Conversely Obama did precipitate a potential cure for the inadequacies of death care through devices that reach beyond "Hope." Casual observance of "conservative" right ideologies congealing in contemporary America demonstrate a growing reactionary position against government and administration. The Obama campaign, following all the progressive elements of political identification and subjectification, is no exception; no one can win without using technologies of an increasingly sophisticated apparatus of voter identification. This is differentiated by Obama's pragmatic style of governance, the executive versus the messianic candidate. By the administration's own admission their information was "ineffectively" communicated.[7] The arguments as to the real appropriation of Reagan's good governance, whatever the case may be, are appropriated today by a radical right that rejects any America whereby its modern institutions survive, part of real fallout in Washington today.

The *bios* that gives force to symbolic power is now oriented toward the thought of these bodies. They have a whole new issue to enforce upon America: governance is no longer acceptable in any civic manifestation where organizing physical bodies was its primary task. These bodies are already in place. Governance would begin in our own blinding vanity as the submission to essence driven by a factored language. The wise counsel of contemporary politicians has less and less to do with how well one knows their leader or their half-baked conspiracies. Today more and more people do not clearly understand what these leaders really say or mean. Regardless of bravado, language contrasts to a general sense of reality these leaders exude once in office. Yet by 2012 it is not a gamble of prophecy to say this general rupture in political messaging will not be corrected and perfected.

---

7 Christopher Beam, "Speech Therapy: Obama Discovers the Limits of Communication," *Slate* (Jan. 27, 2010): http://www.slate.com/id/2242741.

Everyone knows revolutionary leaders are insane, yet to be insane is generally a mode by which one has little way of confronting its suppositionary notions. We live in a time of demented and hallucinogenic language inherited from the post-war America of the 1950s, yet that phenomenon has begun to transpire into nothingness and along with it any revolutionary possibility. Would the new emergence of far right leaders really qualify for a whole group of insane revolutionary leaders appearing in such prolific numbers? This question rests upon the disappearance and emergence of something like an iconographic scaffold whereby our ability to read depends on our aesthetic health, that is, grasping the death in speaking, which would be the ineffable fact of language itself. Our "conservative" leaders of the day are not full lunatics, yet. It seems they believe what they say and what they say is authenticated by invoking the storyteller of Reagan who holds the mantle as the most malleable blazon in American political lexicography. This diction or literacy-shaping is buttressed by nearly countless amounts of data crunching and micro-targeting, the goal, as it has been since the formal introduction of social and information sciences in the early 20th century, is to find a way into the subjectification processes of human *bios*.[8] Walter Lippmann, a pioneer on journalistic ethics and social sciences defines the goal of seeing images forming in people's head in uncomfortably similar terms:

> The pictures inside the heads of these human beings, the pictures of themselves, of others, of their needs, purposes and relationship, are their public opinions [...] we shall inquire first into some of the reasons why the picture inside often misleads men in their dealings with the world outside [...] we shall consider first the chief factors which limit their access to the facts [...]. They are the artificial censorships, the limitations of social contact, the comparatively meager time available in each day for paying attention to public affairs, the distortion arising because events have to be compressed into very short messages, the difficulty of making a small vocabulary express a complicated world, and finally the fear of facing those facts which would seem to threaten the established routine of men's lives.[9]

Hallucinogenic experience inherited something from the percussive shocks that shattered the body. Benjamin's shattered human, as he thought it in "The Storyteller" was one undergoing a decline in valuable experience. Lippmann's cynical attitude stands in contradistinction to any progressive goal of educating and informing everyone by the merits of information and newspapers. Benjamin's stance was quite similar to that. Despite the percussive assault of modern life and its loosing of biological sanctity, human-beings retained an ability to redress progressive obliteration. Benjamin therefore

---

8   I refer here to Walter Lippmann's *Public Opinion* (New York: Harcourt, Brace and Company, 1922), whereby the goal was to see the pictures in people's heads.
9   Lippmann, *Public Opinion*, 30.

sought an "-ability" to think creatively against a desubjectification presaging the ascension of total war fascism. Would this form of desubjectification fully manifest today depends upon whether or not we are able to observe appearances proximate to death, or to authenticate the end of our personal world. The crises of finitude for the subject are linked to Benjamin's analysis of a final review. A dying body allowed a necessary life-affirming transmission critical to human society.[10] This seems a society we conserve less and less of today. How do we engage technological claims on bios and the use of our imaginations by political regimes who exploit those "plugged-in" to the system? Benjamin's general prognosis aligns with this in a rather interesting way. The incessant wiring of the world digs into the destructive currents of our unknowable nature whereby our capacity to grasp our finite existence has few ethical stabilizations.

In Benjamin's thought one could attempt to strike against this type of historical determination. This observation was linked to the electro-mechanical experience of the human body. Today it takes place at an aesthetic level he named aura, yet requires a new articulation. How do we desubjectify with "smart" technologies and conserve the dignity and nature of our own language? How do we smash them without destroying our own bodies and imaginations?[11] If we follow a type of linguistically driven empiricism language is the last place whereby a sensible conversation takes place. Postwar America is a continuity of digital migration of the most remote reflections. This is the enigma by which Obama will secure reelection. It is based upon means of a synthetic authentication through accessing a human based temporality we are quickly losing touch with. This will not secure us from a governance already taking position, the new governance Benjamin proposed is by "spectrum analysis."[12] This mnemonic shift would drive death from language and throw it about the mediated world. It would, in effect, have to be supposed before imagined. Is this best addressed by whatever we are calling post-human? Is it merely an excrescence of writing that demands a more efficacious recovery? Would mourning for authentic language finally been overcome or does this post-human merely obscure it? Only a new art and poetry could emerge as a way to articulate it.[13]

---

10 In "The Storyteller," Benjamin assigns this to anyone, including the "wretch," where after death was swept from view presaging the asylum mentality of the disciplinary society. See "The Storyteller: Observations on the Works of Nicolai Leskov," in *Selected Writings* 3, 1935–1938 (Cambridge/London: The Belknap Press of the University of Harvard Press, 2002).
11 In fact one may begin the conversation of imagination as body forming rather than bodies forming imagination.
12 Benjamin's concept of material theology as he articulates it in the "Paralipomena to 'On the Concept of History,'" in *Selected Writings* 4, 1938–1940 (Cambridge/London: The Belknap Press of the University of Harvard Press, 2006).
13 I reject the narratives of non-anthropocentric thinking. Any thinking is only human thinking even if by proxy.

Legibility in the Age of Sustained Beings:
Thoughts on a Post-Human Militancy

Today it seems language is completely packaged on a level of thought-utterance. Recovering the dignity and nature of authentic speaking, or dare I say "organic" voice, is a move toward the smashing of historical determination. From the inside-out language seems ripped apart from being, and conversely, from the outside-in death is inhaled through endless objects of commodified life. Aisle after aisle of produced thinking we ceaselessly inhabit a neo-bourgeois ideology of moderation. Profane thinkers of the day have yet to turn to novel tactics that are sustaining fronts of resistance. How does one address something that we cannot even see? Paradoxically this ends in the destruction of the imagining body if the aim of any determinative machine would truly want anything at all. But what it really hints at is the reflection of a real body more available than we think. If Benjaminian shock served as a positioning agent for the "sustainability" regime we have now entered, would we not benefit from seriously engaging a project of esthetic rebellion, for the body revealed in global positioning? If we inherited shock from the long term incubation with the technology of writing we should have access to its claim on imagination. That would need to be tempered by the fact that writing has begun a type of disappearance. In the sense of its general "legibility" the essence of writing could be what powers the affect of canonized authenticity.[14] If the ancient human today dissolves in the wake of the shock and awe by a disappearing writing, its own natural propellant (voice and the mystery of nature) would obtain an appearance. Would this new phenomenon have already begun a decline?

Discourse for constructing communities would be one recovered through media that attempts to claim synthetic reason from thought. Discourse is therefore not directly from bodies in a sense of transmission which would handle any effective construction of synthetic reason or moderation, say Burkean calculation or post-Humean passion. Though clearly an issue of the posthumous it is in this death-notion that we surrender to our leaders appearing in devices. Whatever resembles of our own dead-death is obscured by vanity. Vanity obscures scintillas of truth in media devices via storytellers by the essence of death itself. No matter what political or ideological identity, language is the device and perhaps the apparatuses of media in general. Powered by the force of death, our death, everyone's dead-death, language is no longer a footnote for philosophical pause: it powers what appears now as political inanity. Imagination is in some sense legible, somewhere, somehow actually represented.

......
14 Benjamin's notebook N, entitled "On the Theory of Knowledge, Theory of Progress" from the *Arcades Project*, trans. Howard Eiland and Kevin McLaughlin (Cambridge/London: The Belknap Press of the University of Harvard Press, 1999) as well as "On the Concept of History," in *Selected Writings* 4, 1938–1940 (Cambridge/London: The Belknap Press of the University of Harvard Press, 2006) attempt to find ways in which historical continuity may be disrupted, either by colliding with this historical penitentiary or by the realization of our suspension in its directional domination of perception.

Does object-oriented philosophy promise to solve this problem through dejected curiosities, or veiled desubjectification? Thinking the claim on imagination would be the only way to confront the attempt to destroy public and civic governance. Yet this is a problem of immanence or waiting. God is a crisis of imagination incredibly difficult to conceive in the self-conceptualization we have today. It would depend upon those entrepreneurs savvy enough to create a type of space to accommodate radical language in an already fully exhibited human body. The affirmative and immediate truth we ignore today, or simply cannot stabilize any further. We stand at a paradoxical crux.[15] I would open a debate about the esthetics of object-oriented philosophy as a proper place for the remnants of capitalist thought, if we are still thinking on terms of commodities. Dead-death is the ripping of imagination from the body and reselling in what is called "wise counsel" from the likes of a used car politician. This has never been the express goal of commodification, yet is the result of late capitalism.

Any new image of language presents a substantiation or claim on our "post-human" future and what type of politics it would produce. Does it appear in the ironic phrase of "Hope," is it something intimate about our conditions with media? Are we in some sense entering a vast hopelessness but at the same time challenged not to fall victim to narratives of salvation? The human's lingering ideal of having a "post" in society finds a possible irony as a type of Loughnerian grammar (the invisibility of constructing reason[16]) and is linked to this pervasive loss or mourning. Indeed we may have fewer positions in society today. Conversely is not having a "post" the militant imperative of liberal democratic thought and its utopian undercurrents? What we have is equality through opposition and war. What was an inner contradiction in the promise of a welfare state was actually a warfare status of privileging groups or individuals in a larger manifestation or correcting apparatus of natural laws. By abusing "diversity," what was concealed were the nefarious elements of economic sciences and the invisible mastery of divisiveness, one that appears internally, as we see in contemporary politics, the most unnatural nature.

This human positioning in liberal democracy is utterly collapsing. Authentic exchanges, friendship, and mutual care for creative destruction and construction are not nourished long on denatured excrement. Our post in contemporary society is thus messianic. The recycling of thinking has an end in itself, this is an end we must overcome. Our uncanny boot camp of psychosis will always obscure the locus of creative acts, that is, where reason or craft enters into the actual by way of reflection. That we all have a "Call of Duty" means the placement of the game controller in the hands of a biped is a direction that ends in the point-of-view. And the space between them

---

15 I refer to Judith Balso's most current work on poetry and ontology whereby an astounding concept of subjectivity introduces a novel conceptualization of history. See *Hölderlin, Mandelstam* (The Hague/Tirana: Uitgeverij, 2012 [forthcoming]).

16 See Justine Sharrock, "Explained: Jared Loughner's Grammar Obsession," *Mother Jones* (Jan. 11, 2011): http://motherjones.com/politics/2011/01/sovereign-citizens-jared-lee-loughner.

presents an opportunity to move this *orienting* post. As for the word "orient," the proverbial East is the last place the West appearing as Western.

Who or what is godlike today has a point of view that projects a world, that is what replaces orientation is the capacity to observe this schematic. First, one could destabilize the ordering of imagination itself by way of the individual imagination. This is our first "profanity."[17] Second, the imagination and the created world are thus voyages into the logic of an image and not the radical productivity of imagination alone. Their integration, or transmogrifying capacity, lends to our need to learn to read what is writing today in our imaginative bodies, that is, to read experience and navigate the punctual claim, its eidetic variations of our own movement in the world. To stop this novel illiteracy of sense from falling into a politicians image of counsel one would have to recognize that any game console is not a true voyage without deference for reading "outside the box." (Here is where object-oriented philosophies may offer thoughts on grammar.) As it relates to its interiority, it, the post-human, must consider both until it is once again human. This is the only conservative position left in the world of thought? Would this describe our musing about a post-ing, positing, or depositing – the punctual orientation of biology? For imagination available to each biological life is an imaginative "access" to their post or point in the world. This posting is what their real point of view could become as the perishing of this point of view; as an interior window to being. Every human has, in the military anyway, a "post." And the post of Sarah Palin among other inane creatures is a twisted language which has no regard for poetic care.

The suppositions we operate on still concern on the imperatives of an "informed citizenry," that is, their entire index of thoughts and thinking as a public property. The idealistic requisite for voting in a representative democracy is precisely what I mean by electro-mechanical profanity now relegated to wet dream in the anti-humid reality of a computer. We are wise therefore to rethink the famous and certainly defunct "Canons of Journalism." The modernist scientific answer of stabilizing information was to have its site in the bodies of thinking human beings. That is, the object of information and the newspaper itself were the plane by which one could reason effectively if they would just learn how to read them correctly. We have long since entered that phase, a time of readers and writers that we now no longer understand as separate elements. This was observed by Benjamin, that the vanity and egoistic desire of readers to be writers was often abused by editors. This is in no case diminished today, that is, "users" have constant reflection in the devices in hand and hackers find themselves committing the errorism of a Flusserian "functionary."

---

17 I refer expressly to Giorgio Agamben's concept of returning to the public by way of profanity from what was sacred. Yet returning to the public also contributes to the contemporary culture of exhibition and therefore has nothing to do with private dignity. See *What is an Apparatus?*, trans. David Kishik and Stephan Pedatella (Stanford: Stanford University Press, 2009).

Perspective, that is, a point-of-view, is the habitation of the object of the paper by imagination, this is only sped up by way of the user comments. More precisely a migration of thinking-bios into information. The newspaper is now a motherboard, everybody reads them and no body understands them, the goal is to standardize the movement of bios. Science, in particular what is called "social science" does not determine democracy as we opined earlier. This cynical attitude toward participatory democracy is a cornerstone of a more accurate and forgotten conservative skepticism of "liberalism." Thus liberalism fosters the correct conditions of warfare in order to gain access to imagination, and if democracy (the want of grammar) demands discursive freedom, we are far from that today. Conservatives today are merely liberal radicals who intentionally or not use information science to further manipulate every biotic form bleeding being into a corrective system of illegible grammar, that is the way to stabilize the orthodoxy of their followers, return the uncared death of language into the image of their regime.

What is the point-of-viewing humans like that? The point-of-view, or the point-of-viewing has in some sense left us with a type of novel mourning. What is post-human is thus still human, a matter of access to positions of every moment of legible and illegible verbiage (the essence of language). We have to determine an increase in legibility that fits a criterion of dignity and privation. One can stop speeding up to outsmart the calculative and programmatic nature of civil machinery and thus find ways to ethically engage ordering. Timing is thus the answer to impossible speed, at least in boxing. This imperative emerges in political want today, as in America and across the world the hard rightward migration toward national origin is based on the loss of a relationship to language and thus aims at destroying what it believes are results of a "big government." The speed that has desubjectified the hobbits and ancient Vikings of a Tea Partying America are equally astounding, yet they too will undergo a perishing of becoming. The masticatory capacity of necrotic capitalism today is a type of political mourning for the a reasonable discourse obscured in essence. But the answer is not by incarnating politicians as storytellers, or creating fictive worlds whereby our narrators emerge in actual certainty versus a general schematic of reality, these are things we merely attend to as objects and essences.

The Negative Kingdom of Sound Being

It was the cultic and exhibitive dialectic that Benjamin thought in consideration of fascism and technology that excavated language, removing its production of wisdom for the finite subject into the device and returning it as something promising actual, infinite capacity. The weigh station remains the human body yet a body that has lost it capacity to handle the radical being concealed in language itself due to the technologicalization of metaphysical thought. If ana-logism or analog life characterized the annihilative expression of "world war" via media and its acceleration into images, what was underwritten was the capacity of seeing.[18] Shock via media has left the body in a missionary-messianic position that indicates this lack of seeing as the site of almost every political utterance guided by the synthetic narrators of false histories. Iterated earlier, the ideological imperative of sustainability solidifies what appears as the imperatives of smart technology: a novel ground of human imagination and the mastery of the ineffable capacity we are no longer able to tacitly handle. Therefore Reagan's post-humous appearances designate the ethics of optical thought as an ethics most inhumane. Reflected in the rise of Obama, the 2004 Republican Presidential Convention was only one site that is not fully consequential of what has since emerged as disquieting behavior exampled by "conservative" politicians and media despots. The emergence of cultic lunacy is built upon the incredible exploitation of language and being. We cannot fully account for these figures who seemingly occupy the fringes of imaginative thought through an inversion of bodily force into a nearly immaculate conception of the signification of wise counsel, that is, they emerge as our modern version of an effective storyteller capable of facilitating what was lost from real conversation and community: creative embellishments (not unlike Leskov for whom Benjamin attributed in some sense of praise).

There is a bit of countermovement that may have an optimistic tenor. Our own recovery of being forces the question of how we recognize a return to being. If we have lost our collective vision, it may be that we have only realized sight has nothing to do with appearances. This first theoretical step would address the ethical need erupting in not only our continuous digital migration, but the colonization of language by media and its claim on being. If our time is not engaged toward the preservation of biological thinking supposing the incredibly elusive element of human experience, it is at the same time an indifference oriented toward the utter destruction of human systems whereby a chaotic outcome would express a negative fecundity unseen, but one we conversely have some type of access to. Would this shift first appear in imagination itself or merely as another testing? Have we truly divorced ourselves from language by the pent-up desire to escape the fact of finitude that has only resulted in near-death testimonies and theosophical doctrines?

---

18 Literary scholar Laurence Rickels identifies this as "not-see," hence "Nazi." See *Nazi Psychoanalysis 1: Only Psychoanalysis Won the War* (Minneapolis: University of Minnesota Press, 2002).

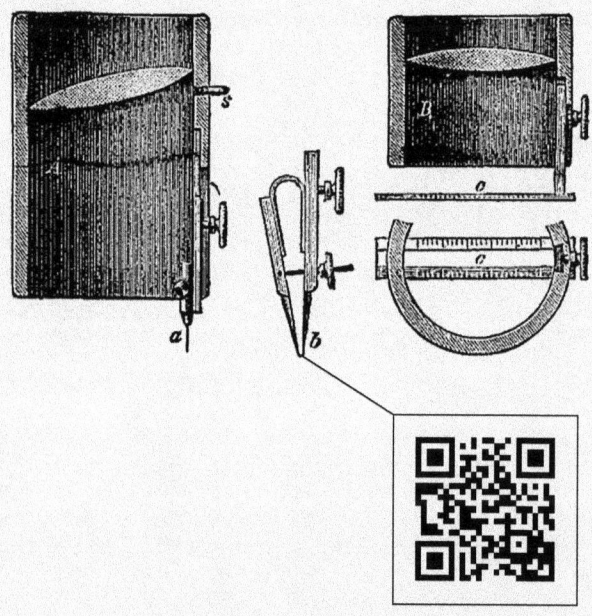

Anders Breivik:
On Copying the Obscure

Vincent W.J. van Gerven Oei

> "This was the moment in any case when 'man,' getting a political pounding, was up against the philosophical wall and steadily losing ground." – Avital Ronell[1]

In the aftermath of the lethal shooting of politically organizing left-wing students and the bombing of Oslo's political center by the Norwegian Anders Breivik, there has been much discussion about the rationale behind his actions in a general sense, and, more specifically, the implications and explications of right-wing, nationalist, racist language which is considerably common in several European nations. In many forum threads and blog posts, analyses are given of Breivik's actions in relation to the current political climate in these environs, which, truth be told, is of an extremely poisonous nature. Ample reflection is given on the 1500+ page manifesto distributed by Breivik, entitled *2083: A European Declaration of Independence; De Laude Novae Militiae Pauperes Commilitones Christi Templique Solomonici*, which appears to have been finished the day before he committed his crimes. This essay aims not so much for a clarification of the content of this manifesto, but attempts to provide a cartography of its rhetorical procedures, hoping to deconstruct some of the discourse that Breivik has managed to create around himself, both before and after his act. It first of all is an attempt to read Breivik as copycat, borrowing left and right, against unstable credit limits and with uncertain debt ceilings, assembling his ideological trust fund from sources as divergent as the Columbine Massacre, American conservative politics, eugenics, post-Luddite ideology, and freemasonry.

The title of his manifesto already gives us the first clues. First, the main title, *2083*, a "prophetic" year,[2] is in its form a clear reference to the apoca-

---

1   Avital Ronell, "The Deviant Payback: The Aims of Valerie Solanas," in Valerie Solanas, *Scum Manifesto* (London/New York: Verso, 2004), 1.
2   Andrew Berwick, [Anders Breivik], *2083: A European Declaration of Independence; De Laude Novae Militiae Pauperes Commilitones Christi Templique Solomonici* (London, 2011), 1098. http://www.liveleak.com/view?i=89a_1311444384. Subsequent references between parentheses.

lyptic overtones related to the year 2012 as promulgated in popular culture. A date is a mark of finitude, of a certain inscription in the regime of time. As for the additional connotations of this year me may refer to the Battle of Vienna, which took place on 11 and 12 September 1683, which according to Breivik or any of his presumed sources "broke the advance of the Ottoman Empire into Europe." In 2083, a similar defeat of Islam might take place, if we would implement the suggestions put forward in his manifesto.

> We must rise and claim what is rightfully ours! By September 11th, 2083, the third wave of Jihad will have been repelled and the cultural Marxist/multiculturalist hegemony in Western Europe will be shattered and lying in ruin, exactly 400 years after we won the battle of Vienna on September 11th, 1683. Europe will once again be governed by patriots. (1412-3)

The first subtitle "A European Declaration of Independence" is copied from a blog post by a writer operating under the pseudonym Fjordman with the same title, and integrally copied in Breivik's manuscript (717–23).[3] The second, Latin subtitle can be translated as "In Praise of the New Knighthood, the poor fellow-soldiers of Christ and of the Temple Solomon" (812; 1335), founded in London, 2002 (832). The first part is taken from a title of text written by Bernard de Clairvaux between 1128 and 1146, entitled *Liber ad milites Templi: De laude novae militiae* (A Book for the Knights Templar: In Praise of the New Knighthood), the second part *Pauperes Commilitones Christi Templique Solomonici*, also abbreviated with PCCTS, was according to Breivik the official name of a Christian military order founded in 1119 also known as the Knights Templar (812). The two Latin parts however do not match grammatically. In his manifesto, Breivik referred to himself as "Justiciar Knight Commander for Knights Templar Europe and one of the several leaders of the National and pan-European Patriotic Resistance Movement" (9). It is unclear to what extent the "Knights Templar Europe" organization actually exists. Chapter 3, "A Declaration of Pre-emptive War," Breivik refers to the "PCCTS, Knights Templar" as a "hypothetical fictional group" (766). As such, the manifesto's title already indicates the variety of sources mined by Breivik and the effects of their juxtaposition: apocalyptic movies, historical narratives and their return, Islamophobia, and Crusader fictions, placed next to each so as to generate the occasional grammatical mismatch.

It has been argued that in comparison to the texts and manifestos written by Islamist Jihadi, Breivik's writings have received too much attention. In other words, there would be a certain, perhaps orientalistically motivated, disproportion in our appreciation of his acts. This may moreover, and in a more general sense, be signaled by the troubled relation of the Western

---

3   The blog entry can also be found on the *Jihad Watch* blog: http://www.islam-watch.org/Fjordman/European-Declaration-Independence.htm. After the Breivik's attacks Jensen claimed never to write again under the Fjordman pseudonym (Jonas Skybakmoen, "Fjordman avviser nye blogg-rykter," *Aftenposten*, August 12, 2011).

media with the word "terrorist," which somehow doesn't seem to stick to Breivik's white-skinned body. Although the accusation of hypocrisy is not entirely unjustified, I think that, if we would provisorily conclude that "terrorism" has become a common shorthand for "terrorism committed by what we perceive as the Muslim other," the source of the slippery nature of Breivik's signifier is that his discourse closely resemble the discourse of the Western media, matching its translational and transpositional skills with an equal disregard for a sense of unity, even though his actions seem to suggest otherwise. Breivik's manifesto provides us with an indication of his "already having failed." Even though I do not deny that a close reading of Jihadi calls and manifestos is of great importance,[4] such reading would have to rely on an intricate knowledge of the context in which they are produced. Instead, by providing one of many possibly productive readings of Breivik's manifesto, I hope to incite others to the same with any call to arms that may resound on this planet.

At the same time I will attempt to relate 2083 to the long history of manifestos reaching from the The Foundation and Manifesto of Futurism, Valerie Solanas's *Scum Manifesto*, Theodore Kaczynski's *Industrial Society and Its Future*, also known as the *Unabomber Manifesto*, and high school shooter manifestos. However, whereas all the above appeal, to certain extent, to originality and authenticity – in fact, the writing of a manifesto seems in all these cases to be expression of a drive toward uniqueness – Breivik's manifesto has no such pretenses, he writes: "I have written approximately half of the compendium myself. The rest is a compilation of works from several courageous individuals throughout the world" (5). However, counting the many unattributed passages, the balance might even more drastically toward the side of the "courageous individuals."

We will take our cues first clues from Valerie Solanas's *Scum Manifesto*, which will have provided one of the most apt descriptions of what we will find to constitute the rhetorical procedure of displacement of Breivik's text, and in general, the so-called debate on Islam as currently articulated in "The West": "The male 'rebel is a farce; this is the male's 'society,' made by him to satisfy his needs. He's never satisfied, because he's not capable of being satisfied. Ultimately, what the male 'rebel' is rebelling against is being male."[5]

---

4   Not only because at several points Breivik refers to or praises Muslim Jihadi organizations for the discipline and faith in their cause.

5   Valerie Solanas, *Scum Manifesto* (London/New York: Verso, 2004), 55. There are many other overlaps between Solanas and Breivik. For example, both had literary aspirations (cf. Ronell, "Deviant Payback," 2). In his "Legal Disclaimer" prefacing the third chapter of his manifesto, Breivik states his intention to "create a new type of innovative writing style. By defining, in a horrifically detailed way, a fictional scenario, the reader will be shocked due to the 'hopefully' credible and extremely detailed elaborations. It should be noted that the author, as a sci-fi enthusiast, wanted to bring and create a complete new writing style that has the potential to shock the reader with an incredibly credible fictional plot (written in first, second and third person narrative). [...] This book is therefore unique in many ways. It is speculated that this type of original approach has the potential to forward and present information in a new and original context. It is therefore no need for concern by any police/state/government prosecutors or intelligence agencies about the content of this book due to its fictional nature. This legal disclaimer was created to remove any doubt whatsoever that the author or anyone chosing [sic] to distribute the book '2083' has any hostile motives or

Breivik did so on many levels, both physical and textual. The steroids that he continued to use until the moment of the massacre,[6] and the muscled-up discourse that "documents through more than 1000 pages that the fear of Islamisation is all but irrational" (4). Just as he tried to "acquire specialized 'aggressiveness' pills on the market" (1464), he acquired his verbal force buy assimilating rhetorical ammo of others. If we may again recall the high school shooters, many of whom used computer games to train themselves for their shooting sprees and to a smaller or larger extent immersed themselves in these environments, we could point at the fact that Breivik consistently used female characters.

> I took a year off when I was 25 and played WoW PvE hardcore for a year. Conservatism – Alliance, human female mage – PvE, Server: Silvermoon Conservative – Horde, tauren female resto druid – PvP, Server: Silvermoon (1408)

In his diary entry of October/November 2010, when he is in seclusion preparing for his actions, he writes: "I'm also going to try the new World of Warcraft – Cataclysm when it is released in December. Time to dust of my mage…" (1424), the mage being a "human female." At the beginning of "the most critical of phases," the "chemical acquirement phase" for the explosives, he writes:

> My concerns and angst relating to this phase impacted my motivation, to a point where I had to initiate specific counter-measures to reverse the loss of morale and motivation. I decided that the correct approach to reversing it was to initiate another DBOL steroid cycle and intensify my strength training. […] In addition; I decided I would allow myself to play the newly launched expansion: World of Warcraft – Cataclysm. (1425)

His steroid use to become more masculine is thus clearly supplemented – "In addition;" – with a female impersonation. This exile to the virtual, as was already suggested by Guy Debord when he stated that "[t]he spectacle is […] a technological version of the exiling of human powers in a 'world beyond'

..... intentions. If any legal authority have reservations against this new and innovative form of writing style, they may address or contact the author, any publisher or distributor and share their concerns which will be taken under consideration. Changes will be considered and implemented. As such, the content in its current form will not incriminate anyone, the author or any distributor" (767–8).

6 As can be inferred from for example the following passage: "I can't possibly imagine how my state of mind will be during the time of the operation, though. It will be during a steroid cycle and on top of that; during an ephedrine rush, which will increase my aggressiveness, physical performance and mental focus with at least 50–60% but possibly up to 100%. In addition, I will put my iPod on max volume as a tool to suppress fear if needed. I might just put Lux Aeterna by Clint Mansell on repeat as it is an incredibly powerful song. The combination of these factors (when added on top of intense training, simulation, superior armour and weaponry) basically turns you into an extremely focused and deadly force, a one-man-army" (1344).

– and the perfection of separation *within* human beings,"[7] will however not be sufficient, or, is perhaps already too much. Whereas Ronell argues in her introduction that Solanas, "[w]hen she couldn't distribute her work, [...] went after the metonymies of her declared targets,"[8] we will find that Breivik couldn't distribute his work in the "world beyond," and mainly had to go after his own signifier. His name "Anders" *signifies* the "other," that is, the other sex: the "Brei-vik," the broad cove, bay, or inlet, the welcoming womb. The contrast with Solanas is therefore one of double negation. Whereas Solanas aimed to destroy the aggressive male figure metonymized by Andy (*anthropos*[9]) War-hol, Anders – and here we may obviously read a slippage from Andy to Anders[10] – Breivik goes after himself, cloaked as a female mage or druid, armed with the powers of transfiguration. It is my intention to show how this is not only visible in the content of Breivik's manifesto, but also in the very style in which he wrote it. In other – yes, other – words, his signifier spilt over in his language.

On the surface, Breivik's actions resemble the shooting sprees as perpetrated by what Jonas Staal and I called the high school shooter movement, which comprised, among others, Eric Harris and Dylan Klebold (Columbine High School, 1999), Cho Seung-Hui (Virgina Tech, 2007), Pekka-Eric Auvinen (Jokela High School, 2007) and Matti Juhani Saari (Seinäjoki University, 2008). In all these cases, high school or college students killed a number of their fellow students and teachers before committing suicide. Every single one of them left manifestos, poems, texts, videos, photographs contextualizing their actions and rendering them fully *their own*. In the text "Follow Us or Die" which accompanied an anthology of their works headed under the same title, we suggested that they "typified the youthful resistance of bodies without a place in a global capitalistic society, and, in the style of this same society, only saw annihilation and self-destruction as possibilities, expressing themselves in *home videos*, which hardly differ in their rhetoric from those of the militant resistance group al-Qa'ida."[11]

All texts and manifestos written by the high school shooters express an existential dilemma: how to perform an act which is fully my own? What is an authentic act? Their violent conclusion must necessarily be self-annihilating, as is becoming once again clear in the aftermath of Breivik's actions, the context created in the aftermath of such traumatic events spins quickly out of control. As Pekka-Eric Auvinen writes in his "Natural Selector's Manifesto": "And remember that this is my war, my ideas, and my plans. Don't blame anyone else for my actions than myself. Don't blame my parents or my friends. I told nobody about my plans and I always kept them inside my

---

7   Guy Debord, *The Society of the Spectacle*, trans. Donald Nicholson-Smith (New York: Zone Books, 1995),18.
8   Ronell, "Deviant Payback," 2.
9   Cf. ibid., 24.
10 We also note that the English pseudonym under which he wrote his manifesto was *Andrew* Berwick.
11 Vincent W.J. van Gerven Oei, ed. *Follow Us or Die: Works from the High School Shooters Selected by Vincent W.J. van Gerven Oei and Jonas Staal* (New York/Dresden: Atropos Press, 2009), 5.

mind only. Don't blame the movies I see, the music I hear, the games I play or the books I read. No, they had nothing to do with this."[12] This type of rhetoric, however, is fully absent in Breivik's manifesto.

On two other points Breivik's case diverges considerably from the high school shooters' one. First of all, he didn't commit suicide – much too everyone's surprise. In fact, the media happily relate how he is willing to testify and thus recruit more crusaders in his war against the Islamization of Europe – in uniform, or red Lacoste sweater.[13] He considers the courtroom to be a stage to perform his persona as a "hero of Europe" (1435).[14] Moreover, contrary to the high school shooters, Breivik doesn't seem to aim for an authentic, singular act. Instead, he considers his act only to be the beginning of a pan-European resistance movement against Islam. It is precisely this aspect that strikes anyone who reads *2083*. The text is a bricolage of blog posts, other manifestos, diaries, manuals, statistics, and news coverage.

According to Breivik, "The compendium/book presents advanced ideological, practical, tactical, organisational and rhetorical solutions and strategies for all patriotic-minded individuals/movements" (4). It is mainly on the "rhetorical solutions and strategies" that I would like to focus in the present essay, as the other topic seem already to have been covered, though certainly not exhaustively, by the ongoing stream of analyses both on- and offline. In order to bring these solutions and strategies to light, I suggest an approach to the core of his argument concerning his "target": "Multiculturalism (cultural Marxism/political correctness) […] is the root cause of the ongoing Islamisation of Europe which has resulted in the ongoing Islamic colonisation of Europe through demographic warfare (facilitated by our own leaders)" (9).

It is an impossible task to provide a reading of over 1500 pages of textual bricolage within the space that is alloted to the average review paper. Therefore I will focus in Breivik's presentation on precisely the two terms that constitute his conception of "multiculturalism," that is, "political correctness" and "cultural Marxism."[15] The pages introducing the concept of political correctness have been copied in their entirety from William S. Lind's online publication *"Political Correctness:" A Short History of an Ideology*, without Breivik mentioning him anywhere in his text.[16] However, he

---

12 Van Gerven Oei, *Follow Us or Die*, 14.
13 His favorite clothing brand (1406).
14 He states so explicitly: "A trial is an excellent opportunity and a well suited arena the Justiciar Knight can use to publicly renounce the authority of the EUSSR/USASSR hegemony and the specific cultural Marxist/multiculturalist regime. […] The accused should use this opportunity to present all available documentation, illustrations and proof included in this compendium (*2083 – A European Declaration of Independence*) to claim his innocence. […] Furthermore, he must demand that that the national parliament immediately transfers all political powers to this newly established tribunal/cabinet" (1103). Indeed Breivik demanded, among other things, that the Norwegian cabinet resign in exchange for a full confession.
15 Breivik defines the concept of multiculturalism as follows: "Multiculturalism (cultural Marxism/political correctness), as you might know, is the root cause of the ongoing Islamisation of Europe which has resulted in the ongoing Islamic colonisation of Europe through demographic warfare (facilitated by our own leaders)" (9).
16 Except for in an unrelated section on fourth generation warfare (1480).

has made several alterations which allow us to read how he interpreted the texts he copied form his online sources. Amendment, supplementation, and deletion are the textual maneuvers that give us insight into Breivik's own theoretical framework; a framework that, as we will see, provides above all the exact textual equivalent of everything he is agitating against. Whereas the high school shooters attempted to contextualize a single authentic act at the cost withdrawing themselves (by means of suicide) from any mediated context, Breivik attempts to universalize his act of resistance by building on rhetorical tactics and strategies that are associated with "his enemy": iteration, duplication, erasure, taking out of context, and reading "too much."

The entire text of *2083* is marked by displacement. Breivik consistently alters the topographical markers of every text he quotes in order to fit them into his context, the context of the European crusade against Islam. Not all of his source material might prove to be resistant to such a treatment. Already in the introduction and first chapter of Lind's book as quoted by Breivik we can discern a systematic suppression of authorship (for example, he deletes the opening phrase "As Russel Kirk wrote," and immediately starts with "One of conservatism's most important insights is that all ideologies are wrong"), and replacement of the continent "America" by "Europe," or sometimes, "EUSSR." For example, the opening sentence of Lind's first chapter is as follows: "Most Americans look back on the 1950s as a good time." Breivik alter this into "Most Europeans look back on the 1950s as a good time."

However, the subsequent paragraphs clearly show the friction caused by this topographical shift. Not only in discordant phrase like "If a man of the 1950s were suddenly introduced in Western Europe in the 2000s, he would hardly recognise it as the same country [*sic*]" (12). Also the picture of "Western Europe" in 1950s that is sketched out in the paragraphs that follow carries little resemblance with the post-war austerity of Western European life: "In the office, the man might light up a cigarette, drop a reference to the 'little lady,' and say he was happy to see the firm employing some coloured folks in important positions" (12). Even the search/replace of American by British English orthography cannot the mask the New York office atmosphere of a "Madmen"-esque scene. In fact, this friction between European and American contexts is anticipated by Breivik himself when he states that "the fundamental factors vary too much" and "What works in the US [...] will not work here" (1365). That it will not work will become clear below.

At first glance, there seems to be no apparent reason for Breivik to relocate a conservative analysis of contemporary American society to Western Europe. However, he has to do so in order to make the introduction of "political correctness" and "cultural Marxism" relevant for a European audience. They would otherwise remain strictly within the realm of American cultural politics: "The ideology that has taken over Western Europe goes most commonly by the name of 'Political Correctness.' [...] Political Correctness in face cultural Marxism (Cultural Communism) – Marxism translated from economic into cultural terms" (12–3). Could it be that the alleged translational drive of Marxism, after having infected the economical body spreading the cultural one, has spilt over in Breivik's discourse, announcing a torrent of translations and transpositions bridging the transcontinental divide?[17]

Breivik's own relations with one of the main lairs of political correctness as an expression of cultural Marxism is without a doubt the practice of deconstruction, to which I already referred briefly above, not in the last place by accommodating two authors that could be placed, if they wouldn't resist, in a deconstructive "canon." According to Lind, deconstruction, together with critical theory, occupies the mediating position between the discourses of Marx and Freud on one side, and the regime of political correctness on the other. "Deconstruction 'proves' that any 'text,' past or present, illustrates the oppression of Muslims, women, homosexuals, etc. by reading that meaning into words of the texts (regardless of their actual meaning)" (13). For Breivik, deconstruction is a cultural force, threatening the "nuclear family" (1208), "European ethnic groups" (1157), the "European Church" (1220), "culture, traditions, norms and moral" (1209), in other words "everything we hold dear" (942). He urges the "patriotic/cultural conservative youth" to "Stop the deconstruction of Christianity" and "the European Cultural Genocide and the deconstruction of European identity" (1240). Any militia or paramilitary group – "MAKE ONE!" – "must ensure that it follows all laws to avoid persecution and deconstruction efforts by the government" (1282).

But Breivik becomes more technical in his approach toward the deconstructive forces threatening Europe. The section "Political Correctness: Deconstruction and Literature" is nearly fully copied from the fourth chapter (with the same title) from Lind's *"Political Correctness."* The chapter offers an overview of the history of deconstruction and its reception in America, but what interests us here, again, are the erasures and supplements provided by Breivik in his manifesto, and not any truthfulness that might be implied or implicated. One sentence is highlighted, forming a paragraph on its own, emphasized by the white space of deletion that surrounds it: "The intelligentsia had forgotten its literature in its haste to promote its politics" (28). Let us take our cue from Breivik and continue to another section in which we will attempt to recall our background in terrorist literature, or, as Ronell would put it, "killer texts," suppressing the politics that we would have liked to promote nonetheless.

The section I would like to consider, "The psychology of cultural Marxists," is nearly entirely copied and amended from Theodore Kaczynski's *Unabomber Manifesto*. As in the case of Lind, Kaczynski's name is nowhere to be found and the text remains signed by default, by Breivik. But whereas the stealth of the Unabomber's attacks allowed him to hide in the woods for

---

17 Such shifts of the signifier are a common trait of the current European discourse on multiculturalism and the influence of Islam in the West. For example, the Dutch extreme right ideologue Martin Bosma consistently writes "(national) socialism" when referring to Hitler's ideology, thus pasting fascism onto Marxism.

over twenty years, Breivik's cover was supposed to be blown upon his first attack. His regime of invisibility and untraceability painstakingly describe in the many pages of his diary appended to his manifesto served only to maximally expose himself. And although, again, superficially, there are many relations between Kaczynski's and Breivik's tactics, the aims differ widely.

Whereas Kaczynski was aiming against a certain economical-industrial-technological acceleration of society and had no immediate political aims,[18] Breivik's aim is to overthrow the perceived cultural hegemony of cultural Marxism and the system of political correctiveness – or should we say political correction – that sustains it. And whereas Kaczynski wrote his "psychological analysis" of leftism[19] in order to sketch the general outlines of modern society and its general psyche, Breivik appropriates the same passages as a depiction of a very precise "enemy": the "cultural Marxist." Let us start at the beginning of his extensive citation[20]:

> 6. Almost everyone will agree that we live in a deeply troubled society. One of the most widespread manifestations of the craziness of our world is leftism, so a discussion of the psychology of leftism can serve as an introduction to the discussion of the problems of modern society in general. [§6]

> 6. Almost everyone will agree that we live in a deeply troubled society. One of the most widespread manifestations of the craziness of our world is **multiculturalism**, so a discussion of the psychology of **multiculturalists** can serve as an introduction to the discussion of the problems of **Western Europe** in general. (373)

From this paragraph we can already induce a number of textual strategies deployed by Breivik. First, he has erased Kaczynski's paragraph numbers throughout. This already provides us an indication of the fact that contrary to the Unabomber's case, we are not dealing with an organized discourse. We are dealing with a textual bricolage that in its essence rejects the linear order of enumeration.

Second, Breivik again erases the opening sentence: "Almost everyone will agree that we live in a deeply troubled society." For Breivik is not concerned with society as such, in which industrialization and leftism go hand in hand, but rather with a typology of the ones who threaten an essentially pure, homogeneous, white, West-European community: the "multiculturalists." Whereas for Kaczynski profiling leftists is a means, it is an end for Breivik. The translation of Kaczynski's "leftism" to "multiculturalism" is thus a transposition of a general condition of modern society to an external threat

---

18 FC (Freedom Club) [Theodore Kaczynski], *The Unabomber Manifesto: Industrial Society and its Future* (Livermore: WingSpan Press, 2009), 6 [§4].
19 Ibid., 6–11 [§§6–23].
20 In the following citations, the *Unabomber Manifesto* excerpts (with paragraph numbers between square brackets) always precede Breivik's altered citation from it.

to it. According to Breivik, modern society is neither "deeply troubled" nor global. It has a very precise location: "Western Europe." In general Breivik's discourse transposes its origins – through his erasure of the origins, the first sentences of Lind's and Kaczynski's texts – to Europe and again this is marked by a generalized British English orthography. As was the case with his appropriation of Lind's text, the American continent is replaced by the European one:

> Leftists tend to hate anything that has an image of being strong, good and successful. They hate America, they hate Western civilisation, they hate white males, and they hate rationality. [...] Thus it is clear that these faults are not the leftist's real motive for hating America and the West. He hates America and the West because they are strong and successful. [§13]

> **Cultural Marxists** tend to hate anything that has an image of being strong, good and successful. They hate Europe, America, they hate Western civilisation, they hate white males, and they hate rationality. [...] Thus it is clear that these faults are not the leftist's real motive for hating **Europe,** America and the West. He hates ~~America and~~ the West because they are strong and successful. (374)

Third, Breivik literally confuses ideology with ideologue by replacing "leftism" the first time with "multiculturalism" and the second time with "multiculturalists." This again points to another feature of Breivik's actions, namely that he actually acted out his manifesto. As in the case of the high school shooters, there is immediate actualization of his textual drive in reality. The force of this drive can be measured along a chronology proposed by the text itself. On the last day of the diary appended to, or, if you will, included in 2083, Friday July 22, or "Day 82" since he started preparing the explosives for his operation on a remote farm, he writes: "First coming costume party this autumn, dress up as a police officer. Arrive with insignias:-) Will be awesome as people will be very astonished:-)" (1470). In fact, he didn't wait till August, but had his "costume party" on Day 83, perhaps once again driven by his obsession with this particular number.

Whereas regular extreme nationalists in Western Europe time after time stress the difference between Islam as "ideology of hate" and "ordinary" Muslims, Breivik's conflation of multiculturalism with multiculturalists and, by extension, Islamism with Muslims allows him immediately to implement his own action plan and massacre 70+ students. But let us not forget that calling for preemptive strikes or embargoes of any sort will make thousands more suffer and die. The next paragraph introduces the necessary shifts to accommodate Kaczynski's discourse for Lind's terminology that Breivik appropriated earlier.

7. But what is leftism? During the first half of the 20th century leftism could have been practically identified with socialism. Today the movement is fragmented and it is not clear who can properly be called a leftist. When we speak of leftists in this article we have in mind mainly socialists, collectivists, "politically correct" types, feminists, gay and disability activists, animal rights activists, and the like. But not everyone who is associated with one of these movements is a leftist. What we are trying to get at in discussing leftism is not so much a movement or an ideology as a psychological type, or rather a collection of related types. Thus, what we mean by "leftism" will emerge more clearly in the course of our discussion of leftist psychology (Also, see paragraphs 227-230). [§7]

7. But what is **multiculturalism or Cultural Communism?** ~~During the first half of the 20th century leftism could have been practically identified with socialism. Today~~ The movement is fragmented and it is not clear who can properly be called a **cultural Marxist**. When we speak of **cultural Marxists** in this article we have in mind mainly **individuals who support multiculturalism;** socialists, collectivists, "politically correct" types, feminists, gay and disability activists, animal rights activists, **environmentalists** etc. But not everyone who is associated with one of these movements **support multiculturalism**. What we are trying to get at in discussing **cultural Marxists** is not so much a movement or an ideology as a psychological type, or rather a collection of related types. ~~Thus, what we mean by "leftism" will emerge more clearly in the course of our discussion of leftist psychology (Also, see paragraphs 227-230)~~. (373)

The first sentence already introduces, by means of a disjunction, the notion of "Cultural Communism" as being identical to "multiculturalism," together replacing Kaczynski's "leftism." But again this can only happen at the cost of an erasure. Whereas in Kaczynski's §6, Breivik replaced a global perspective with local considerations, this paragraph aims for stasis, not only suppressing the historical aspect of Kaczynski's discourse ("During the first half..." and "Today,"), but also by erasing the discursive arch of the *Unabomber Manifesto* in which a definition of "leftism" would "emerge more clearly" in the last paragraphs.

Something similar is at stake when in the next paragraph, his copy of §8 of Kaczynski's text, where he deletes the sentence "We leave open the question of the extent to which our discussion could be applied to the leftists of the 19th and early 20th century." For Breivik this question is not open at all, and the break enacted by modernity in Kaczynski's analysis, which is often signaled by the adjective "modern" preceding "leftist" or "leftism" is actively repressed. Either "leftist" or "modern leftist" is replaced by the eternal "multiculturalist."

Breivik's next move is to introduce the figure of the enemy at the gates, which he imports from the orientalist discourse that has been haunting

America and Europe alike since 9/11, namely the figure of the Muslim (terrorist), whose only aim is to conquer the West, impose the *shari'a*, and found a new Caliphate. This figure has been productive of an entire vocabulary that if anything expresses his intense influence on certain segments of the occidental mediated subconscious, surfacing in neologisms like *dhimmedia*. Specifically this insertion into Kaczynski's manifesto will prove difficult, as the figures that the Muslim is supposed to replace are by no means the "enemies" in the Unabomber text.

> 13. Many leftists have an intense identification with the problems of groups that have an image of being weak (women), defeated (American Indians), repellent (homosexuals), or otherwise inferior]. The leftists themselves feel that these groups are inferior. They would never admit it to themselves that they have such feelings, but it is precisely because they do see these groups as inferior that they identify with their problems. (We do not suggest that women, Indians, etc., ARE inferior; we are only making a point about leftist psychology). [§13]

> ~~13.~~ Many **cultural Marxists** have an intense identification with the problems of groups that have an image of being weak (women), **"so called" oppressed minorities**, repellent (homosexuals), **and other groups in the "victim hierarchy"**. The **cultural Marxists** themselves feel that these groups are inferior. They would never admit it to themselves that they have such feelings, but it is precisely because they do see these groups as inferior that they identify with their problems. (We do not suggest that women, **Muslims**, etc., ARE inferior; we are only making a point about **cultural Marxist** psychology). (374)

First we encounter the erasure of the typically American figure of the Indian or Native American, who finds himself replaced by "'so called' oppressed minorities." We should be attentive here to the curious placement of the quote marks. Instead of placed around "oppressed minorities," as one would expect from the rest of Breivik's discourse, they are placed on the ironizing speech act itself: "'so called.'" How many quote marks would have been enough? Or is he pointing out the practice of "calling" them oppressed minorities, thus opening the extensive directory of missed calls and broken connections that have not only haunted the many post-terror situations in recent years but has structured much of philosophical and by extension ideological discourse as such? But not only Indians are called off stage, Blacks are next.

> For example, if one believes that affirmative action is good for black people, does it make sense to demand affirmative action in hostile or dogmatic terms? Obviously it would be more productive to take a diplomatic and conciliatory approach that would make at least verbal and

symbolic concessions to white people who think that affirmative action discriminates against them. But leftist activists do not take such an approach because it would not satisfy their emotional needs. Helping black people is not their real goal. Instead, race problems serve as an excuse for them to express their own hostility and frustrated need for power. In doing so they actually harm black people, because the activists' hostile attitude toward the white majority tends to intensify race hatred. [§21]

For example, if one believes that affirmative action is good for **Muslims**, does it make sense to demand affirmative action in hostile or dogmatic terms? Obviously it would be more productive to take a diplomatic and conciliatory approach that would make at least verbal and symbolic concessions to **non-Muslims** who think that affirmative action discriminates against them. But **cultural Marxist** activists do not take such an approach because it would not satisfy their emotional needs. Helping **Muslims** is not their real goal. Instead, **problems related to Islam** serve as an excuse for them to express their own hostility and frustrated need for power. In doing so they actually harm **Muslims**, because the activists' hostile attitude toward the **non-Muslims** tends to intensify **the irritation or hatred**. (375–6)

The replacement of "race problems" with "problems related to Islam" clearly summarizes ideological shift that is taking place in these sections, moving from race to religion. The emphasis on the critique of religion as replacing race has constituted much of the nationalist and anti-Arab rhetoric in the West, which has always defended itself against the "racism" argument by quickly pointing out that Islam is not a "race" but an "ideology." But that we are dealing with the same mechanisms of racial exclusion becomes immediately clear upon inspection of Breivik's adaptation of Kaczynski's text. Breivik's "Muslims" are Kaczynski's "black people" and the former's "non-Muslims" are the latter's "white majority." In spite of much rhetoric against the racism inherent in the "Muslim debate," Breivik's textual tactics, and sometimes even his content,[21] show the contrary.

The final emendation in the paragraph, however, suggest that there is more at stake than a simple replacement. Breivik disposes of Kaczynski's "race hatred," and supplements the gap with "the irritation or hatred." What is this "irritation" that suddenly slips into his discourse? There is no immediately reason for it to appear, neither his own logic nor the text itself

---

21 For example when he meditates his "ideological journey" "from indoctrinated multiculturalist zealot to Conservative Revolutionary": When I first started on this compendium more than three years ago I had already decided to only cover issues relating to Islamisation and mass-Muslim immigration out of the fear of being labeled as a racist. I have always been terrified of the prospect of being labeled as a racist, to such a degree that I have put significant restrictions on myself, not only verbally but concerning all aspects of my social image. And I know this is the case for a majority of Europeans. I would say I have allowed myself to be paralyzed by this fear. I was inclined not to bring up WW2, the relevance of ethnicity or mention the word race at all. Unfortunately for me, I found out through the years of research and study that everything is connected" (761).

necessitate it. It would have been sufficient just to delete "race." The rest of his manifesto gives us little clue about this sudden appearance of an ideological itch. All the other four appearances of the root "irritate" are located in fully quoted blog posts.

Perhaps it is an expression, not so much of a tendency in society to be "irritated" by Muslims on the street or the multicultural ideology that he perceives all around him, but of a textual annoyance; the fact that the Kaczynski text doesn't fully fit his own "Islam-critical" discourse. This textual wardrobe malfunction culminates to the point that Breivik suddenly starts to politically correct anaphors. Whereas Kaczynski throughout his text uses masculine anaphors to refer to any human being in general, Breivik introduces the "he/she" when referring to the cultural Marxist's "inferiority complex":

> The leftist's feelings of inferiority run so deep that he cannot tolerate any classification of some things as successful or superior and other things as failed or inferior. [§18]

> The **cultural Marxist** feelings of inferiority run so deep that **he/she** cannot tolerate any classification of some things as successful or superior and other things as failed or inferior. (375)

This first occurrence is clearly marked, not only because the cultural Marxist is feminized in immediate relation to his/her "inferiority complex," but also because this feminization is ungrammatical. Breivik refers to "The cultural Marxist feelings" and not "The cultural Marxist's feelings" as suggested by Kaczynski's original. In other words the grammaticality of the text starts to break down in Breivik's attempt to feminize and suppress the cultural Marxist. He wouldn't be the first to do so, as it has been common in recent years to call multiculturalism and related ideological viewpoints "soft," or "for pussies," and opposed to the masculine bombast of reawakened national conscience and ethnic identity. But it would be difficult to find an example so minimal in its displacement, yet so clearly manifesting the textual mechanisms at work. Breivik continues.

> The leftist is not typically the kind of person whose feelings of inferiority make him a braggart, an egotist, a bully, a self-promoter, a ruthless competitor. This kind of person has not wholly lost faith in himself. He has a deficit in his sense of power and self-worth, but he can still conceive of himself as having the capacity to be strong, and his efforts to make himself strong produce his unpleasant behavior. [§19]

> The **cultural Marxist** is not typically the kind of person whose feelings of inferiority make **him/her** a braggart, an egotist, a bully, a self-promoter, a ruthless competitor. This kind of person has not wholly lost faith in himself. He has a deficit in his sense of power and self-worth, but he can still

conceive of himself as having the capacity to be strong, and his efforts to make himself strong produce his unpleasant behaviour. (375)

The tactic of feminization is quite precise here. The first replacement – "The cultural Marxist is not typically the kind of person whose feelings of inferiority make him/her a braggart,…" – is not repeated once we are speaking of the "braggart," "bully," or "ruthless competitor." At this point Breivik returns to the masculine "himself" and "he."

> But the leftist is too far gone for that. His feelings of inferiority are so ingrained that he cannot conceive of himself as individually strong and valuable; hence the collectivism of the leftist. He can feel strong only as a member of a large organization or a mass movement with which he identifies himself. [§19]

> But the cultural Marxist is too far gone for that. His feelings of inferiority are so ingrained that he cannot conceive of himself as individually strong and valuable; hence the collectivism of the cultural Marxist. She can feel strong only as a member of a large organisation or a mass movement with which she identifies herself. (375)

In a most literal sense "the cultural Marxist is too far gone for that." The feelings of inferiority he might have as mere "bully," which do not rob him from his masculinity ("he," "himself") have become "so engrained" that they start to behave as a collective. At the introduction of this "collectivism" Breivik rapidly drops the masculine pronoun: "She can feel strong only as a member of a large organisation or a mass movement with which she identifies herself." In the end, the cultural Marxist or multiculturalist, in other words, Breivik's *enemy* is woman, the broad-caved mage. Other interpreters of his manuscript have already pointed at his all too apparent misogyny, and it is not my intention to remain on the level of such statement of the obvious. Misogyny appears not to be an aspect of Breivik's thought, but, as I will argue, one of the main ideological components of the so-called Islam debate.

The signifier "woman" actually allows Breivik to tie back together the various displacements that constitute his text. Let us review them briefly. The key term to the introduction of 2083 is "political correctness," which arrives with a discourse borrowed from the American William Lind. In order to match Lind's discourse with his own, American society is displaced to Europe. Once the American issues of "political correctness" as imposed by "cultural Marxists" have been successfully transplanted into the European context, these can be supplemented by Kaczynski's analysis of "leftism" which is replaced by Lind's "cultural Marxism" or "multiculturalism," which has do be cleaned from any linear logic (paragraph numbers), global perspective (the target is "The West"), and the historical framework of modernity. These displacement should finally furnish the stage for the final *pièce de resistance* of switching race for religion. All of this is done under the auspices of a feminization of the cultural Marxist – the one who has "feminized European males," which allows Breivik to fold Kaczynski back onto Lind, connecting their misogynist subtexts. Woman, and by extension the "Feminist movement" are the bearers of political correctness, or the "feminisation of European culture." (29)

> Perhaps no aspect of Political Correctness is more prominent in American life today than feminist ideology. Is feminism, like the rest of Political Correctness, based on the cultural Marxism imported from Germany in the 1930s? While feminism's history in America certainly extends longer than sixty years, its flowering in recent decades has been interwoven with the unfolding social revolution carried forward by cultural Marxists.[22]

> Perhaps no aspect of Political Correctness is more prominent in **Western European** life today than feminist ideology. Is feminism, like the rest of Political Correctness, based on the cultural Marxism imported from Germany in the 1930s? While feminism's history in **Western Europe** certainly extends longer than sixty years, its flowering in recent decades has been interwoven with the unfolding social revolution carried forward by cultural Marxists. (28)

In this sense, Lind, Kaczynski, nor Breivik escape the condemnation of feminism that was already expressed by the fascistically inclined Futurists, who proclaimed to "glorify war […] militarism, patriotism, the destructive act of the libertarian, beautiful ideas worth dying for, and scorn for women. We wish to destroy museums, libraries, academies of any sort, and fight against moralism, feminism, and every kind of materialistic, self-serving cowardice."[23] Compare this for example with Breivik's §3.153 "Interview with a Justiciar Knight Commander of the PCCTS, Knights Templar," an interview with himself:

> Approximately 70% of European males support our cause while only 30% of European women. As a consequence, when this is all over we must significantly reduce these women's influence on political issues relating to national security, social structures, penal policies, border control, immigration, assimilation, certain cultural issues – national cohesion and procreation (birth) policies. This is perhaps the most important lesson we must learn, the betrayal by so many of our own women. It is not really a betrayal as a majority of our women only thinks and acts in accordance with how nature created them – in a suicidal compassionate manner. But it is essential that we prevent our women from propagating their suicidal compassion in "safe and more controlled environments" in the future.

---

22 Lind, "Political Correctness," n.p.
23 F.T. Marinetti, "The Foundation and Manifesto of Futurism," in *Critical Writings*, trans. Doug Thompson, 11–17 (New York: Farrar, Straus and Giroux, 2006), 14.

Sure, this is sexist policies but nature itself is sexist and you cannot defy primary natural laws.

Whenever obscure revolutions are proclaimed, scorn for the feminine is never far away. Thus we have tentatively determined the signifier "Anders Breivik" that binds together the multiple displacements enacted in his discourse, albeit not without auto-immune reactions of the texts which he cut into, resulting in occasional ungrammaticality and an invading notion of "irritation": another word of the obsession of nationalist, racist, or, if you like, "Islam-critical" discourse with the female Muslim body.[24]

As I suggested above, this properly ideological point emerges not only explicitly in the Breivik's manifesto, but also manifests itself in the way in which the text juxtaposes its signifiers, their collisions, incidents, and the grammatical debris that is the result of it. Even though he admits, by commenting on himself from the perspective of himself fifteen years ago, to will have been captured by conspiracy theories,[25] it seems as if they turn toward him, that his texts, implanted from various strange, external bodies conspire against him and everything he stands for. Breivik's *2083: A European Declaration of Independence; De Laude Novae Militiae Pauperes Commilitones Christi Templique Solomonici* not only exposes itself as complex assemblage of displacements, falling apart at the seams, it also casts in full light on the discourse of the obscure forces in Europe – those who were the first to displace Breivik to the realm of insanity or even the obscurity of Islamic Jihadism. However, their own language, even when in the obscurity of plagiarism, does not fail to emerge in broad, albeit fragmented, daylight.

---

24 This tendency has already been explicitly established by for example Alain Badiou. In his sardonic essay "Behind the Scarfed Law, There is Fear," he points to the fact that "everyone" can rally behind such an easily obtainable victory against the spreading of Islam. A first step, so to say, in Breivik's plan to deport all Muslims from Europe. (See §2.104 of Breivik's manifesto: "Future deportation of Muslims from Europe" [753].) The control that the French state, as Badiou puts it, intends to exert over the female body by imposing a law banning the headscarf thus in the end comes uncomfortably (or not so uncomfortably) close to Breivik's own dreams of dominating the female sex.

25 "If I had met myself 12 years ago I would probably think I was an extreme and paranoid nut, who believed in conspiracy theories: 'Our school institutions are brainwashing us and our media are systematically lying to us you say? Lol, you're, paranoid! Get a grip'" (761), and: "Q: How would you view your own current political standpoints 15 years ago? A: I would most likely think I was a complete nut job due to the fact that I was ignorant about most issues then" (1382).

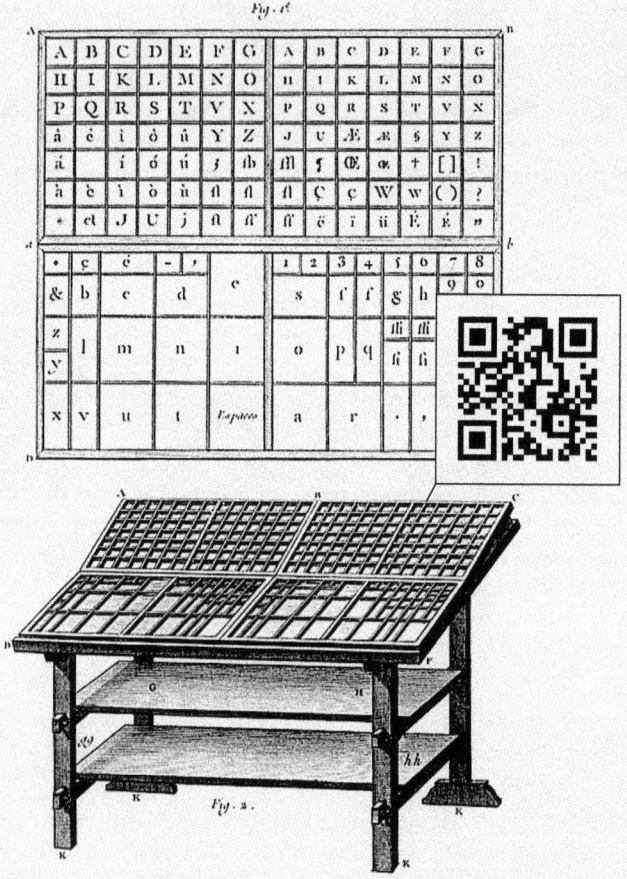

A Playful Reading of the Double Quotation in *The Descent of Alette* by Alice Notley

Feliz Lucia Molina

> "We read (reread) the poems that keep the discourse with ourselves going." – Wallace Stevens

> "We have to break open words or sentences, too, and find what's uttered in them."– Gilles Deleuze

A word about the quotation marks. People ask about them, in the beginning; in the process of giving themselves up to reading the poem, they become comfortable with them, without necessarily thinking precisely about why they're there. But they're there, mostly to measure the poem. The phrases they enclose are poetic feet. If I had simply left white spaces between the phrases, the phrases would be read too fast for my musical intention. The quotation marks make the reader slow down and silently articulate – not slur over mentally – the phrases at the pace, and with the stresses, I intend. They also distance the narrative form myself. I am not Alette. Finally they may remind the reader that each phrase is a thing said by a voice: this is not a thought, or a record of thought process, this is a story, told.[1]

"*The Descent of Alette*" "is an allegorical poem" "in four books" "first published" "in 1992" "by Alice Notley." "In *The Descent of Alette*," "the double quotation mark" "is wrapped around" "words, phrases, sometimes whole sentences, and utilized as bones for structure and tonality." "The winged" "dbl quotation" "like angels or devils" "descending from elsewhere" "function as" "poetic feet." "Distance" "in the text through the use of dbl quotes," "according to Notley," "was a way to distance" "her self" "from the narrative."

---

1   Alice Notley, "Author's Note," in *The Descent of Alette* (New York: Penguin Poets, 1996).

I know someone who tattooed double quotes on her shoulder blades. In other words, the body is quotable. To be able to say that one is quotable. A body filled with other's sayings. I never asked her what for, what is the double quote tattoo for and why on the shoulder blades? I prefer my own interpretation that keeps shifting every time I see her.

First Words of Every Poem in Every Book

Book One

One … On … A … There … I … We … An … A … A … I … At … A … When … When … There … I … In … At … I … Once … A … A … In … A … A … Two … I … I … Eyeball … In … I… A … I … I … On … I … There … What … As … As

Book Two

I … When … I … I … As … I … I … There … I … There … I … A … I … I … I … I … I … I … I … I … I … I … I … I … I … I … I … I … I … I … I … I … I

Book Three

The … Presently … I … I'm … I … We … What … My … I … Who … But … Lay … My … I … The … Your … The … I … It's … As … The … Talon's … When … We … I … Slowly … I … I … The … How … The

Book Four

I … I … You … The … Now … She … The … There … As … Then … The … All … Let's I … You … The … Thus … The … I … The … I … There … Have … The … As … The

Defamiliar Object

"Poetry is a defamiliarized language, whose formations, so far from being simply formations of meaning, are aesthetic structures…."[2] "The same can be" "irresponsibly associated" "with the use of punctuation." "The dbl quotation as a measure" "of poetic feet" "is treated as such" "because the author" "injects artfulness into it." "The dbl quote is an object –" "a joystick" "to control breadth" "(of breath.)" "To de-familiarize" "said sign" "is also to" "impart the sensation of [it] as [it is] perceived and not as they are known."[3] "The dbl quote" "nests previous words, phrasings and sayings." "How many have come and gone" "through the doorway of this punctuation sign."

---

2   Gerald L. Bruns, "From Intransitive Speech to the Universe of Discourse," in *Modern Poetry And The Idea of Language* (New Haven & London: Dalkey Archive Press, 1974), 75.
3   Ibid., 77.

"There are also air quotes and virtual quotes." "There is emphasis and there's irony." "It would be aggravating" "or interesting" "to watch a reading of" "*The Descent of Alette*" "with someone" "raising and curling" "fingers" "bent out of shape" "in what could be used as" "peace signs." "I am trying to avoid" "scare quotes." "I looked up" "what they are" "and supposedly they arose" "in the early 20th century." "The scare quote" "is a mark around a word or phrase to indicate that it doesn't signify conventional or literal meaning." "This isn't how Notley" "intended to use them" "in *The Descent of Alette*." "The characters, places, and things" "signify nothing" "beyond" "their literal meaning" "within the allegory." "I'd like to stress" "within the allegory;" "that's why it's" "italicized." "It is told through" "the main character/voice of" "Alette." "The author reminds us she is not Alette." "The author marvelously found a way" "to distance" "her self" "from the narrative." "This was attempted" "by tonal and intimate" "affect of the dbl quote" "used as poetic feet." "It's as though" "punctuation in this regard" "becomes a magical toy." "Arguably, punctuation" "(as perceived)" "undergoes a kind of" "defamiliar" "make-over." "The text" gently forces the reader" "to slow down," "read slowly." "At some point" "one begins to sense" "lines of text" "moving on its own." "Broken words, phrases, and sentences" "shuttling left to right" "like a subway" "that stops" "from station to station;" "open quote to end quote."

Double Quote Occupied
"There are two worlds; one above ground" "and one underground." "The world above ground is where," "the tyrant" "with a capital t" "lives." "(The "T" gets tangled in the claws of the dbl quote.)" "Alette becomes an owl and kills him." "In the last book the tyrant dies."

> " "…the tyrant" "a man in charge of" "the fact" "that we were" "below the ground" "endlessly riding" "our trains, never surfacing" "A man who" "would make you pay" "so much" "to leave the subway" "that you don't" "ever ask" "how much it is" "It is, in effect," "all of you & more" "Most of which you already" "pay to live below" "But he would literally" "take your soul" "Which is what you are" "below the ground" "Your soul" "your soul rides" "this subway" "I saw" "on the subway a" "world of souls" "[4]

"New York;" "the city of cities" "and its subways –" "worlds underground," "above ground," "& above the above ground." "Skyscrapers," "Wall Street," "old money," "new money," "and falling further down a cleavage;" "the middle class" "slipping away." "Contemporary artist " "Ligorano Re-

---
[4] Alice Notley, *The Descent of Alette*, 3.

ece" "recently made" "a sculpture of ice " "a block of ice" "carved to read" "middle class" "(in all upper case letters)" "and let it melt" "naturally" "for however long – " "hours," "days." "It didn't take very long to melt."

> A global uprise of mass demonstrations; a cacophony of bodies on the street, in parks and universities, on City Hall lawns, coastal ports, neighborhoods, etc., and for what? The reasons are endless and finite. Not a single body is unaffected by the movement even when not "occupying."

"Occupiers" "stormed into a Sotheby's auction" "protesting" "via human microphone" "that the CEO takes home" "about" "six thousand dollars" "a day." "(The a/Art market" "is not a reflection" "of a desire" "for a/Art" "but a reflection" "of a desire" "for money" "confused with a/Art.)"

> What could it mean to occupy that which has been written or said? Someone with double quotes tattooed on both shoulders attempts to reclaim the sign; re-invent it privately-publicly since the body is always split between both spheres. A genre of hide-and-seek; the speaking and silent body which can never mean what it says even while it so desires to mean something. To nest (and hold hostage) someone in double quotes is an act of violence; a gesture of displacement where one is arrested, dislocated, and scrutinized under a distant gaze.

"The air quote" "also known as" "finger quote or ersatz quote" "supposedly" "harks back to" "1927." "The brevity of this gesture" " as something invisible" "like virtual money or credit" "doesn't really exist" "though it take up space;" "it's the ghostliest of all punctuation signs" "and one that requires the presence and appearance of a body."

> " "she made a form" "in her mind" "an imaginary" "form" "to settle" "in her arms where" "the baby" "had been" "We saw her fiery arms" "cradle air" "She cradled air…" "[5]

"The air" "gets occupied" "by one or two hands" "with thumb, forefinger, and middle finger" "which alternately could be used" "to shoot rubber bullets," "pepper spray," "tear gas." "How three fingers" "could be responsible for so much:" "satire, sarcasm, irony" "and ultimately" "bruises, blood, death." ("The violence of the dbl quote is to eagerly to place oneself inside a tornado.)" "The violence of this" "embodied punctuation mark" "stems from a discordance with others." "Is the name, word, or phrase" "placed in dbl quotes" "heroic" " or brave?" "An act of displacement;" "must there always be" "bright or negative lights –" "a leaderless act" "to inhabit, to occupy" "space removed" "from normative use." "Of course" "I'm also wondering" "what it means to re-occupy" "public/private space – the street,

---
5   Alice Notley, *The Descent of Alette*, 10.

neighborhood or page" "policed" "by laws, limits, and" "to some extent" "punctuation."

Echo, Mirror

"There are first, second, and third voices interwoven." " "Braid of voices,"[6] " "Some lines read as internal thoughts," "dialogues," "and scene descriptions," "all of which make up the allegory." "It seems appropriate" "for the word" "allegory" "to nest in dbl quotes" "for perhaps it might be" "a gesture to echo on and on" "eternally referencing" "whatever came before."

> I notice the first tooth of the double quote, when paying too close attention, gets caught in the hook of the "f". I space bar to untangle them; the f does not resist the closed bite of "deaf" and I resist to know what it could mean, because it could doubly mean nothing.

" "He looked" "so familiar" "to me...."[7] " "The second-person" "echoes in one of two directions:" "further into" "or farther from" "me." "It's as though" "the second-person amplifies" "or else the opposite" "in which he," "who looks so familiar," "retreats further" "like stars in a telescope." "The dbl quote" "has this kind of affect" "concerning distance and dimension" "as also illusory" "as something twice removed" "and unreal" "in a similar way" "movie stars are unreal and far away."

> " "I entered" "a car" "in which I seemed" "to see double" "Each person I" "looked at seemed" "spread out" "as if doubled" "Gradually" "I perceived that" "each person" "was surrounded by a ghostly" "second image" "was encased in it" "& each" / "of those images," "those encasings," "was exactly the same" "each was in fact" "the tyrant…" "[8]

A daydream of a mirror-less world while staring through window blinds; a palm tree behind. It was dark with nothing there. A world with no mirrors "in my mind," though my mind could only reflect what it knew: a palm tree. Naturally then, palm trees multiplied; a world of palm trees reflected the daydream with no mirror in sight.

"The mirror" "(prior to obsidian manufacturing ca. 6000 BC)" "was wherever water" "could be found." "It's interesting" "mirrors have been around" "before humans – it's funny" "animals and humans" "get born into" "a world of mirrors," "therefore, simulation" "is always already" "a given –" "a sparkly consequence to be born with a dbl."

------
6   Ibid., 9.
7   Ibid., 16.
8   Ibid., 12.

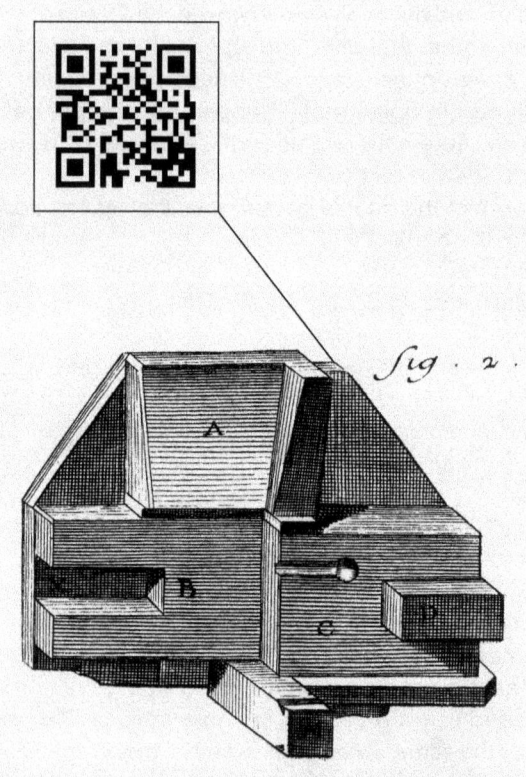

Objects as Temporary Autonomous Zones

Timothy Morton

"The world is teeming. Anything can happen." – John Cage

Autonomy means that although something is part of something else, or related to it in some way, it has its own "law" or "tendency" (Greek, *nomos*). In their book on life sciences, Medawar and Medawar state, "Organs and tissues […] are composed of cells which […] have a high measure of autonomy."[1] Autonomy also has ethical and political valences. De Grazia writes, "In Kant's enormously influential moral philosophy, *autonomy*, or freedom from the causal determinism of nature, became prominent in justifying the human use of animals."[2] One of the oldest uses of autonomy in English is a description of the French civil war from the late sixteenth century: "Others of the […] rebellion entred in counsell, whether they ought to admit the King vpon reasonable conditions, specially hauing their autonomy."[3]

Life, and in particular human life, and in particular human politics, is well served by the usages of *autonomy*. What about the rest of reality, however? Should it be thought of, if it's even considered real and mind-independent, as pure stuff for the manipulation or decorative tastes of truly autonomous beings? We tend to think of things such as paperweights and iPhones as mere tools of human design and human use. To use them is to cause them to exist as fully and properly as they can. But according to Martin Heidegger, when a tool such as a paperweight is used, it disappears, or withdraws (*Entzug*). We are preoccupied with copying the page that the paperweight is holding down. We are concerned with an essay deadline, and the paperweight simply disappears into this general project. If the paperweight slips, or if the iPhone freezes, we might notice it. All of a sudden it becomes *vorhanden* (present-at-hand) rather than *zuhanden* (ready-to-hand).[4]

1 P. B. Medawar and J. S. Medawar, *The Life Science: Current Ideas in Biology* (London: Wildwood House, 1977), 8.
2 David DeGrazia, *Animal Rights: A Very Short Introduction* (Oxford: Oxford University Press, 2002), 5.
3 Antony Colynet, *A True History of the Civil Warres in France* (London, 1591), 480.
4 Martin Heidegger, *Being and Time*, trans. Joan Stambaugh (Albany: SUNY Press, 1996) 62–71.

Yet Heidegger is unable to draw a meaningful distinction between what happens to a paperweight when it slips from the book I'm copying from and what happens to the paperweight when it presses on the still resilient pages of the thick paperback itself. Further still and related to this point, even when I am using the paperweight as part of some general task, I am not using the entirety of the paperweight as such. My project itself selects a thin slice of paperweight-being for the purposes of holding down a book. Even when it is *zuhanden* the paperweight is withdrawn. Graham Harman is the architect of this way of thinking.[5] Harman discovered a gigantic coral reef of withdrawn entities beneath the Heideggerian submarine of Da-sein, which itself is operating at an ontological depth way below the choppy surface of philosophy, beset by the winds of epistemology, and infested with the sharks of materialism, idealism, empiricism and most of the other isms that have defined what is and what isn't for the last several hundred years.

At a moment when the term ontology was left alone like a piece of well chewed old chewing gum that no one wants to have anything to do with, object-oriented ontology (OOO) has put it back on the table. The coral reef isn't going anywhere and once you have discovered it, you can't un-discover it. And it seems to be teeming with strange facts. The first fact is that the entities in the reef – we call them "objects" somewhat provocatively – constitute all there is: from doughnuts to dogfish to the Dog Star to Dobermans to Snoop Dogg. People, plastic clothes pegs, piranhas and particles are all objects. And they are all pretty much the same, at this depth. There is not much of a distinction between life and non-life (as there isn't in contemporary life science). And there is not much of a distinction between intelligence and non-intelligence (as there is in contemporary artificial intelligence theory). A lot of these distinctions are made by humans, for humans (anthropocentrism). And the concept *autonomy* has come into play in policing such distinctions. In this essay I shall to try to liberate autonomy for the sake of nonhumans. I shall do so by parsing carefully the title, which is taken from Hakim Bey's work *The Temporary Autonomous Zone*.[6] First we shall explore the term *autonomous*. Then we shall explore what the full meaning of zone is. Finally, we shall investigate what *temporary* means. Each of these terms is of great value.

An object withdraws from access. This means that its very own parts can't access it. Since an object's parts can't fully express the object, the object is not reducible to its parts. OOO is anti-reductionist. But OOO is also anti-holist. An object can't be reduced to its "whole" either, "reduced upwards" as it were. The whole is not greater than the sum of its parts. So we have a strange irreductionist situation in which an object is reducible neither to its parts nor to its whole. A coral reef is made of coral, fish, seaweed, plankton and so on. But one of these things on its own doesn't embody part of a

---

5   Graham Harman, *Tool-Being: Heidegger and the Metaphysics of Objects* (Peru: Open Court, 2002).
6   Hakim Bey, *TAZ; The Temporary Autonomous Zone: Ontological Anarchy, Poetic Terrorism* (Brooklyn: Autonomedia, 1991): http://hermetic.com/bey/taz_cont.html

reef. Yet the reef just is an assemblage of these particular parts. You can't find a coral reef in a parking lot. In this way, the vibrant realness of a reef is kept safe both from its parts and from its whole. Moreover, the reef is safe from being mistaken for a parking lot. Objects can't be reduced to tiny Lego bricks such as atoms that can be reused in other things. Nor can be reduced upwards into instantiations of a global process. A coral reef is an expression of the biosphere or of evolution, yes; but so is this sentence, and we ought to be able to distinguish between coral reefs and sentences in English.

The preceding facts go under the heading of *undermining*. Any attempt to undermine an object – in thought, or with a gun, or with heat, or with the ravages of time or global warming – will not get at the withdrawn essence of the object. By essence is meant something very different from *essentialism*. This is because essentialism depends upon some aspect of an object that OOO holds to be a mere appearance of that object, an appearance-for some object. This reduction to appearance holds even if that object for which the appearance occurs is the object itself! Even a coral reef can't grasp its essential coral reefness. In essentialism, a superficial appearance is taken for the essence of a thing, or of things in general.

In thinking essentialism we may be able to discern another way of avoiding OOO. This is what Harman has christened *overmining*.[7] The overminer decides that some things are more real than others: say for example human perception. Then the overminer decides that other things are only granted realness status by somehow coming into the purview of the more real entity. When I measure a photon, when I see a coral reef, it becomes what it is. But when I measure a photon, I never measure the actual photon. Indeed, since at the quantum scale *to measure* means "to hit with a photon or an electron beam" (or whatever), measurement, perception (*aisthēsis*), and doing become the same. What I "see" are deflections, tracks in a diffusion cloud chamber or interference patterns. Far from underwriting a world of pure illusion where the mind is king, quantum theory is one of the very first truly rigorous realisms, thinking its objects as irreducibly resistant to full comprehension, by anything.[8]

So far we have made objects safe from being swallowed up by larger objects and broken down into smaller objects – undermining. And so far we have made objects safe from being mere projections or reflections of some supervenient entity – overmining. That's quite a degree of autonomy. Everything in the coral reef, from the fish to a single coral life form to a tiny plankton, is autonomous. But so is the coral reef itself. So are the heads of the coral, a community of tiny polyps. So is each individual head. Each ob-

---

7   Graham Harman, *The Quadruple Object* (Ripley: Zero Books, 2011), 7–18.
8   This is not the place to get into an argument about quantum theory, but I have argued that quanta also do not endorse a world that I can't speak about because it is only real when measured. This world is that of the reigning Standard Model proposed by Niels Bohr and challenged by De Broglie and Bohm (and now the cosmologist Valentini, among others). See Timothy Morton, "Here Comes Everything: The Promise of Object-Oriented Ontology," *Qui Parle* 19.2 (Spring–Summer, 2011): 163–90.

ject is like one of Leibniz's monads, in that each one contains a potentially *infinite regress* of other objects; and around each object, there is a potentially *infinite progress* of objects, as numerous multiverse theories are now also arguing. But the infinity, the uncountability, is more radical than Leibniz, since there is nothing stopping a group of objects from being an object, just as a coral reef is something like a society of corals. Each object is "a little world made cunningly" (John Donne).[9]

We are indeed approaching something like the political valance of *autonomy*. The existence of an object is irreducibly a matter of coexistence. Objects contain other objects, and are contained "in" other objects. Let us, however, explore further the ramifications of the autonomy of objects. We will see that this mereological approach (based on the study of parts) only gets at part of the astonishing autonomy of things. Yet there are some more things to be said about mereology before we move on. Consider the fact that since objects can't be undermined or overmined, it means that there is strictly *no bottom object*. There is no object to which all other objects can be reduced, so that we can say everything we want to say about them, hypothetically at least, based on the behavior of the bottom object. The idea that we could is roughly E.O. Wilson's theory of *consilience*.[10] Likewise, there is no object from which all things can be produced, no *top object*. Objects are not emanations from some primordial One or from a prime mover. There might be a god, or gods. Suppose there were. In an OOO universe even a god would not know the essential ins and outs of a piece of coral. Unlike even some forms of atheism, the existence of god (or nonexistence) doesn't matter very much for OOO. If you really want to be an atheist, you might consider giving OOO a spin.

If there is no top object and no bottom object, neither is there a *middle object*. That is, there is no such thing as a space, or time, "in" which objects float. There is no environment distinct from objects. There is no Nature (I capitalize the word to reinforce a sense of its deceptive artificiality). There is no world, if by world we mean a kind of "rope" that connects things together.[11] All such connections must be emergent properties of objects themselves. And this of course is well in line with post-Einsteinian physics, in which spacetime just is the product of objects, and which may even be an emergent property of a certain scale of object larger than 10^{-17} cm).[12] Objects don't sit in a box of space or time. It's the other way around: space and time emanate from objects.

---

9   John Donne, "Holy Sonnet 15," in *The Major Works: Including Songs and Sonnets and Sermons*, ed. John Carey (Oxford: Oxford University Press, 2009).
10 Edward O. Wilson, *Consilience: The Unity of Knowledge* (New York: Knopf, 1998).
11 Martin Heidegger, *What Is a Thing?*, trans. W.B. Barton and Vera Deutsch (Chicago: Henry Regnery, 1967), 243.
12 Albert Einstein, *Relativity: The Special and the General Theory* (London: Penguin, 2006); Petr Horava, "Quantum Gravity at a Lifshitz Point," arXiv:0901.3775v2 [hep-th]: http://arxiv.org/abs/0901.3775v2

How does this happen? OOO tries to produce an explanation from objects themselves. Indeed, the ideal situation would be to rely on just one single object. Otherwise we are stuck with a reality in which objects require other entities to function, which would result in some kind of undermining or overmining. We shall see that we have all the fuel we need "inside" one object to have time and space, and even causality. We shall discover that rather than being some kind of machinery or operating system that underlies objects, causality itself is a phenomenon that floats ontologically "in front of" them. In so doing, we will move from the notion of autonomy and begin approaching a full exploration of the notion of *zone,* which was promised at the outset of this essay.

Since an object is withdrawn, even "from itself," it is a self-contradictory being. It is itself and not-itself, or in a slightly more expanded version, there is a *rift between essence and appearance* within an object (as well as "between" them). This rift can't be the same as the clichéd split between *substance* and *accidents,* which is the default ontology. On this view, things are like somewhat boring cupcakes with somewhat less boring sugar sprinkles on them of different colors and shapes. But on the OOO view, what is called *substance* is just another limited slice of an object, a way of apprehending something that is ontologically fathoms deeper. What is called *substance* and what is called *accidence* are just on the side of what this essay calls appearance.

The rift (Greek, *chōrismos*) between essence and appearance means that an object presents us with something like what in logic is known as the Liar: some version of the sentence "This sentence is false." The sentence is true, which means that it is a lie, which means that it is false. Or the sentence is false, which means that it is telling the truth, which means that it is true. Now logic since Aristotle has tried desperately to quarantine such beasts in small backwaters and side streets so that they don't act too provocatively.[13] But if OOO holds, then at least one very significant thing in the universe is both itself and not-itself: the object. An object is $p \wedge \neg p$. To cope with this fact, we shall need some kind of paraconsistent or even fully dialetheic logic, one that is not allergic to dialetheias (double-truthed things).

Yet if we accept that objects are dialetheic $p \wedge \neg p$, we can derive all kinds of things easily from objects. Consider the fact of motion. If objects only occupy one location "in" space at any "one" time, then Zeno's paradoxes will apply to trying to think how an object moves. Yet motion seems like a basic, simple fact of our world. Either everything is just an illusion and nothing really moves at all (Parmenides). Or objects are here and not-here "at the same time."[14] This latter possibility provides the basic setup for all the motion we could wish for. Objects are not "in" time and space. Rather, they "time" (a verb) and "space." They produce time and space. It would be better to think

---

13 Graham Priest, *In Contradiction* (Oxford University Press, 2006), passim: the most notable recent quarantine officers have been Tarski, Russell, and Frege.
14 Priest, *In Contradiction,* 172–81.

these verbs as intransitive rather than transitive, in the manner of *dance* or *revolt*. They emanate from objects, yet they are not the object. "How can we know the dancer from the dance?" (Yeats).[15] The point being, that for there to be a question, there must be a distinction – or there must not be ($p \wedge \neg p$).[16] It becomes impossible to tell: "What constitutes pretense is that, in the end, you don't know whether it's pretense or not."[17]

In this notion of the emergence of time and space from an object we can begin to understand the term *zone*. *Zone* can mean *belt*, something that winds around something else. We talk of temperate zones and war zones. A zone is a place where a certain action is taking place: the zone winds around, it radiates heat, bullets fly, armies are defeated. To speak of an *autonomous zone* is to speak of a place that a certain political act has carved out of some other entity. Cynically, Tibet is called TAR, the Tibetan Autonomous Region, for this very reason. In this phrase, *Region* tries to emulate *zone*: it sounds as if the place has its own rules, but of course, it is very much under the control of China.

What action is taking place? "[N]ot something that just is what it is, here and now, without mystery, but something like a quest [...] a tone on its way calling forth echoes and responses [...] water seeking its liquidity in the sunlight rippling across the cypresses in the back of the garden."[18] If as suggested earlier there is no functional difference between substance and accidence; if there is no difference between perceiving and doing; if there is no real difference between sentience and non-sentience – then causality itself is a strange, ultimately nonlocal aesthetic phenomenon. A phenomenon, moreover, that emanates from objects themselves, wavering in front of them like the astonishingly beautiful real illusion conjured in this quotation of Alphonso Lingis. Lingis's sentence does what it says, casting a compelling, mysterious spell, the spell of causality, like a demonic force field. A real illusion: if we knew it was an illusion, if it were just an illusion, it would cease to waver. It would not be an illusion at all. We would be in the real of noncontradiction. Since it is like an illusion, we can never be sure: "What constitutes pretense..." A *zone* is what Lingis calls a *level*. A zone is not entirely a matter of "free will": this concept has already beaten down most objects into abject submission. Objects are far more threateningly autonomous, and sensually autonomous, than the Kantian version of autonomy cited in the first paragraph of this essay. A zone is not studiously decided upon by an earnest committee before it goes into action. One of its predominant features is that it is *already happening*. We find ourselves in it, all of a sudden, in the late afternoon as the shadows lengthen around a city square, giving rise to an uncanny sensation of having been here before.

......

15 William Butler Yeats, "Among School Children," in *Collected Poems*, ed. Richard J. Finneran (New York: Scribner, 1996).
16 Paul de Man, "Semiology and Rhetoric," *Diacritics* 3.3 (Autumn, 1973): 27–33, at 30.
17 Jacques Lacan, *Le séminaire, Livre III: Les psychoses* (Paris: Editions de Seuil, 1981), 48. See Slavoj Žižek, *The Parallax View* (Cambridge, Mass.: MIT Press, 2006), 206.
18 Alphonso Lingis, *The Imperative* (Bloomington: Indiana University Press, 1998), 29.

Objects emit zones. Wherever I find myself a zone is already happening, an autonomous zone. It is the nonautonomous zones that are impositions on what is already the case. Or rather, these zones are autonomous zones that exclude and police. They are brittle. Every object is autonomous, but some objects try to maintain themselves through rigidity and brittleness, like (and such as) a police state. Paradoxically, the more rigidly one tries to exclude contradiction, the more virulent become the dialetheias that are possible. I can get around "This sentence is false" by imagining that there are metalanguages that explain what counts as a sentence. Then I can decide that this isn't a real sentence. This is basically Alfred Tarski's strategy, since he invented the notion of metalanguage specifically to cope with dialetheias.[19] For example we might claim that sentences such as "This sentence is false" are neither true nor false. But then you can imagine a strengthened version of the Liar such as: "This sentence is not true"; or "This sentence is neither true nor false." And we can go on adding to the strengthened Liar if the counter-attack tries to build immunity by specifying some fourth thing that a sentence can be besides true, false, and neither true nor false: "This sentence is false, or neither true nor false, or the fourth thing." And so on.[20]

It seems as if language becomes more brittle the more it tries to police the Liars of this world. Why? I believe that this increasing brittleness is a symptom of a deep fact about reality. What is this deep fact? Simply that there are objects, that these objects are withdrawn, and that they are walking contradictions. This means indeed that (as Lacan put it) "there is no metalanguage," since a metalanguage would function as a "middle object" that gave coherency and evenness to the others.[21] Since there is no metalanguage, there is no rising above the disturbing illusory play of causality. This may even have political implications: no global critique is therefore possible, and attempts to smooth out or totalize are doomed to fail.

To think the zone is to think the notion of *temporary*, which we shall now begin to discuss in greater detail. The zone is not in time: rather it "times." But because a zone is an emanation of an object, it is based on a wavering fragility, since objects are $p \land \neg p$. When an object is born, that means that it has broken free of some other object. An object can be born because it and other objects are fragile. If not, no movement would be possible. Objects contain the seeds of their own destruction, a dialetheic sentence that says something like "This sentence cannot be proved."

Kurt Gödel argues that every true system of propositions contains at least one sentence that the system cannot prove. In order to be true, the system must have a minimum incoherence. To be real, it has to be fragile. Imagine a record player. Now imagine a record called *I Cannot Be Played on This Record Player*. When you play it on this record player, it produces sympa-

---

[19] Priest, *In Contradiction*, 9–27.
[20] See Graham Priest and Francesco Berto, "Dialetheism," *The Stanford Encyclopedia of Philosophy* (Summer 2010 Edition), ed. Edward N. Zalta: http://plato.stanford.edu/entries/dialetheism/
[21] Jacques Lacan, *Écrits: A Selection*, trans. Alan Sheridan (London: Tavistock, 1977), 311.

thetic vibrations that cause the record player to shudder apart. No matter how many defense mechanisms you build in, there will always be the possibility of at least one record that destroys the record player.[22] That is what being physical is. An object is inherently fragile because it is both itself and not-itself. When the rift between appearance and essence collapses, that is called destruction, ending, death.

When an object breaks, several new objects are born. An opera singer sings a loud note in tune with the resonant frequency of a wine glass. (See the movie included here.) The singing is a zone, an autonomous level of intensity, opening a rift between appearance and essence. The glass ripples – for a moment it is nakedly a glass and a not-glass – almost as if it were having an orgasm, a little death. It is caught in the rift of the singing. Then its structure can't handle the coherence of the sound waves, and it breaks. It is incoherence and inconsistency that is the mark of existence, not consistency and noncontradiction. When things break or die, they become coherent. Essence disappears into appearance. I become the memories of friends. A glass becomes a dancing wave. Instantly, there are glass fragments, new temporary autonomous zones. The fragments have broken free from the glass. They are no longer its parts, but emanate their own time and space, becoming perhaps accidental weapons as they bury themselves in my flesh.

Thus Hakim Bey's instructions on creating temporary autonomous zones oscillate disturbingly between performance art and politics, circus clowning and revolution. To play with the aesthetic is to play with causality, to rip from the sensual ether emanating from things new regions, new zones. Anarchist politics is the creation of fresh objects in a reality without a top or a bottom object, or for that matter a middle object:

> Everything in nature is perfectly real including consciousness, there's absolutely nothing to worry about. Not only have the chains of the Law been broken, they never existed; demons never guarded the stars, the Empire never got started, Eros never grew a beard. [...] There is no becoming, no revolution, no struggle, no path; already you're the monarch of your own skin – your inviolable freedom waits to be completed only by the love of other monarchs: a politics of dream, urgent as the blueness of sky.[23]

Bey imagines that this is because chaos is a primordial "undifferentiated oneness-of-being." A Parmenides or a Spinoza or a Laruelle would read this a certain way. Individual objects, or decisions to talk about this rather than that, are just maggot-like things crawling around on the surface of the giant

---

22 The analogy can be found at length in Douglas Hofstadter, "Contracrostipunctus," in *Gödel, Escher, Bach: An Eternal Golden Braid* (New York: Basic Books, 1999), 75–81.
23 Bey, "Chaos: The Broadsheets of Ontological Anarchism," in *Temporary Autonomous Zone*: http://hermetic.com/bey/taz1.html#labelChaosSection

cheese of oneness.²⁴ Yet he also describes chaos as "Primordial uncarved block, sole worshipful monster, inert & spontaneous, more ultraviolet than any mythology." This image is of an inconsistent object, not of an undifferentiated field. An object, indeed, that can be distinguished from other things. If not, then the first part of *The Temporary Autonomous Zone*, subtitled "The Broadsheets of Ontological Anarchism," is a kind of onto-theology. Ontotheology proclaims that some things are more real than others. Bey, however, is writing poetically, and thus ambiguously. We are at liberty to read "undifferentiated oneness-of-being" as something like the irreducibility of a thing to its parts and so forth (undermining and overmining). This certainly seems closer to the language in the following paragraph: "There is no becoming [...] already you're the monarch of your own skin."²⁵

On this view, there is no difference between art and politics: "When ugliness, poor design & stupid waste are forced upon you, turn Luddite, throw your shoe in the works, retaliate." Since Romanticism this has been the war cry of the vanguard artist.²⁶ To say to is to fall prey to the tired axioms of the avant-garde, and we think we know how the game goes. But OOO is not simply a way to advocate "new and improved" versions of this shock-the-bourgeoisie boredom. Bey's text is certainly full enough of that. Rather, since causality as such is aesthetic, and since nonhumans are not that different from humans, the new approach would be to form aesthetic–causal alliances with nonhumans. These alliances would have to resist becoming brittle, whether that brittleness is right wing (authoritarianism) or left wing (the endless maze of critique). No "ism," especially not the ultimate forms, nihilism and cynicism, is in any sense effective at this point. All forms of brittleness are based on the mistaken assumption that there is a metalanguage and that therefore "Anything you can do, I can do meta."

I will not be listing any approaches here, as Bey does. Such lists and manifestos belong to the vanguardism that no longer works. Why? Not because of some marvelous revolution in human consciousness, but because nonhumans have so successfully impinged upon human social, psychic and aesthetic space. It is the time after the end of the world. That happened in 1945, when a thin layer of radioactive materials was deposited in Earth's crust. Geology now calls it this era the *Anthropocene*. Ironically, this period, named after humans, is the moment at which even the most thick headed of us make decisive contact with nonhumans, from mercury in our blood to manta rays to magnesium.

Richard Dawkins, Pat Robertson, and Lady Gaga all have to deal with global warming and mass extinction, somehow. We now live in an *Age of Asymmetry* marked by a skewed, spiraling relationship between vast knowledge and vast nonhuman things – both become vaster and vaster because

---
24 This is closest to the language of François Laruelle in *Philosophies of Difference: A Critical Introduction to Non-Philosophy* (New York: Continuum, 2011) 179.
25 Bey, "Chaos: The Broadsheets of Ontological Anarchism," in *Temporary Autonomous Zone*:
26 Peter Bürger, *Theory of the Avant Garde* (Minneapolis: University of Minnesota Press, 1984).

of one another and for the same reasons.²⁷ This means that coming up with the perfect attitude or the perfect aesthetic prescription just won't work any more. Even the most hardened anthropocentrist now has to pay through the nose for basic food supplies, and has to use more sunscreen. Whether he knows it or acknowledges it, he is already acting with regard to nonhumans.

There is nothing special to think, no special critique that will get rid of the stains of coexistence. The problem won't fit into the well-established modern boxes, which is why the "mystical," "spiritual" quality of Bey's prose is welcome. Of course, when I put it this way, you may immediately close up and decide that I am talking about perfect attitudes after all, or something outside of politics, or other ways that the radical left marshals to police its thinking of the nonhuman. Because that is what is really at stake in all this: the nonhuman in its coexistence with the human – bosons, gods, clouds, spirits, lifeforms, experiences, the sunlight rippling across the cypresses. Bey begins to get at this in a Latour litany in the second part of *The Temporary Autonomous Zone*, "The Assassins":

> Pomegranate, mulberry, persimmon, the erotic melancholy of cypresses, membrane-pink shirazi roses, braziers of meccan aloes & benzoin, stiff shafts of ottoman tulips, carpets spread like make-believe gardens on actual lawns – a pavilion set with a mosaic of calligrammes – a willow, a stream with watercress – a fountain crystalled underneath with geometry – the metaphysical scandal of bathing odalisques, of wet brown cupbearers hide-&-seeking in the foliage – "water, greenery, beautiful faces."²⁸

This will be conveniently dismissed as orientalism. If we're never allowed to escape the crumbling prison of modernity for fear of imperialism there is truly no hope. In a similar way, the fear of anthropocentrism and anthropomorphism is very often staged from a place that just is *anthropocentrism*.²⁹ Critique turns into *ressentiment*.

An object radiates a zone that is aesthetic and therefore causal. Because objects "time" they are temporary. Not because they exist "in" time that eventually gets the better of them. Their very existence implies the possibility of their non-existence. Since objects are not consistent, they can cease to exist. But nothing, no one, will ever be able to insert a blade between appearance and existence, even thought there is a rift there. Now that's what I call autonomy.

---

27 For further discussion see Timothy Morton, "From Modernity to the Anthropocene: Ecology and Art in the Age of Asymmetry," The International Social Science Journal 209 (forthcoming).
28 Bey, "The Assassins," in *Temporary Autonomous Zone*: http://hermetic.com/bey/taz1.html#labelTheAssassins
29 Timothy Morton, *The Ecological Thought* (Cambridge: Harvard University Press, 2010), 75–6.

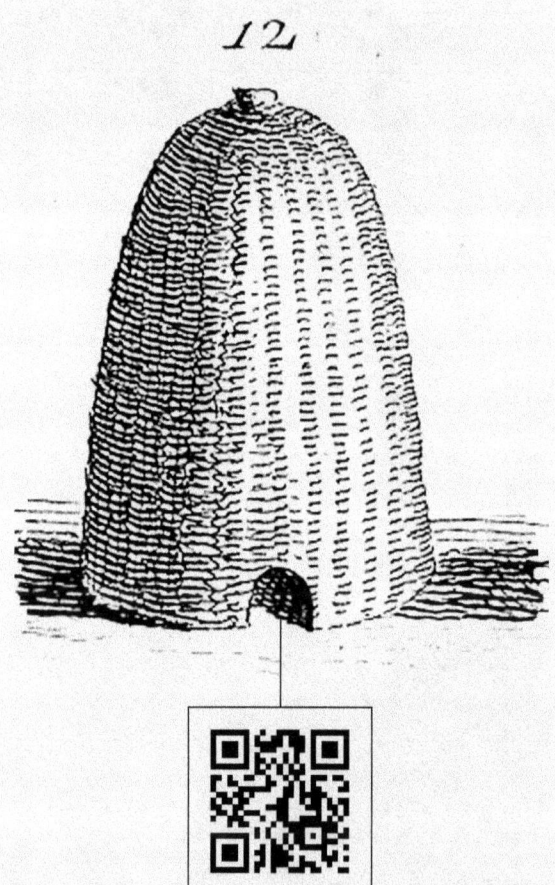

Money as Media: Gilson Schwartz on the Semiotics of Digital Currency

Renata Lemos-Morais

From the multifarious subdivisions of semiotics, be they naturalistic or culturalistic, the realm of semiotics of value is a field that is getting more and more attention these days. Our entire political and economic systems are based upon structures of symbolic representation that many times seem not only to embody monetary value but also to determine it. The connection between monetary and linguistic exchanges is self-evident: the former requires the latter and develops in direct relation to it. Creative experimentation and design of digital systems of value exchange are blossoming on the web. Dr Gilson Schwartz, an economist turned media theorist and professor at the University of São Paulo, adopted the concept of "iconomics," originally created by Michael Kaplan, an author concerned with the linguistics of economic value. Empowering local communities and unlocking new levels of value creation and representation via digital technologies are the main goals of dr Schwartz's projects, aiming at the re-designing of our relationship to the economic value of imagination and the social control of property. Schwartz is Assistant Professor at the School of Communication and Arts of the University of São Paulo, a former Chief Economist at BankBoston, Brazil and Advisor to the President of the National Social and Economic Development Bank (BNDES).[1]

Renata Lemos-Morais (RLM): You have recently produced and directed a short documentary about Creative Currencies in Latin America. Could you tell us a bit about its process and its findings?

Gilson Schwartz (GS): The "Creative Currencies" project is a work-in-progress platform which unfolds as an action research agenda connected both to the production of audiovisual content and the development of social cur-

---

[1] For further reading see Michael Kaplan, "Iconomics: The Rhetoric of Speculation," *Public Culture* 15.3 (2003): 477–93.

rency software. The initiative dates back to 2003 when I led an experimental project supported by the Presidency of Brazil. At that time, we issued paper currency in a small, touristic village in the Northeast Region which stimulated local cultural projects. But it was only in 2009 that the Central Bank of Brazil acknowledged "social currencies" as a legitimate economic agenda, calling for more debate at the Financial Inclusion Forum. This year, the monetary authorities organized a second forum that also opened the room to discussions on mobile payment systems and new perspectives on poverty alleviation via State subsidies. The Ministry of Culture funded the "Creative Currencies" project in 2009–2010 and our next stage in this discovery process is to be supported by the National Social and Economic Development Bank (BNDES). In short, there is genuine interest among public officials in different areas and public funding for social currencies is on the rise in Brazil.

However, after all these years we are still at a very early stage of research and practice. Some of the most successful initiatives (such as Banco Palmas) actually evolved out of local monetary creation to become correspondent banking operations for commercial banks and other financial groups. After eight years of price stability and social inclusion, Brazil stands out as a major opportunity for social experimentation, even the Grameen Bank is now entering the Brazilian market and many NGOs are geared towards different forms of entrepreneurialism in the base of the pyramid, riding solidarity economic models, microfinance and microcredit for local development. It is yet to be seen, however, whether these developments are just one more stage of "bankarization," that is to say, an extension of regular banking services or actually a new form of social and symbolic self-determination at the local level. So far, the Central Bank of Brazil is open to new forms of credit and local finance as long as they are strictly territorial and very close to barter among the poor.

In other words, whether the process of monetary creation could be made to fit an open source paradigm is yet to be seen. Community banking and social currencies might as well end up as just another channel for access to and use of banking services. The "Creative Currencies" project aims at promoting the discussion of more fundamental issues, such as the limits of central banking, the prospects for local financial development and the possibility of creating and managing financial icons as cultural assets. The purpose of this project is to produce short documentaries that will bear testimony to this evolving regulatory framework while inducing more discussion about the fundamental iconomic issues concealed in the process of money and wealth creation.

RLM: What new potential is there in applying digital technologies to currency creation?

GS: Globalization is a result of the virtualization of money, that is, the overcoming of illusions such as the "gold standard." Money is an icon created by institutions, not on supposedly natural or material foundations but out of political and financial interests. The "dollar standard" is an outstanding evidence of this phenomenon and Kaplan's paper, the first to use the expression "iconomics," insists on the rhetoric and semiotic effects associated to a supposedly scientific model of money creation and management. This is a fundamental change that was perceived and discussed much before the digitalization of the world by unorthodox economists such as John Maynard Keynes since the early 20th century. The digitalization of global financial flows accelerated this immateriality and the creation of the Euro was yet another evidence of the political foundations of currencies.

The banking establishment, however, is keen on the idea that scientific formulae hold the key to sound money creation. Keynesianism has been repeatedly associated to "inflationism" while the supposedly sound monetary policies of the Orthodoxy serve well the political and financial interests of a technocratic elite. Corporate media also serve this fictitious depiction of the monetary process despite the cyclical bust of monetary rules and financial regulations. The internet, however, has created numerous opportunities for the disintermediation in industries such as film, music and commodities. There is no reason to doubt that the financial industry can also be transformed by Peer-to-Peer (P2P) infrastructures. Money is media as well. Credit is but confidence. Once people realize that the distributed computing power of networks can also be the platform to weave new monetary and credit operations, there is room for grassroots emancipation out of the established owners of monetary institutions.

So far, however, there has been a privatization of monetary management and there is not a clear path or model for the emergent (P2P) property democratization that is inherent to the internet. Digital assets, however, clearly have an inherent potential to escape central control and proprietary regulatory frameworks.

> RLM: How are social networks transforming the ways in which we exchange value? Do you believe that online influence and reputation might be translated into a new kind of currency?

GS: The foundation for social currencies as envisaged by solidarity economics is the territory. Authorities are willing to concede local monetary creation as long as it is restricted to poor neighborhoods, as a proxy to barter. In this relevant but limited context, reputation, personal knowledge and informal ties form the matrix of local or "proximity" finance which are expected to keep credit and leverage to a sustainable level. Anything beyond that should and would lead to an integration of local finance into the established banking system. However, inasmuch as the internet promotes virtual territories and reputation is now subject to all sorts of digital manipulation and stardom becomes an everyday cultural process among teenagers and elders alike, the territorial "foundation" is substituted for more complex patterns of solidarity, cooperation and exchange that reach beyond the physical territory and even the "human."

Digital assets embody knowledge, technology, cultural and educational values that are exchanged at a global scale beyond the control of democratic States (Chinese-like intervention is the exception, not the rule). Hacktivism is unstoppable and so is monetary hacktivism. Especially in the Third World, mobile communications fast became conveyors of money transfers and other appropriation strategies. Banking and telecom sectors already battle for the control of these emerging markets and, as a matter of fact, have so far contributed to the containment of these processes. Governments serve these moguls and have usually adopted a wait-and-see attitude. If open source hardware and grassroots social movements combine to challenge these proprietary battles, then social networks may evolve into new forms of social capital and thus form the ground on which to design and implement social currencies.

The global financial crisis, as well as the dollar demise, are an event of such a proportion that social networks may open the path for emancipator subjects to seize the opportunity.

> RLM: What are some of the social experiments that you think are revolutionizing the way in which value is exchanged?

GS: There is a broad evolution of economic systems towards the valuation of intangible assets such as knowledge, reputation and sustainability. There are many examples of local as well as global events that call the traditional systems of exchange into question, from carbon credits to educational bonuses, digital barter frameworks and locally based solidarity and fair trade networks. These emerging examples, no matter how different in nature or scale, represent a challenge to the traditional value creation schemes and theories which are based on use and exchange value, supply and demand.

This is not to say that utility and labour or scarcity are to be totally dismissed, but there is now an emerging perception that value is also a function of behavioral codes, symbolic patterns and the energy of institutional frameworks. The plasticity of digital platforms is relevant insofar as intellectual property becomes the central source of value creation. But when you discuss the property rights of public goods such as the environment or basic social rights (of minorities or localities), then a new paradigm seems to emerge.

> RLM: Are gaming and online storytelling digital practices that might have an impact on the way new currencies are created and developed?

GS: "Play money" has been one of the early and most intriguing phenomena associated to the diffusion of virtual worlds. These virtual currencies have also been prone to "boom and bust" dynamics, speculation and pure theft (Second Life scams were common and led to "intervention" by the owners of the game). Storytelling is a major source of value, that is, the value of attention and the markets for audience. There are plenty of private monies created and managed by corporate entertainment groups, telecom operators (via mobile virtual network operators) and marketing frameworks.

The casino economy, as already depicted by Keynes and other unorthodox economists, is always storytelling about future states of the world, confidence building and leverage of animal spirits. The novelty of current events is not the fictitious nature of any form of capital, but the potential for digital democratization of controls over the imaginary nature of value creation. But this is just a potential, a possibility, a figment that more often than not is appropriated by centralized and opaque private powers. The game industry is a testbed for new connections between storytelling and money creation.

> RLM: Monetary value was originally connected to the scarcity of precious metals, such as gold. Our entire monetary system seems therefore to function according to a logic of scarcity. Do you believe it is possible to reverse this logic into a logic of abundance?

GS: The gold standard was a fiction itself, the "scarcity" is always produced by institutions that regulate confidence and access to credit. The key issue is not to fabricate abundance, but to question the institutions which produce scarcity out of any standard, gold or whatever. Central banks are at the service of private banks in the creation and management of scarcity.

> RLM: The promise that nanotechnology holds for our future is one of radical abundance (or so say transhumanists). The possibility of creating any kind of material substance through nanoengineering seems each day more feasible. What would this possibility entail in terms of systems of value exchange?

GS: Nanotechnology, environmental concerns and grassroots appropriation of distributed knowledge are the frontiers of a new horizon of energy creation and management. Social groups in charge of managing scarcity for the sake of wealth and power concentration must be held accountable for the destruction of our future. Once this key political conundrum is accounted for, new systems of value exchange and even a non-mercantile society will come into existence. Revolutionary theorists such as Marx envisaged transformation via the extreme clash of contradictions between capital and labour. This approach has never led to a change in the systemic logic of scarcity for the sake of social control.

We are once again facing the threshold of large scale societal change, but the outcome of the current crisis should come from our imagination, not from yet another paradox of abundance and scarcity. As long as we remain attached to the materiality of value, the illusion of freedom will but reinforce the massive manipulation of necessity.

RLM: What do you think is the role of crowdfunding in this context?

GS: Crowdsourcing as well as crowdfunding are examples of the peer to peer opportunities that come along with distributed computer power. However, the power structure behind wealth and scarcity creation may or may not be changed by crowd management. But it should not be taken at face value, so to speak. The stock market of course is an early form of crowdfunding without calling into question the proprietary framework of the companies offering their investment projects to the market.

Any market is a form of crowdsourcing, that is to say, of distributed forms of supply and demand matchmaking. The wealth of networks, however, depends on the contractual ecosystem, the institutional framework, the channeling of social imagination, not on the purely quantitative distribution of bids and offers. I see economics as supply, demand and code. Once you have access to the code, once openness becomes part of the game, then there is a chance of crowd behavior becoming collective intelligence and sustainable imagination.

RLM: Is the development of digital currencies headed towards a pluralistic ecology in which many micro currency systems co-exist, or is it penetrating the mainstream monetary system? If it is affecting the mainstream financial system, what would be its effect in the long-term?

GS: The same issue is at stake both at local and global levels. The global system is, as a matter of fact, an unstable ecosystem of "micro currencies" whereas the dollar has so far exerted an overwhelming influence. Local currencies and private monies coexist with national currencies only to the extent that the Central Bank admits, for instance, that grassroots monetary emissions remain territorial and strictly connected to poverty. However, the question of how new developments in digital technologies and nanotechnologies might alter not only our current monetary systems but also our understanding of value in itself, is still an open question.

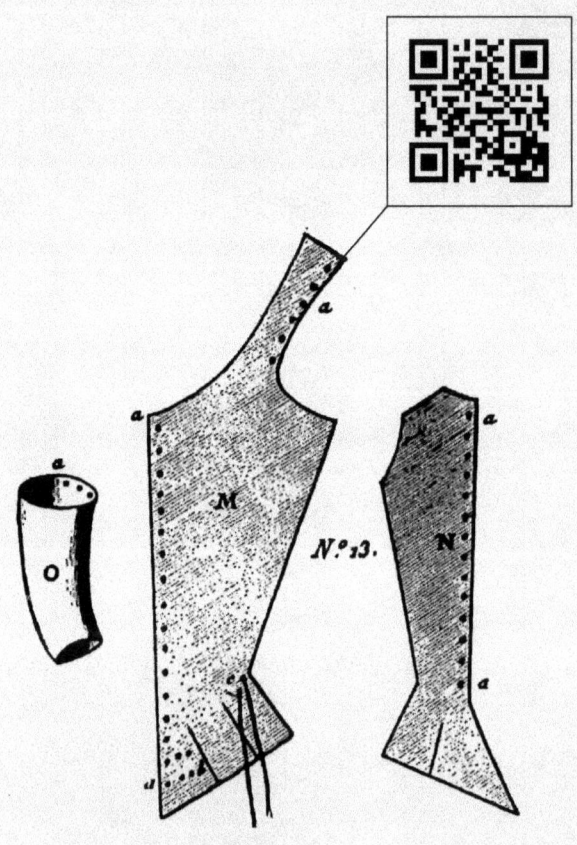

The Afterlives of Queer Theory

Michael O'Rourke

> *"All experience open to the future is prepared or prepares itself to welcome the monstrous arrivant, to welcome it, that is, to accord hospitality to that which is absolutely foreign or strange […]. All of history has shown that each time an event has been produced, for example in philosophy or in poetry, it took the form of the unacceptable, or even of the intolerable, or the incomprehensible, that is, of a certain monstrosity."*
> – Jacques Derrida[1]

Post-Continental Queer Theory

In an interview with Paul Ennis in *Post-Continental Voices*, Adrian Ivakhiv is asked about his opinion concerning the future of post-continental philosophy and he responds that:

> In an increasingly global context, I'm not sure if either 'continental philosophy' or "analytical philosophy" have much of a future except as carriers of certain legacies; they're carry-overs from a time when philosophy seemed exclusive to the North Atlantic world. In a globally mediated, technologically shaped world of shifting and intersecting biocultural contexts, philosophy will have to be more hybrid, viral, and shapeshifting if it's to remain efficacious as a motivating and inspirational force for cosmopolitical world-making – which, to my mind, is what lies ahead of us.[2]

Ivakhiv goes on to prescribe what such a post-continental philosophy would need to be: "post-analytical, post-feminist, post-Marxist, post-postcolonial, post-constructivist"[3] and so on. He does not explicitly mention queer theory here but we might ask, and this essay sets out to ask, what queer theory might look like if we were to consider it as a hybrid, viral, shapeshifting,

---

1 Jacques Derrida, "Passages – from Traumatism to Promise," in *Points: Interviews 1974–1994*, ed Elisabeth Weber, trans. Peggy Kamuf et al. (Stanford: Stanford University Press, 1995), 387.
2 Adrian Ivakhiv, "Interview with Adrian Ivakhiv," in *Post-Continental Voices: Selected Interviews*, ed. Paul J. Ennis (Winchester, UK: Zer0 Books, 2010), 97.
3 Ibid.

post-continental philosophy with cosmopolitical world-making aspirations. Lauren Berlant and Michael Warner's essay "What does Queer Theory Teach us about X?" a guest column written for the PMLA in 1995 was already talking about queer theory in ways which we might now recognize as resonating with the term "post-continental." The first thing we might notice about their essay is a refusal to succumb to the need to pin things down, to say what exactly queer theory *is* and *does* and to be entirely clear about what precisely it is that queer theorists *do*. Berlant and Warner are equally reluctant to accord a specific time to queer. For them, queer is radically anticipatory; it holds out a promise, a utopian aspiration, and occupies a time out-of-joint. Perhaps the appeal and the lasting power of queer theory then (and now) is that it is non-delimitable as a field and non-locatable in terms of a chrononormative temporal schema.[4] Part of, perhaps all of, the attraction of queer theory is its very undefinability, its provisionality, its openness, and its not-yet-here-ness. Queer occupies a strange temporality; it is always, like Derrida's monstrous *arrivant*, to-come, whether from the past or from the future. And it has a ghostly formlessness too. Berlant and Warner write that, in their view, "it is not useful to consider queer theory a thing, especially one dignified by capital letters. We wonder whether *queer commentary* might not more accurately describe the things linked by the rubric, most of which are not theory."[5] It cannot, they insist, "be assimilated to a single discourse, let alone a propositional program" (343). I share their desire "not to define, purify, puncture, sanitize, or otherwise entail [pin a tail on to] the emerging queer commentary" or to fix a "seal of approval or disapproval" (344) on anyone's claims to queerness as I begin to think about the many and various afterlives of queer theory, if there is such a thing. Furthermore, I agree with them that we ought to prevent the reduction of queer theory to a speciality or a metatheory and that we ought to fight vigorously to "frustrate the already audible assertions that queer theory has only academic – which is to say, dead – politics" (344).

And, as we shall see shortly, there is a certain discourse which propagates the idea that queer theory (and not just its politics) is always already dead, buried, over, finished. For me, much of queer thinking's allure is its openness, its promissory nature, and that much of what goes under its name has been "radically anticipatory, trying to bring a [queer] world into being" (344). Because of this very provisionality, and an attendant welcomeness to its own revision, any attempt to "summarize it now will be violently partial" (343). But we might see some value in the violently partial accounts, the short-lived promiscuous encounters, cruising impersonal intimacies, I will be trying to stage here in this article as I ruminate upon the post-continental afterlives of queer theory.

---

4   The term "chrononormative" is one of the many brilliant formulations in Elizabeth Freeman's *Time Binds: Queer Temporalities, Queer Histories* (Durham: Duke University Press, 2010).
5   Lauren Berlant and Michael Warner, "What Does Queer Theory Teach Us About X?," PMLA 110.2 (1995): 343–9, at 343. Subsequent references between parentheses.

If, for Berlant and Warner, "Queer Theory is not the theory *of* anything in particular, and has no precise bibliographic shape" (344) then I would like to suggest – with a willful disingenuousness since after all Queer Theory [dignified by capitals] does have a working bibliographical and anthologizable shape which one can easily constitute – that queer theory is *not solely* the theory of nothing in particular. We might, a little hyperbolically to be sure, say that queer theory is (and always has been) the theory of *everything*. However, if we turn queer theory into a capital-t Theory (as we are often wont to do [and I cannot exclude myself from this urge]) we risk forgetting the differences between the various figures associated with it and the variegated contexts in which they work (as we shall soon see). As Berlant and Warner caution, "Queer commentary takes on varied shapes, risks, ambitions, and ambivalences in various contexts" (344) and if we try to pin the tail on the donkey by imagining a context (theory) in which queer has "a stable referential content and pragmatic force" (344) then we are in danger of forgetting the "multiple localities" (345) of queer theory and practice. No one corpus of work (Judith Butler's for example) or no one particular project should be made to stand in for the whole movement, or what we might more provisionally – and more openly, perhaps a possible alternative to Berlant and Warner's queer *commentary* – call the "culture" of queer theory (small-q, small-t).

If queer thinking were simply reduced to being the province of one particular thinker (say Judith Butler or Eve Kosofsky Sedgwick[6]) then its multiple localities would be worryingly narrowed and its localities would become merely parochial like "little ornaments appliquéd over real politics or real intellectual work. They [would] carry the odor of the luxuriant" (345). If the works of Butler or Sedgwick, were made into a metonym for queer theory or queer culture (or world-building) itself, and if they are held to be exemplary cases (either for good or for bad) then what we lose is the original edgy impetus behind queer theory in the first place. We lose, as Berlant and Warner state, that "wrenching sense of re-contextualization it gave" (345). And then we would really leave queer theory open to charges of political uselessness and glaciation, "the infection of general culture by narrow interest" (349).

The Many Deaths of Queer Theory

Were we to accept recent commentators, Queer Theory, is over, passé, moribund, stagnant; or, at worst, dead, its time and its power to wrench frames having come and gone. Almost since it began we have been hearing about the death(s) of Queer Theory. Stephen Barber and David Clark wrote in 2002 that, "it is not especially surprising to hear that the survival of queer theory has been questioned or its possible 'death' bruited,

---

6   Although I would argue that both have been read *less and less well* and indeed less and less as queer theory.

however questioningly."[7] However questioning this may have been, a year later Judith Halberstam wrote, "some say that queer theory is no longer in vogue; others characterize it as fatigued or exhausted of energy and lacking in keen debates; still others wax nostalgic for an earlier moment."[8] One year later Heather Love reports that some suspect that "queer theory is going downhill."[9] Andrew Parker and Janet Halley, who edited a special issue of *South Atlantic Quarterly* in 2007 entitled "After Sex: On Writing Since Queer Theory," invited their contributors to share some "after" thoughts on what it might mean to be "after queer theory" since they had, "been hearing from some quarters that queer theory, if not already passé, was rapidly approaching its expiration date."[10]

Yet, despite the rumors of extinction, Queer Theory continues to tenaciously hold on to life, to affirm the promise of the future, even despite the dominant influence of Lee Edelman's book *No Future: Queer Theory and the Death Drive* which encourages us to fuck the future and its coercive politics which are, he tells us, embodied in the fascist face of the Child. With each new book, conference, seminar series, each new masters program, we hear (yet again) that Queer Theory is over. Some argue that the unstoppable train of queer theory came to a halt in the late nineties having been swallowed up by its own fashionability. It had become, contrary to its own anti-assimilationist rhetoric, fashionable, very much included, rather than being the outlaw it wanted to be. But the books and articles still continue to appear, the conferences continue to be held. And, if it were true that Queer Theory has been assimilated completely, become sedimented, completely domesticated (or at least capable of being domesticated) then it really would be over. Nobody would be reading any more for we would already know what was to come (And I would argue that this is actually what has really been happening: does anyone actually read Judith Butler's work now *as* queer theory or even of relevance *to* queer theory?). In a fascinating conclusion to her article "Busy Dying" Valerie Rohy suggests that we need not necessarily "resist the death of queer theory, or not in the way one might think." She explains:

> While it is ironic that queer theory should also be enlivened by prophecies of its death [...] there is no reason why that conversation should not continue. If we choose to accept the humanizing trope that gives life to queer theory, it must therefore be dying, like all of us: after all, the condition of life is its ending. And if so, the question becomes how long

---

7   Stephen M. Barber and David L. Clark, eds. "Queer Moments: The Performative Temporalities of Eve Sedgwick," in *Regarding Sedgwick: Essays on Queer Culture and Critical Theory* (Durham: Duke University Press, 2002), 4.
8   Judith Halberstam, "Reflections on Queer Studies and Queer Pedagogy," *Journal of Homosexuality* 45.2–4 (2003): 361–4.
9   Heather K. Love, "Oh, The Fun We'll Have: Remembering the Prospects for Sexuality Studies," *GLQ: A Journal of Lesbian and Gay Studies* 10.2 (2004): 258–61.
10 Janet Halley and Andrew Parker. "Introduction: After Sex? On Writing Since Queer Theory," *South Atlantic Quarterly* 106.3 (2007): 421–32.

and how richly queer theory can live that dying, busy with the work of its time.[11]

Of course, to speak of afterlives, as I do here, is to suggest that queer theory has already died and has come back as a ghost or ghosts. Certainly, this gestures some way towards the hauntological survival of queer theory and its weird temporalities. But, if it is already-dead (and queer theory does tend to get anthropomorphized in these accounts of its demise) then its ghost comes from the future as well as from the past. But, Queer Theory, stubbornly vital as specter, revenant, ghost, took a strange twist in the late nineties and early noughties (or whatever we might awkwardly name our present queer age). Suddenly, queer theorists were interested in ethico-politics, in world politics, in events outside of the texts they were so busy subverting. And it was this political turn which led David Ruffolo to call for a renaming of queer thinking as *post-queer politics*.

In Ruffolo's book *Post-Queer Politics* we catch a glimpse of what queer as a post-continental theory might look like and it is useful to read it alongside John Mullarkey's *Post-Continental Philosophy: An Outline*. At the beginning of his book Mullarkey admits that he is writing about something, the philosophical event of post-continental thought, which does not yet have a shape, has not yet come into existence:

> This book may have been written too early. It is not about something, or some idea, that has actually occurred as yet, an objective event. It is about something that is unfolding, an event in the making. The "Post-" in "Post-Continental" is not an accurate description of what is, but a prescription for what could be.[12]

Similarly, the "post-" in David Ruffolo's book operates not as a description of something which has already happened in response to the "peaking" of queer theory,[13] but rather describes (or prescribes) what could be, if queer theory were to undergo significant renewal. Ruffolo's primary concern is to immanentize queer theory which, for him, remains rooted in subjectivity, language, representations, discourses, identities, and so on. Ruffolo rejects the queer theoretical insistence on transcendence which he finds primarily in the work of Foucault and Butler – where acute attention is placed on representations, significations, and identifications – and he aims to kindle a neomaterialist (in the spirit of Elizabeth Grosz's work) post-queer thinking which is open rather than closed to the world. In my preface "TwO (Theory without Organs)" to *Post-Queer Politics* I gestured toward the idea that Ruffolo is reanimating queer theory, plateauing it in ways that can be diagrammed: he

---
11 Valerie Rohy, "Busy Dying," in *Sex, Gender and Time in Fiction and Culture*, eds. Ben Davies and Jana Funke (Basingstoke: Palgrave, 2011), 205-219, at 219.
12 John Mullarkey, *Post-Continental Philosophy: An Outline* (London: Continuum, 2006), 1.
13 David V. Ruffolo, *Post-Queer Politics* (Farnham: Ashgate, 2009), 1.

puts queer theory *on the line* and he maps the plane of consistency of queer theory as a kind of free-floating space that is formless, without subject, without development, without centre or structure, without beginning or end.[14] Mullarkey's wager is that post-continental thought (which he associates with the philosophies of Deleuze, Laruelle, Badiou and Henry) embraces "absolute immanence over transcendence."[15] Each of these philosophers insist, Mullarkey tells us, upon "a return to the category of immanence if philosophy is to have any future at all" (2). In "rejecting both the phenomenological tradition of transcendence (of consciousness, the Ego, Being, or Alterity), as well as the post-structuralist valorization of language" (2) these four French philosophers take continental philosophy "in a new direction that engages with naturalism with a refreshingly critical and non-reductive approach to the sciences of life, set theory, embodiment and knowledge. Taken together, these strategies amount to a rekindled faith in the possibility of philosophy as a worldly and materialist thinking" (2).

Although Deleuze is the central figure in both Mullarkey's and Ruffolo's texts, it is perhaps Derrida (and his notion of the *à-venir*, the to-come) which springs to mind when we try to think about the attempt to make immanence supervene on transcendence in queer studies. The queer theory to-come (which Ruffolo refers to as post-queer dialogical becomings) is impossible to discern, to outline, to give precise shape too. If queer theory has reached an abyss (the heteronormativity–queer dyad Ruffolo problematizes) then re-mapping the co-ordinates of the field depends on an aporetic impossibility, a crossing of the uncrossable, a passing through the impassable.

For Mullarkey, Derrida's later thinking was marked by an inability to stay still and a shift from the undermining of the "possibility of experience" to "the experience of impossibility" (9) in the later writings on the aporetics of ethical, religious and political experience. The queer theory to-come, we might wager, then, is an experience of aporetic impossibility and Mullarkey gives us a clue as to how Derrida's writing on/about aporias might be useful for thinking about the regime of philosophical immanence:

> In his own work entitled *Aporias*, Derrida tells us that the term's philosophical use comes to us from Aristotle's *Physics IV* and concerns the problematics of time. But it also concerns the issue of regress, Aristotle taking the view in the Categories that any relation (like time) must have distinct *relata* lest there be infinite regress. The *relata* need to be distinct if their relation is to be defined. And here is where we can begin to see a way out of our entanglement in immanence. (9)[16]

Mullarkey contends that, "the regress, aporia, or 'vertigo' of immanence" can never be undone, "indeed, it can never even be said, strictly speak-

---

14 And this for me is exemplified by Masoud Ghaffarian-Shiraz's cover image, "The Droplet."
15 Mullarkey, *Post-Continental Philosophy*, 1. Subsequent references between parentheses.
16 Patricia MacCormack's resonant phrase "becomings to-come" seems to me to be a very useful one in this context. See her book *Cinesexuality* (Farnham: Ashgate, 2008).

ing" (9). Rather, we show it by *unwriting* it. He turns to Deleuze for a theory of abstraction that, "would provide the key to how a discourse of immanence might be possible – namely the theory of the diagram or philosophical drawing" (9). He explains that the diagram operates metaphilosophically in that it is a moving outline which takes both "a transcendent view (*representing* immanence) while also remaining immanent: it does this by diagrammatising itself – it reiterates itself as a drawing that is perpetually re-drawn, and so materializes its own aporia" (9). Ruffolo's post-queer politics is perhaps only capable of being captured spatially, or rather diagrammatically, and not chronologically. Post-queer does not mean *after* queer or leaving queer behind, the post-queer remains, after all, forever tethered to the queer genealogically. Mullarkey sums up his project in ways which are strikingly similar to Ruffolo's central concerns about the stagnation or death of queer theory, "the news this nascent event brings is effectively the following: not only was the report of Continental philosophy's death at the hand of self-inflicted *aporia,* obscurantism and anti-scientism an exaggeration, but a recent change has taken place that will allow it to regenerate and renew itself with unexpected consequences" (11).

The Many Afterlives of Queer Theory

The news of queer theory's death (or many deaths) at the hands of "self-inflicted aporia" also came too soon, was a gross exaggeration. And, echoing Mullarkey, I would argue that recent changes to the shape of the field promise its regeneration and renewal with many unexpected (and indeed unforeseeable consequences). So, in the remainder of this article I would like to speculate about some of Queer Theory's afterlives by taking a look at some recent texts (all from the past two years and each committed to re-imagined queer futurities) which take the field in new directions and open up new spaces of enquiry, new worlds: José Esteban Muñoz's *Cruising Utopia: The Then and There of Queer Futurity* (2009) on critical idealism, aesthetics and a Blochian educated hope; Sara Ahmed's *The Promise of Happiness* (2010) on affect; Tim Dean's *Unlimited Intimacy: Reflections on the Subculture of Barebacking* (2010) on barebacking, HIV, and intimacies; Kathryn Bond Stockton's *The Queer Child; Or Growing Sideways in the Twentieth Century* (2009) on queer childhood, and finally, Lynne Huffer's *Mad for Foucault: Rethinking the Foundations of Queer Theory* (2010) which is a landmark text for queer studies because it shifts the emphasis away from Foucault's three-volume *History of Sexuality* to his *Madness and Civilization*.

My "violently partial"[17] readings of these five important texts and the immemorial currents sweeping Queer Theory towards new headings, new

---

17 Elizabeth Freeman embraces the queerness of close reading encounters. She writes that the narratives she assembles in *Time Binds* (Durham: Duke University Press, 2010) are, "practices of knowing, physical as well as mental, erotic as well as loving 'grasps' of detail that do not accede to

futures, suggests not only that there is life after death for Queer Theory, a future for queer thinking, but that, Queer Theory *is* the future, a theory *of* the future, one which still has much to teach us about the urgent cultural and political questions of today.¹⁸

Queer Theory and/as the Future

From its very "beginnings"¹⁹ Queer Theory has, like its pervert twin, deconstruction, been turned toward the future, a theory permanently open to its own recitation, re-signification and revision. It has always been a hopeful and hope-*full* theory. We see this in its earliest incarnations as the AIDS activism of ACT UP and Queer Nation, both of which are privileged by utopian political thought that promises an unmasterable future,²⁰ and the "foundational" theorizations of Eve Kosofsky Sedgwick and Judith Butler (among many others), queer theory has *always already* been of, for, and promised, given over to, the future, to futurality as such. It has curved, "endlessly toward the realization that its realization remains impossible,"²¹ as Lee Edelman wrote in 1995, the same year as Berlant and Warner's guest column in PMLA. So, in the early to mid 1990s Edelman himself was able to celebrate the utopic negativity, and asymptotic, incalculable futurity of queer thinking as a site of permanent becoming. But what his *No Future* has almost single-handedly instantiated is a turn away from the future, or what he more recently has called the "Futurch"²² as it is embodied in the saccharine-laden figure of the Child.

In the wake of Edelman's book there has been an almost universal rejection of, a resounding "fuck you," to the future and what has come to be called the 'anti-social thesis' now dominates the *post-political, post-futural, anti-or post-relational* landscape of queer studies. On the one side, the side of anti-utopianism and hopelessness you have figures like Edelman, Jonathan Goldberg and Madhavi Menon, and (much more problematically and equivocally) Judith Jack Halberstam, for whom hope is imbued with and unable to be dislodged from a heteronormative logic. Theirs is a project calculated to give up on hope and by extension to refuse both the political

---

existing theories and lexicons but come into unpredictable contact with them: close readings that are, for most academic disciplines, simply too close for comfort" (xx-xxi).

18 We might note that the death of Theory itself has been repeatedly announced. A recent collection edited by Derek Attridge and Jane Elliott, entitled *Theory After "Theory"* (New York: Routledge, 2011) argues that far from being dead that theory has adapted itself to the most pressing political and cultural problems of our time.
19 It is interesting that the subtitle to Huffer's *Mad for Foucault* is *Rethinking the Foundations of Queer Theory* as if queer theory had foundations, as if it were not suspicious of all origins.
20 See Michael Hardt and Antonio Negri, *Multitude: War and Democracy in the Age of Empire* (New York: Penguin, 2004).
21 Lee Edelman, "Queer Theory: Unstating Desire," *GLQ: A Journal of Lesbian and Gay Studies* 2.4 (1995): 343–6, at 346.
22 Lee Edelman, "Antagonism, Negativity and the Subject of Queer Theory," *PMLA* 121.3 (2006): 821–2, at 821.

and the futural. In a sense then the anti-social theorists are on the side of death, or of a logic which loudly proclaims *and* embraces the traumatized death drivenness of both queer theory and politics, raising a specter which has haunted it from the very start.

On the other side, on the side of affirmation, utopianism and socio-political hope, very much *on the side of life,* we have figures such as Tim Dean, Michael Snediker, Sara Ahmed, and José Esteban Muñoz (a thinker such as Heather Love falls somewhere in the middle but I don't think an optimistic queer theory can afford to dwell for very long on loss, melancholia, trauma at the expense of feeling forward as her work does). These theorists, a little bit in love with queer theory as lure, return us to the affirmative, revolutionary potential of queer studies, and seek to re-imagine a hopeful, forward-reaching, world-making queer theory that matters as the future, as the telepoietic queer event, as the always already not-yet of the democracy to-come and the justice to-come. We might even say, affirming the far-from-dead politics of queer theory, that queer theory *is* radical democracy, that queer theory *is* justice, is all about futurity and hope. And it is worth remembering here that for Eve Kosofsky Sedgwick, whose death in April 2009 occasioned a new round of assertions that the work of queer theory which she inspired was over and done with, queerness is "inextinguishable."[23] And, to quote Beth Freeman, "as much as sexual dissidents have suffered, lived as objects of contempt or oblivion, endured physical and emotional punishment, we have also risked experimentation with our bodies and those of others, with affiliation, and with new practices of hoping, demanding, and otherwise making claims on the future."[24]

Revolt, We Said

Those who take up the anti-social argument (a position usually incorrectly attributed to Leo Bersani's *Homos*[25]) refuse to make claims on the future and so refuse queer theory as future dawning promise. To do so is to betray a certain spirit of Derridean deconstruction which has always animated queer thought. To take this anti-social argument is to give up on a Derridean understanding of the event as prospective and to remain in thrall to an onto-chrono-temporality. I would quite seriously suggest that we need to avoid this wrong turn by mobilizing a Derridean understanding of historicity, temporality (and by extension spatiality), relationality and the event. The latter

---

23 Eve Kosofsky Sedgwick, *Tendencies* (Durham: Duke University Press. 1993), xii.
24 Freeman, *Time Binds*, xxi.
25 Incorrectly because Bersani's work has everywhere been committed, like Eve Kosofsky Sedgwick's, to recreating the world and letting it be. For Bersani everyone relates to everyone and everything else through formal correspondences and there is a marked shift from the anti-relational to ever-proliferating new relational modes and forms of being in his later work, cf. *Homos* (Cambridge: Harvard University Press, 1995) and *Forms of Being: Cinema, Aesthetics, Subjectivity* (co-authored with Ulysse Dutoit, London: BFI, 2004).

being understood as that which ruptures onto-chrono-phenomenological temporality and is faithful to, or welcomes, that which arrives but which cannot be known or grasped in advance. This theoretical gesture, a reparative one, is in the service of what I have called elsewhere queer theory as a weak force, queer theory as revolt.[26] Julia Kristeva in *Revolt, She Said* understands the event as revolutionary, emphasizing there the etymological roots – which overlap with queer's own etymological ones – of the word revolt, meaning "return, renewing, returning, discovering, uncovering, and renovating."[27] This renovation is possible because at the moment of revolution, according to Kristeva, "I revolt, therefore we are still to come."[28] Kristeva considers thinking as, "a revelation, an exploration, an opening, a place of freedom."[29] Similarly, José Esteban Muñoz, in his *Cruising Utopia*, sees queerness as, "a structuring and educated mode of desiring that allows us to see and feel beyond the quagmire of the present."[30]

For Muñoz, "Queerness is also a performative because it is not simply a being but a doing for and toward the future."[31] Following Muñoz, queerness occupies the space of the not-yet, is always promissory, horizontal. He begins *Cruising Utopia* by stating:

> Queerness is not yet here. Queerness is an ideality. Put another way, we are not yet queer. We may never touch queerness, but we can feel it as the warm illumination of a horizon imbued with potentiality. We have never been queer, yet queerness exists for us as an ideality that can be distilled from the past and used to imagine a future. The future is queerness's domain.[32]

I am not suggesting that it is easy to unmoor ourselves from linear temporalities, from what Elizabeth Freeman in her important recent book on erotohistoriographies calls "chrononormativities," but I would like to draw attention to the way in which this capitulation in the end refuses and forecloses the promise of the future. In the remainder of this paper I would like to take a glimpse at some forward-glancing texts (or particular moments in those texts which we might encounter closely, even over-closely)[33] which can be shored up against the so-called ruin(s) or death(s) or queer theory.

---

26 See Michael O'Rourke, "History's Tears" in *Sex, Gender and Time in Fiction and Culture*, eds. Ben Davies and Jana Funke (Basingstoke: Palgrave, 2011), 53–69.
27 Julia Kristeva, *Revolt, She Said* (Los Angeles: Semiotext(e), 2002), 85.
28 Ibid., 42.
29 Ibid., 114.
30 Muñoz, *Cruising Utopia*, 1.
31 Ibid.
32 Ibid.
33 For Freeman a commitment to "overcloseness" informs her sense of "queer" which, for her, "cannot signal a purely deconstructive move or position of pure negativity" (*Time Binds*, xxi).

Child's Delay

Firstly, let us take a sideways look at the child, from a parallax angle which Edelman's *No Future*, with its rejection of the child and of the possibility for queer children or queer childhood to even exist, explicitly disallows. Kathryn Bond Stockton's *The Queer Child* asserts that "if you scratch a child, you will find a queer."[34] In her readings of fiction and films from the twentieth century she returns the shadowy, ghostly, penumbral figure of the queer child to a central place. She will, she boldly claims, show throughout "how every child is queer."[35] What this might suggest to us is that queer children stubbornly refuse to grow up, to follow arborescent, vertical, even Oedipalized models of development.[36] Rather they make lateral, rhizomatic, sideways moves. The child is post-queer, then, in Ruffolo's sense. It is important to note that these sweeping lateral shifts are also as such a rejection of the coercive politics of "reproductive futurism."[37] But, having said that, the temporality Stockton's queer children occupy is the time of Derrida's *différance*, a time of delay. Their "supposed gradual growth, their suggested slow unfolding, which, unhelpfully, has been relentlessly figured as vertical movement upward (hence 'growing up') toward full stature, marriage, work, reproduction and the loss of childishness."[38] The temporality of delay is, Stockton admits, a tricky one. Like the speeds of Derridean *différance*, the child's delay "spreads [...] sideways and backwards," rather than simply accelerating and thrusting "toward height and forward time."[39] As a queer strategy, maneuvering sideways has the virtue of mobilizing the frame-wrenching unruliness of Berlant and Warner's queer thinking, but also the power to bend the hetero-chrono-normative frames of temporality and History we are used to working with. These complicated asynchronicities, these luminescent moments of queer refusals to grow *up,* carve open new futures for queer childhood. If queer childhood – and here queer childhood becomes synecdochal for the childlike wonder of queer theory itself – is only ever recognizable after its death, retroactively, then this delaying or stalling of the forward-propulsion of growing up, allows the queer child, or simply queerness *tout court,* to live on, inextinguishably.

Utopia's Propulsions

In his manifesto-like *Cruising Utopia*, José Esteban Muñoz enacts another sideways re-temporalizing move and makes a compelling argument for the *anti*-anti-relational thesis. We must, he states, "vacate the here and now for

---

34 Kathryn Bond Stockton, *The Queer Child; Or Growing Sideways in the Twentieth Century* (Durham: Duke University Press, 2009), 1.
35 Ibid., 3.
36 And childhood, as Eve Sedgwick so acutely taught us, need not necessarily adhere *only* to children.
37 Lee Edelman, *No Future: Queer Theory and the Death Drive* (Durham: Duke University Press, 2004),
38 Stockton, *The Queer Child*, 4.
39 Ibid.

a then and there,"[40] leaving behind the contested present and its quagmire, for a re-imagined futurity. If Edelman emphasizes the lonely figure of the *sinthomosexual* who refuses relationality, then Muñoz wishes for, wants a "collective temporal distortion." This is a Kristevan revolt: "Individual transports are insufficient. We need to engage in a collective temporal distortion. We need to step out of the rigid conceptualization that is a straight present."[41] In a way Stockton's queer child occupies Muñoz's space (although the future is both a spatial and a temporal destination) of the "not yet here." Rather than refusing the future's pull in the way that Edelman rejects the tow of the *à-venir* (to-come), Muñoz reminds us that, "what we need to know is that queerness is not yet here but it approaches like a crashing wave of potentiality. And we must give in to its propulsion, its status as a destination,"[42] or we might say its status as a horizonless horizon. In a rather compelling conclusion to his book Muñoz imagines this capitulation to the inexorable propulsive tug of the future-as-promise in terms of the ecstatic: "we must take ecstasy." This has a whole range of possible registers from the pharmaceutical to the carnal but I want to place it alongside (or sideways with) Lynne Huffer's more ecstatic moments in *Mad for Foucault*, in which she is mad about *her* Foucault. She engages in moments of rapturous cross-temporal vibration with him in terms redolent of Muñoz's own *ekstasis* (a Heideggerian standing outside of oneself which ruptures, tears up the linearities of straight time). Muñoz's injunction, or request, for us to take ecstasy with him, to encounter a queer temporality thus

> becomes a request to stand out of time together, to resist the stultifying temporality and time that is not ours, that is saturated with violence both visceral and emotional, a time that is not queerness. Queerness's time is the time of ecstasy. Ecstasy is queerness's way.[43]

It is in these ecstatic moments that we arrive (or move inexorably toward) "collective potentiality."[44] These ecstatic moments often take place in encounters with certain objects, objects like Warhol's coke bottle which harbor potentiality and are illuminated by "the affective contours of hope itself."[45]

Queer *Ekstasis*
Those objects, which are illuminated by future- or forward-dawning-promise, can also be texts themselves. These are texts which take on qualities of the sentient as they vibrate with us across time and space. Lynne Huffer's *Mad*

---
40 Muñoz, *Cruising Utopia*, 185.
41 Ibid.
42 Ibid.
43 Ibid., 187.
44 Ibid., 189.
45 Ibid., 7.

for *Foucault* dramatizes a feverish moment which she shares in the archive with Foucault, where she takes ecstasy with him. Her argument throughout this field redefining book is that we cannot properly understand Foucault's work on sexuality until we learn to (re)read *The History of Madness*. This project of "re-queering Foucault"[46] actually turns on a rejection of the now-sanctified versions of his ideas which dominate queer theory.[47] Huffer bravely suggests that our understanding of Foucault occupies the time of ecstatic queerness: if we have yet to read (or understood) his work properly, then another Foucault, a futural Foucault is always potentially dawning. She glimpses this wave of potentiality for unsettling the object-event that Foucault has become in the Normandy archive where Foucault's unpublished texts are held.

While perusing a 400-page interview between Roger Pol Droit and Foucault, Huffer chances upon a moment of suppressed self-disclosure. Foucault had refused to publish this long interview text, embarrassed by how it forced him to resort to biographical answers, to a *moi* that his work – and the queer theory it has inspired – so assiduously moved to decenter. Foucault tells Droit that madness has always interested him, that "for twenty years now I've been worrying about my little mad ones, my little excluded ones, my little abnormals."[48] At this point, Droit presses him to explain the motivation for writing *The History of Madness* in the first place and he responds:

> in my personal life, from the moment of my sexual awakening, I felt excluded, not so much rejected, but belonging to society's shadow. It's all the more a problem when you discover it for yourself. All of this was very quickly transformed into a kind of psychiatric threat: if you're not like everyone else, it's because you're abnormal, if you're abnormal, it's because you're sick.[49]

Huffer admits that she is "immediately thrilled," to have "discovered such a 'confession'" from Foucault.[50]

This is a moment where, for Foucault, "individual transports are not enough."[51] Rather he engages in a "collective temporal distortion" in which he declares his solidarity with his "little mad ones, my little abnormals."[52] Huffer calls this moment a "*coup de foudre*" which sparks a "fever" in her and engenders "a loyal kind of disloyalty to Foucault,"[53] who after all wanted to suppress this "confessional" text that she erotically vibrates toward, or

---

46 Lynne Huffer, *Mad for Foucault: Rethinking the Foundations of Queer Theory* (New York: Columbia University Press, 2010), 24.
47 No figure more than Foucault – except perhaps Freud – has exerted such a deep influence on queer thinking since its "inception."
48 Huffer, *Mad for Foucault*, 23.
49 Ibid.
50 Ibid.
51 Muñoz, *Cruising Utopia*, 185.
52 Ibid.
53 Huffer, *Mad for Foucault*, 24.

even with. Perhaps, she says, "it can be received as an event of discovery that engenders what Deleuze called a resistant thinking, 'a thought of resistance' to the despotic readings that refuse to see Foucault's queer madness."[54] Huffer's queer theory takes it chances with that which has been repressed but in so doing goes where Muñoz tells us queer theory needs to go: into the queer time of ecstasy and archive fever. Huffer's encounter with Foucault, her queer "touch" which crosses temporal lines, reveals the inherent strangeness which inhabits the chrono-normative rhythms of time. And her seeming "disloyalty," her overcloseness discloses what Freeman says is the "messiest thing about being queer," that is, "the actual meeting of bodies with other bodies and with objects."[55]

The Promise of Affect

Huffer's ecstatic moment, her stepping outside of herself in a moment of happy stance, a chancy happenstance, should remind us that we know, as Muñoz puts it, "time through the field of the affective, and affect is tightly bound to temporality."[56] Sara Ahmed's *The Promise of Happiness* turns its attention to an affect which has been downplayed in queer studies which has up until recently preferred to wallow in bad feelings such as shame (by far the most dominant affect in queer cultural studies), hate, fear, anger, disgust and so on. Negative affect, melancholy and trauma, as Michael Snediker points out in his gorgeous dance of a book *Queer Optimism*, have preoccupied queer theorizing at the expense of or to the detriment of positive affect, happiness, optimism, hope, utopianism. In his review of Ahmed's book Snediker avers that, "arguments for or against happiness arise most provocatively in the field of queer theory," which suggests to him that "queer persons bear an acutely salient relation to happiness as that from which they've been excluded, but furthermore, that they bear an exemplary relation to a happiness always requiring sacrifice and compromise, a shady bittersweetness from which no persons are exempt."[57]

Most queer theory has found itself cleaving to pernicious versions of happiness over and against its capacity for fungibility (there are many forms of happiness) and its constitutive (or at the very least etymological) potentiality for surprise. Happiness, then, occupies the strange temporality of Stockton's child and his or her delay (and of Muñoz's then-and-there, a not-yet-here). Ahmed imagines an affective relation that can be both happy or unhappy; there is, after all, no pure form of either happiness or unhappiness as these tend to "equivocate around each other's edges" to an "experienced past as structurally analogous to a futural affect which we can speculate about

---

54 Huffer, *Mad for Foucault*, 24.
55 Freeman, *Time Binds*, xxi.
56 Muñoz, *Cruising Utopia*, 187.
57 Michael D. Snediker, *Queer Optimism: Lyric Personhood and Other Felicitous Persuasions* (Minneapolis: University of Minnesota Press, 2009), n.p.

but haven't yet encountered": "Nostalgic and promissory forms of happiness belong under the same horizon, insofar as they imagine happiness as being somewhere other than where we are in the present."[58] The anti-social theorists argue that, if one is to be queer, happiness is ontologically risky and therefore should be refused, given up. However, Ahmed much more promisingly (and promissorily) mines those times and spaces where we can in fact find forms of happiness beyond those we presently "trust and mistrust."[59] In this brighter, more expansive world, Ahmed promises a differently theorized happiness, which we might allow to migrate across other affects, both positive and negative. As Snediker concludes, Ahmed gratifyingly allows that, by swerving away from happiness's compulsions and coercions and being drawn into near-proximity, "we might wish to be happy, without feeling theoretically unhappy in the wishing."

Unlimited Promiscuity

Muñoz's *Cruising Utopia* imagines what we "can possibly see, let alone know, here, and now, of future social relations, how we can dream and enact new and better pleasures, other ways of being in the world, and ultimately new worlds."[60] The *then and there* of his subtitle insists on the now central question of how to bring about utopian futures from within a negating and seemingly hopeless present, how to introduce or bring exuberant futures (what Michael Warner would call "queer planets" maybe) into being. It may seem perverse to look for and to find ballast for what we can know of future social relations that would induce ebullient queer futurities in Tim Dean's *Unlimited Intimacy: Reflections on the Subculture of Barebacking*, the opening chapter of which bears the confessional epigraph, "I like to bareback – to fuck without condoms." But for Dean barebacking "concerns an experience of unfettered intimacy, of overcoming the boundaries between persons, that is far from exclusive to this subculture or, indeed, to queer sexuality."[61] What this might mean, of course, is that barebacking occupies the queer time and space of the not-yet-here. It also promises a shattering of the identitarian structures which presently underpin our theories of sexuality and potentializes the thinking of new relational modes or forms-of-life (an important point to make about a book which has the virtue of bringing HIV, AIDS, and death back into focus without falling under the sway of the death driven queer post-politics).[62] If Foucault needs to be re-queered, unleashing his queer unreason or madness, then Dean suggests that queer theory itself needs to be re-queered. Barebacking (which he refuses to endorse or condemn) al-

---

58 Sara Ahmed, *The Promise of Happiness* (Durham: Duke University Press, 2010), 160–1.
59 Snediker, *Queer Optimism*.
60 Muñoz, *Cruising Utopia*, 1.
61 Tim Dean, *Unlimited Intimacy: Reflections on the Subculture of Barebacking* (Chicago: University of Chicago Press, 2010), 2.
62 I mean post-politics here in terms of Edelman's position of pure oppositionality to politics.

lows him "to defer judgement about it in order to open a space in which real thinking can occur."[63] If for Stockton growing sideways is a queer strategy in practice, and for Muñoz taking ecstasy is a queer strategy in motion, then for Dean promiscuity occupies that re-opened space where real thinking and patient forms of attention can take place. In lieu of the politics of identification he argues for an impersonal ethics in which one cares about others (strangers in the Levinasian sense), "even when one cannot see anything of oneself in them." So, in "contradistinction to the politics of identification, we have the ethics of alterity."[64]

This post-continental approach which moves beyond the subject in favour of what Elizabeth Grosz calls a "process of opening oneself up to the otherness that is the world itself [...] that makes us unrecognisable,"[65] might also be diagrammed using Lacan's graphs of sexuation as Levi Bryant does in his work on the democracy of objects and what he has termed object-oriented ontology (OOO). Lacan plays a crucial role in both Dean's *Beyond Sexuality* and *Unlimited Intimacy* as well as in Bryant's onticology, his "flat ontology." Bryant's theory of withdrawal is one which, in conversation with Tim Morton, asserts that we must oppose any "phallocentric totalization."[66] This is what Bryant has recently called "phallosophy."[67] Instead of interpreting Lacan's graphs in terms of sexuation, he understands them in terms of ontology. He explains that, "on both the masculine and the feminine side of the graph of sexuation, what we get are two different ways of handling the withdrawal at the heart of being. The left side of the graph refers to masculine sexuation, while the right side of the graph refers to feminine sexuation."[68] And in Bryant's post-phallosophical onticology, queer theory is to be found on the feminine ("not-all") side of the graph.

If David Ruffolo is determined to theorize queer desiring machines to counter an unproductive focus on lack then Bryant is equally attuned to the ways in which we ought to swerve away from Lacan's phallic function (which of course refers to castration or lack). Bryant explains:

> rather than referring to a masculine and feminine side of the graph, we can instead refer to a side of the graph that refers to object-oriented ontologies (the feminine [and subsequently he has placed the queer here too]). Moreover, rather than treating *phi* as the phallic function, we should instead treat *phi* as withdrawal. [...W]hat we get in this schema are two fundamentally different ways of discoursing about being.[69]

---

63 Dean, *Unlimited Intimacy*, 3.
64 Ibid., 25.
65 Elizabeth Grosz, "The Future of Feminist Theory: Dreams for New Knowledges." Keynote Address at Duke University, Durham, NC (March, 2007).
66 Timothy Morton, "Queer Objects," ecologywithoutnature.blogspot.com (March 15, 2011).
67 Levi Bryant, "Lacan's Graphs of Sexuation and OOO," larvalsubjects.wordpress.com (June 28, 2010).
68 Ibid.
69 Ibid.

Bryant reformulates the schemas for masculinity and femininity in terms of philosophies of presence where, "all are submitted to withdrawal with one exception," and object-oriented ontologies where, "not all are submitted to withdrawal. But there is no exception. There is none which is not submitted to withdrawal." What Bryant is getting at here is that there is no master signifier outside the set of all objects and there is no top or bottom object anywhere to be found. He goes on to say that:

> if the graphs of sexuation are rewritten in terms of ontology and withdrawal we can see how we get radically different ontologies depending on whether or not we're dealing with a metaphysics of presence or an object-oriented ontology. What the metaphysics of presence seeks and is always dependent upon is an exception or an entity that is not subject to withdrawal. In other words it seeks an entity that is *fully present* without any withdrawal whatsoever.[70]

However, OOOs give us a completely different schematization because, as Bryant argues, there is "no exception to withdrawal." He explains that, "it belongs to the being of all beings to withdraw without exception. Not only do beings withdraw from one another, but they also necessarily withdraw *from themselves*." In his democratization of objects Bryant develops the thesis that objects have a dual nature, that they simultaneously withdraw and are, "self-othering in and through their manifestations."

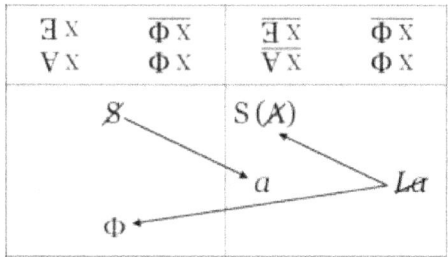

If we look at Lacan's graphs of sexuation we see a series of arrows traversing the two sides of the graph. As Bryant explains, on the masculine side we see an arrow pointing from the barred subject (*S*) to *objet a* (*a*) and the "logic of metaphysics of presence" generates a situation in which "withdrawal is seen as a loss rather than as a constitutive dimension of being." However, on the feminine side of the graph, which is on the side of object-oriented ontologies, there is a very different logic at work (something like Ruffolo's creative lines of flight, a multiplicity of flows). The feminine article (*La*) is represented as a constitutively split subject. "On the one hand," Bryant tells us, "we see an arrow pointing to the symbol for withdrawal (Φ) indicating an orientation

---

70 Ibid.

not to the presence or actuality of entities, but the manner in which an entity is always in excess of its manifestations. Likewise, we see yet another arrow directed at S(A) [...] the signifier for the barred Other." But, Bryant rethinks that barred other:

> The arrow pointing to the barred object would thus indicate a desire oriented to welcoming the stranger or that which disrupts the familiar world of local manifestations. Where the logic of desire underlying metaphysics of presence is predicated on overcoming a loss and thereby attaining presence, the logic of desire underlying object-oriented ontology would emphasize the excess of all substances over their local manifestations (the arrow pointing to *phi*), and therefore the *contingency* of all local manifestations (there's always more), and would welcome difference or those eruptions within stable regimes of local manifestation where the strange stranger surprises and indicates this excess.[71]

Bryant rethinks that barred other in terms of what Timothy Morton has called in various places the strange stranger,[72] a figure akin to Derrida's monstrous *arrivant*, and also in terms of Graham Harman's distinction between the real and sensuous properties of objects:

> the arrow pointing to the barred object would thus indicate a desire oriented to welcoming the stranger or that which disrupts the familiar world of local manifestations. Where the logic of desire underlying metaphysics of presence is predicated on overcoming a loss and thereby attaining presence, the logic of desire [we might call it post-queer desire with Ruffolo] underlying object-oriented ontology would emphasize the excess of all substances over their local manifestations (there's always more) and would welcome difference or those eruptions within stable regimes of local manifestation where the strange stranger surprises and indicates this excess" ("Phallosophy").[73]

This is perhaps how we might diagram the virtuality of queer theory's being constitutively open (to the world itself, and to go further, constitutively open to its future) and undomesticatable. If for Bryant, every "entity is a becoming that promises to become otherwise" then this is why entities are not only strange strangers to other entities but are also strange strangers to *themselves.*"[74] Morton has in his essay "Queer Ecology" extended his idea of the strange stranger to queer objects, guaranteeing a theory of with-

---

71 Bryant, "Lacan's Graphs of Sexuation and OOO."
72 See in particular, "Queer Ecology" PMLA 125.2 (March 2010): 273–82; *The Ecological Thought* (Cambridge: Harvard University Press, 2010).
73 Ibid.
74 Ibid.

drawn objects which recognizes the strange strangeness to *everything*.[75] Any state an entity, say queer theory, happens to be in is merely provisional and there is always an excess or remainder beyond phallic identification and totalization. Bryant asks if his non-phallosophical thought deserves the title of a queer ontology "in addition to a feminist ontology?" and the answer he provides is yes. His theory of withdrawal shares a great deal with Derrida's abyssal aporetics, moving as it does beyond any epistemological limitation and "inscribing itself in the very being of the object itself." If the object is withdrawn because "it is never present either for-itself or for-another," then we might begin to redraw queer theory as an entity which also deserves the name "strange stranger."[76] And we might now see Dean's unlimited intimacy as a withdrawal from and reaching out towards strangers.

In the concluding chapter, "Cruising as a Way of Life" (a clear nod to the later Foucault and the invention of new alliances, modes of life and unforeseen lines of force) to *Unlimited Intimacy* Dean writes that, "cruising entails a remarkably hospitable disposition towards strangers. Insofar as that is the case, the subculture of bareback promiscuity, far from being ethically irresponsible, may be ethically exemplary."[77] Barebacking, as he makes very clear throughout, is a practice which anyone can perform and may not have any particular attachment to or origin in gay sexualities. Cruising, which also is not a gay-specific practice, "exemplifies a distinctive ethic of openness to alterity and that – irrespective of our view of the morality of barebacking – we all, gay and non-gay, have something to learn from this relational ethic."[78] Barebacking disintricates us, then, from the identitarian (or in Dean's terms "identificatory") focus of lesbian and gay studies and opens up a space for queer sexualities and relationalities. Barebacking, we might say, is a queer strategy in practice. Methodologically – not that queer theory is a methodology, it is just what happens – this relates to a certain promiscuity, to "thinking promiscuously about promiscuity itself," extending promiscuity beyond the sexual realm to the philosophico-theoretical (queer not as a sexual orientation but as a theoretical one). If for Lauren Berlant and Michael Warner queer commentary was attuned to the opening up of a world then for Dean, fifteen years later, it is pleasurable yet risky openness to contact with others, with strangers which opens up to the world. "Cruising" for Dean "involves not just hunting for sex but opening oneself to the world"[79] and we might add, to a recalibrated futurity and erotico-relational ethic(s). Erotic impersonality, experimenting with viruses, for Dean, is an exploration of the ways in which we may, "relate to others and even become intimately engaged with them

---

75 See also Morton's "Here Comes Everything: The Promise of Object-Oriented Ontology," *Qui Parle* 19.2: 163–90.
76 Bryant, "Lacan's Graphs of Sexuation and OOO."
77 Dean, *Unlimited Intimacy*, 176.
78 Ibid.
79 Ibid., 210.

without needing to know or identify with them."⁸⁰ And this, I think, is what Bryant means by his own onticology of withdrawal which discloses the

> relation that is a non-relation to the strange stranger. Such is the (non)relational ethics, the posthuman ethics of difference, that onticology and [Morton's] dark ecology strive to think, an ethics where the "non" must be placed in parentheses precisely because it is oddly both a relation and an absence of relation, precisely because it is proximity and the impossibility of any proximity.⁸¹

> Queer Theory, in moving outline (capable of being endlessly redrawn), we might say, could be diagrammed as a post-continental theory of precisely everything, a madly erotically impersonal mode of opening up to and meshing with the strangeness of others, of opening up to the incalculable strangeness of the future to-come, of opening up to aesthetic and political practices that do not yet exist but need to be envisioned as necessarily ecstatic modes of stepping out of this enmired place and time to something cosmopolitically "fuller, vaster, more sensual and brighter."⁸²

---

80 Dean, *Unlimited Intimacy*, 211.
81 Bryant, "Lacan's Graphs of Sexuation and OOO."
82 Muñoz, *Cruising Utopia*, 189.

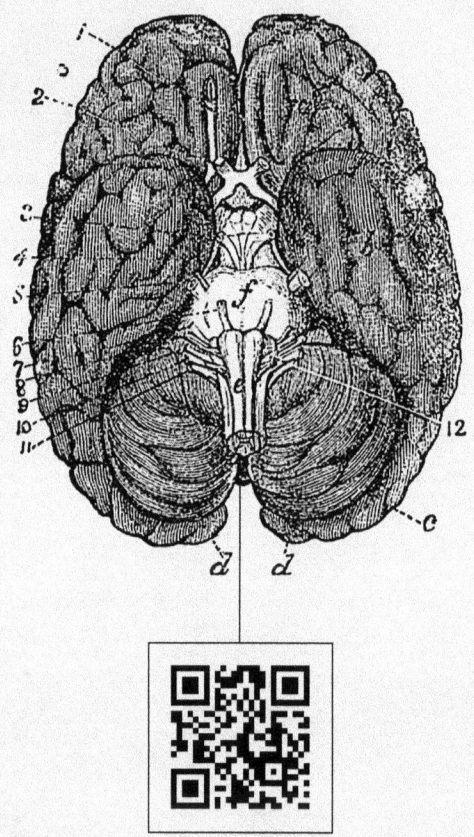

Please Mind the Gap: How to Podcast Your Brain[1]

Karen Spaceinvaders

Please scan the QR code to access the mp3 files of deep brain recordings of individual brain cells, the smallest unit of the brain, in a whole, intact living brain. Each brain region's cells possess an electrical signature. During recordings electrical signals are transformed into sound to facilitate auditory identification of cells during a process called "mapping."

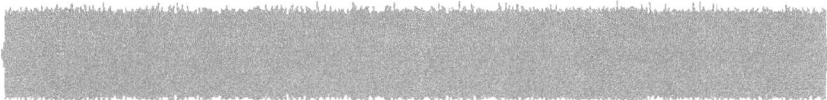

Subthalamic Nucleus

Cortex

Mapping is an important step in successfully identifying and localizing the appropriate target site in the brain for an experimental therapeutic procedure called deep brain stimulation which has been used for patients with movement disorders and, more recently, for patients with psychiatric disorders.

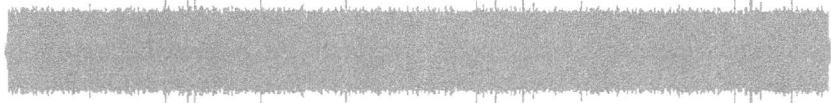

Thalamus

---

1 Editor's suggested resources: Michael Gazzaniga's lecture, "Free Yet Determined and Constrained" at Edinburgh University Gifford Lectures on October 19, 2009 is an excellent discussion of the field. It can be viewed on Edinburgh University's YouTube channel: https://www.youtube.com/watch?v=aGtZek7RPts; Patricia A. Reuter-Lorenz, Kathleen Baynes, George R. Mangun, and Elizabeth A. Phelps (eds), *The Cognitive Neuroscience of the Mind* (Cambridge: MIT Press, 2010).

I have pursued a career as a neuroscientist for the past decade because I wanted to learn about the mind. In my most recent research, I record electrical activity from individual cells in the brain, and look at individual brain cells with a high resolution, electron microscope.

Globus Pallidus (internal segment)

Globus Pallidus (extrenal segment)

The closer I examine the brain, the less I learn about the mind. Rather, what has been most informative about the mind is how people – neuroscientists and non-neuroscientists alike – interpret neuroscience data. Some cognitive neuroscientists have proposed the qualities we hold most precious as humans, like morality and free will, exist only in the context of human interaction. Likewise, I propose that the mind does not exist in a vacuum and one's mind only necessitates distinction in a social context, and the mind's existence may only be relevant due to its relative relationships. In sum, bodies have brains. People have minds.

Striatum

I invite readers to reflect on and/or refute these statements after listening to these recordings of the brain in action. These regions are part of the cortico-basal ganglia-thalamo-cortical circuit, which is thought to possess parallel, functionally segregated loops including a motor-movement circuit and limbic-emotional circuit which work together to generate behavior (e.g. motivated movements) and have been researched for their role in Parkinson's disease as well as Obsessive Compulsive Disorder.

continent. 1.3 (2011): 158–70

The Fragment as a Unit of Prose Composition: An Introduction

Ben Segal

The fragment, the note, the idea, the aphorism even: there are many names and as many uses for such small shards of free-floating text. Typically fragments are less works than gestures, arrows pointing in the direction a person might research, meditate on or develop. Unlike paragraphs or sentences, they do not flow directly from and into their bordering text. Instead they are independent, defined by their singularity, by the white space that encases them on a page – even when they are cobbled together and marshaled into service as the contents of a book.

Still, though not exceedingly common, books of fragments (or notes or what-have-yous) do exist. However they are labeled, the very aloofness of disconnected micro-texts allows them certain privileges and possibilities that a writer can employ and exploit. In such instances, the book of fragments may, almost paradoxically, gain a coherence as a singular work, all the more satisfying for its fractures.

Two such books are Maggie Nelson's BLUETS *and Evan Lavender-Smith's* From Old Notebooks. *We are pleased to present a series of excerpts from each of these books, a selection of 'outtakes' – fragments that did not make it into the final manuscripts – from each,[1] and short interviews with both Nelson and Lavender-Smith about the fragment as a literary device.[2]*

---

1 Since this feature includes excerpts and outtakes from both *BLUETS* and *From Old Notebooks*, I chose to ask both Nelson and Lavender-Smith similar questions about working with the fragment as the building-block of a larger work. This means that the questions are, for the most part, more concerned with things like form than about specific passages from the books.
2 In both interviews, I ask a question that cites Philippe Lacoue-Labarthe and Jean Luc Nancy's *The Literary Absolute: The Theory of Literature in German Romanticism*, trans. Philip Barnard and Cheryl Lester (Albany: SUNY Press, 1988). It should be noted that *The Literary Absolute* is concerned with the fragment as developed and understood in the context of the Jena Romantics (the Schlegel brothers, Novalis, etc.), not necessarily the fragment in general.

Maggie Nelson

Ben Segal (BS): "Bluet" conjures a constellation of similar words. These include Blue, Bullet, and the flower to which the word actually refers. I'm wondering if this range is intentional and if there's anything I'm leaving out. Or, more simply, can you talk a little about the title?

Maggie Nelson (MN): I first got interested in the word BLUETS via the painter Joan Mitchell, about whom I'd written earlier in my book on women and the New York School. LES BLUETS is the name of one of my very favorites of all her paintings; she painted it the year I was born. Later the poet Jimmy Schuyler wrote a lovely prose poem about this painting, which I also adored, and which I've also written about. So the word had been in my mind for some time, as had her amazing painting (which is in several panels, so also in parts – i.e. in dialogue with questions of parts/wholes).

While it was in progress, I always called BLUETS "The Blue Book." But I knew I always wanted an eventual title that referred, however obliquely, to the book's form. In this case, the form is notably PLURAL, as is BLUETS, which seemed right. Also, I have always pronounced BLUETS "bluettes," which is kind of a personal joke about feminization. Like, "majorettes," etc. It's a joke because I think the book has a lot to do with the robustness of being a female human, so I found irony in the diminutive nature of the suffix. I also liked the fact that the word means a kind of flower, as it allowed each proposition, or whatever you might call each numbered section, to be thought of as a single flower in a bouquet. This sounds cheesy here, but I think I talk about this idea in a less cheesy way in the book itself, near the end, when I'm ruminating on its composition, and its surprising (to me) slimness, or "anemia."

BS: I know you've thought (and taught) about the fragment as a mode of writing. I'm wondering how your study of the form influences the way you use it.

While writing a book, I'm influenced by things the same way I would imagine most writers are: I look for what I want to steal, then I steal it, and make my own weird stew of the goods. Often while writing I'd re-read the books by Barthes written in fragments – *A Lover's Discourse, Roland Barthes by Roland Barthes* – and see what he gained from an alphabetical, somewhat random organization, and what he couldn't do that way. I mostly read Wittgenstein, and watched how he used numbered sections to think sequentially, and to jump, in turn. I read Shonagon's *The Pillow Book*, and tried to keep a pillow book about blue for some time. (It didn't last long, as an exercise, but some of the entries made it into BLUETS.) I re-read Haneke's *Sorrow Beyond Dreams*, which finally dissolves into fragments, after a fairly strong chronological narrative has taken him so far.

In the course I taught on the fragment, which was somewhat after the fact of writing BLUETS, but conceived in relation to it, we studied a kind of taxonomy of fragments: the decayed fragment (Sappho); the contemporary fragment (text messages, twitter, blog posts, etc.); the modernist fragment (T.S. Eliot; fragment as mark of psychological disintegration); Freud's fragment (dreams, slips, etc. as thruways to the unconscious; the sampled or plagiarized fragment; fragment as waste, excess, or garbage; the footnote; fragment as frame (Degas, Manet); life narrative as fragment: we can't see the whole until we're dead, and then we can't see it (pathos); fragment as psychological terror (castration, King's head); fragment as fetish, or as "organ-logic," as pornography; fragment as metonym & synecdoche; fragment as that which is preserved, or that which remains; fragment as the unfinished or the abandoned; and so on and so forth.

I think, in the back of my mind, I was aware of all these categories while writing BLUETS, and put them each into play as needed while writing. The book seems to me hyper-aware of the fragment as fetish, as catastrophe, as leftover, as sample or citation, as memory, and so on. Many of the anecdotes in the book (such as about the decay of blue objects I've collected, or my memory of a particularly acute shade of blue, or the recountings of dreams) perform these concepts quite directly.

> BS: In *The Literary Absolute,* Philippe Lacoue-Labarthe and Jean-Luc Nancy write that "each fragment stands for itself and for that from which it has been detached."[3] They go on to explain that the fragment is both "sub-work" (in the obvious sense of being only a small piece of the Work), but also "super-work", as it stands, complete in itself, outside the work and calls up the plural potentiality of the work. What do you make of this idea and how do you understand the relation of the fragment to the Work as a whole?

MN: I like the idea of the "super-work," the fragment that indicates the whole it has been excised from. However, on a concrete level, I don't think that's really true of BLUETS. Some of the propositions are very much in dialogue with the ones that have come before it, acting as rebuffs, or conclusions, or swerves. To detect their motion, one has to already be in the car. Often they are as short as: "*Disavowal,* says the silence," or "As if we could scrape the color off the iris and still see," or "In any case, I am no longer counting the days." These don't make much sense outside of their context. Although, now that I've isolated just these few, I can see that they might gesture to the whole – but I think you'd have to know what the whole was, for the exercise to feel full.

I am interested, however, in the notion of collecting, of a collection – and how to know when to stop, when you've amassed enough. While writing

---

3   Lacoue-Labarthe and Nancy, *The Literary Absolute,* 44.

BLUETS, I thought of Joseph Cornell as the ultimate teacher in this respect: he collected enormous amounts of junk, he "hunted" for treasures all over the city, but each box or collage or even film has a certain minimalism, each feels as if it's been distilled to become exactly as specific as it should be. In other words, the composition emanates from the piles of junk left in its wake, but it in itself becomes perfect. It may be unfashionable, but I'm interested in this sense of perfection.

> BS: Fragments collected together become a whole that gestures to dozens of other, potential wholes. How, if at all, do you think about your book in relation to the preservation of potentiality?

MN: I have to admit, I don't entirely understand this question. Preservation of potentiality – that's what I don't quite understand. I will say this, though: writing a book, especially a book of this kind (i.e. I'd wanted to write a book on the color blue for my whole life), has a certain pain in it – the pain of manifestation. Every word that gets set down, every decision made – form, content, sentence structure, image – begins to define a work that previously was a kind of infinitely indeterminate mental cloud, or beautifully diffuse physical sensation. As the book comes into being, I'm often thinking, "this is it? this is all it's going to be?" For me, I think it's this feeling, rather than that of not having anything to say, or a terror of the blank page, that can bring a sort of writer's block. Think of Lily Briscoe at the end of Woolf's *To the Lighthouse* – after her long reverie, she eventually must make the mark on the canvas. She brings the brush down, then sighs: "There, I have had my vision." To have made the mark, to have manifested the vision, brings with it a certain satisfaction, a certain euphoria and relief – but also a brand of pathos. Of all the possible books, you wrote this book. Of all the possible brush strokes, you made this one. How very strange!

The good news is, you're usually so tired when you finish a book that you don't care anymore – you're just happy it's finished, and that you can move on. And if you're lucky, you may eventually marvel at the specificity of the result, feel the magic and largesse in its specificity, in its singularity. I feel this way about BLUETS.

> BS: Can you talk a little about the way traditional prose standbys like character and narrative develop out of distinct and disconnected fragments? I feel like this definitely happens in Bluets as well as other texts that use a similar approach.

MN: BLUETS always had a specific set of dramatic personae, and also a sort of narrative arc. It begins by saying, "Suppose I were to begin," which places the whole book, at least for me, in the realm of the novelistic, or at least the speculative. That freedom was important to me while writing. I have a lot of issues, for lack of a better word, with narrative, but I also have no problem with trying to structure a work so that it acts as a page-turner. I wanted there to be a lot of momentum in this book, as well as plenty of opportunities for eddying out into cul-de-sacs. That was the tension – how to make some chains of propositions that pull you forward, and then allow for some to bring you so far afield that you might find yourself wondering, "why are we talking about this here?" before remembering how you got there, and why it might matter.

While some of the fragments may seem disconnected or distinct, the truth is that they each had to fall into one the book's major categories, which included love, language, sex, divinity, alcohol, pain, death, and problems of veracity/perception. If I truly couldn't tether an anecdote or factoid to the thread, it eventually had to go. I also spaced out the distinct threads fairly methodically, and had the characters reappear at a fairly regular rate. There's even a kind of "where are they now?" section at the end, announced by my injured friend's letter to her friends, in which she tells them how her spinal cord injury has affected her life, and how she feels today.

I'm sure one could write a book of very disconnected fragments that didn't so overtly weave into a whole – I've read many of them – but it's also true that the mind will always work overtime to put disparate things together; the Surrealists mined that tendency for all it was worth. I think that's a cool approach, to let the reader make the connections, but it's important to me as a writer to make sure that the connections, when made, actually point toward what I want to be pointing at, rather than just reflecting the human brain's capacity to make a bridge.

> BS: To what extent does how you label your texts matter? What is the difference between notes, fragments, bluets, and aphorisms? Basically, is taxonomy important?

MN: Taxonomy, hmm. At some point I was very compelled by issues of taxonomy, but over the years I've grown less interested in the question, as the notion of the "hybrid" or the "cross-genre" seems to have become its own kind of jargon or pitch. I got very excited some time ago when I was trying to subtitle my book JANE, and I came across Brian Evenson's book *Dark Property: An Affliction* I thought – of course! A book can be a *condition* rather than a *genre*. So I subtitled JANE "A Murder," with this concept in mind. My most recent book, THE ART OF CRUELTY, I subtitled "a reckoning," using the same logic. This has been one means of skirting the whole genre issue.

On the other hand, I don't really like it when people called BLUETS "notes" or "aphorisms," or "fragments," because it's not really any of those things. Aphoristic philosophy – which was one of this book's inspirations – is not made up of just aphorisms per se. There may be great aphorisms to be found in Nietzsche or Wittgenstein, for example, but neither is writing a series of one-liners. Their projects are bigger than that. They are in dialogue with argumentation as much as with impression. Likewise, I don't really see

BLUETS as poetry. I mean, I don't care if someone wants to call it that – if they do, it happily expands the notion of poetry – but I've written enough poetry to have a lot of respect for its particular tools, which include the line break, and forms of logic unavailable to prose. BLUETS thinks in prose; it is written in prose. It sometimes thinks in images, and sometimes in sound, but essentially it is about sentences, and about trains of prose logic and their limits. But if someone wants to call it poetry, I wouldn't go to the mat about it.

BS: Are there other texts (of or about fragments) that you'd like to recommend?

MN: Texts about fragments to recommend: Here are the ones that come immediately to mind: *The Notebooks of Joseph Joubert*; Anne Carson's *If Not, Winter*; Stevie Smith, "The Person from Porlock"; the poetry of Lorine Niedecker, Lucille Clifton, and Paul Celan; Tom Phillips's *A Humument*; Ann Lauterbach's essay on "the whole fragment"; Linda Nochlin, *The Body in Pieces*; Mary Ann Caws, *The Surrealist Look*; Heather McHugh, *Poetry and Partiality*. And the drawings of David Shrigley.

BS: And finally, is there anything you wish I would have asked? Please ask/answer if so.

MN: No, I'm happy with these questions!

The Beginning of Maggie Nelson's BLUETS

1. Suppose I were to begin by saying that I had fallen in love with a color. Suppose I were to speak this as though it were a confession; suppose I shredded my napkins as we spoke. *It began slowly. An appreciation, an affinity. Then, one day, it became more serious.* Then (looking into an empty teacup, its bottom stained with thin brown excrement coiled into the shape of a sea horse) *it became somehow* personal.

2. And so I fell in love with a color – in this case, the color blue – as if falling under a spell, a spell I fought to stay under and get out from under, in turns.

3. Well, and what of it? A voluntary delusion, you might say. That each blue object could be a kind of burning bush, a secret code meant for a single agent, an X on a map too diffuse ever to be unfolded in entirety but that contains the knowable universe. How could all the shreds of blue garbage bags stuck in brambles, or the bright blue tarps flapping over ever shanty and fish stand in the world, be, in essence, the fingerprints of God? *I will try to explain this.*

4. I admit that I may have been lonely. I know that loneliness can produce bolts of hot pain, a pain which, if it stays hot enough for long enough, can begin to stimulate, or to provoke – take your pick – an apprehension of the divine. (*This ought to arouse our suspicions.*)

5. But first, let us consider a sort of case in reverse. In 1867, after a long bout of solitude, the French poet Stéphane Mallarmé wrote to his friend Henri Cazalis: "These last months have been terrifying. My Thought has thought itself through and reached a Pure Idea. What the rest of me has suffered during that long agony, is indescribable." Mallarmé described this agony as a battle that took place on God's "boney wing." "I struggled with that creature of ancient and evil plumage – God – whom I fortunately defeated and threw to earth," he told Cazalis with exhausted satisfaction. Eventually Mallarmé began replacing "le ciel" with "l'Azur" in his poems, in an effort to rinse references to the sky of religious connotations. "Fortunately," he wrote Cazalis, "I am quite dead now."

6. The half-circle of blinding turquoise ocean is this love's primal scene. That this blue exists makes my life a remarkable one, just to have seen it. To have seen such beautiful things. To find oneself placed in their midst. Choiceless. I returned there yesterday and stood again upon the mountain.

7. But what kind of love is it, really? Don't fool yourself and call it sublimity. Admit that you have stood in front of a little pile of ultramarine pigment in a glass cup at a museum and felt stinging desire. But to do what? Liberate it? Purchase it? Ingest it? There is so little blue food in nature – in fact blue in the wild tends to mark food to avoid (mold, poisonous berries) – that culinary advisers generally recommend against blue light, blue paint, and blue plates when and where serving food. But while the color may sap appetite in the most literal sense, it feeds it in others. You might want to reach out and disturb the pile of pigment, for example, first staining your fingers with it, then staining the world. You might want to dilute it and swim in it, you might want to rouge your nipples with it, you might want to paint a virgins robe with it. But you still wouldn't be accessing the blue of it. Not exactly.

8. Do not, however, make the mistake of thinking that all desire is yearning. "We love to contemplate blue, not because it advances to us, but because it draws us after it," wrote Goethe, and perhaps he is right. But I am not interested in longing to live in a world in which I already live. I don't want to yearn for blue things, and God forbid, for any "blueness." Above all, I want to stop missing you.

9. So please do not write to tell me about any more beautiful blue things. To be fair, this book will not tell you about any, either. It will not say, *Isn't x beautiful?* Such demands are murderous to beauty.

10. The most I want to do is show you the end of my index finger. Its muteness.

Bluets that did not make the final version of BLUETS

We think of a glowing chunk of sapphire, for instance, or a pane of Chartres stained glass, as luminous, and God knows they are. But such luminosity doesn't necessarily have anything to do with *clarity*.

To call something a false idol is to elevate it to the company of deities, even if one eventually casts it down (cf. Milton giving Lucifer the best speeches).

For the truth is that I have never really understood what *love* and *will* have to do with each other. Following the blue, as if tracking a trail of decomposing crumbs left in the woods by a benevolent or absentminded stranger, is, at times, the best I can do.

Joan Mitchell: so beautiful and athletic when young; so craggy and indomitable as she aged – in both cases, *without vanity* – like my Swedish grandparents, whom I barely knew, but whom I remember as being tan and fair at the same time, prematurely decimated by morning vodka with OJ and an endless boil of cigarettes.

Do not think, however, that this is a scrapbook in which blue is the star and I its delirious fan. For it is a mistake to think of blue as separate from us. It is the bulge of the carotid against the bracket of your skin. It is the matrix of veins that enlaces your heart.

At one point during this period, Klein – no stranger to grandiosity – "signed the sky." He also arranged performances at which he dipped naked women from head to toe in IKB blue, rolled an enormous canvas out on the floor, and instructed the women to drag each other around on top of it while a string quartet played nearby. He called the women "human paintbrushes."

In both cases, I have arguably been nothing more than a child of illusion.

Beethoven felt differently. "Can you lend me the *Theory of Colours* for a few weeks?" he wrote to a friend in 1820. "It is an important work. His last things are insipid."

There would seem to be a lesson here, but I am not prepared to describe it.

"They feel as though if you fell into them you would be trapped and unable to breathe, choked and suffocated by the powdery pigment," wrote Berger of Klein's IKB monochromes.

At times I look forward to this ravaging, if only because it represents all that I am supposed to fear, and because, if one manages to live long enough, it seems something of an inevitability, and looking forward to an inevitability seems at least an approximation of spiritual wisdom.

In the far-off blue places, one finds oneself face to face with one's stupidity. The cradle of it. It is a tremendous relief. Instead of sputtering forth a gargle, a howl, or an assertoric proposition, one can remain silent, stupefied. It is as if one's tongue had been sewn, at long last, into its den.

For one does not just seek oblivion. One can also find it. Sometimes one can even purchase it.

Of the oblivion seekers themselves, Eberhardt says simply: "They are people who like their pleasure."

Caravaggio is a serious painter. He does not use blue. Neither does Goya, nor Velasquez. They are *tenebrists*, not denizens of the carnival. The blues of Picasso and Matisse, even in their most melancholy applications, do not strike me as altogether serious. The blues of Joseph Cornell, Hiroshige, Fra Angelico, and Cézanne, on the other hand, strike me as quite serious. The blue of Vermeer is simply too painful to discuss here. Let us leave the woman in blue alone with her letter. Let us leave her transfixed, standing on the bright edge of the earth, about to fall.

In the Middle Ages, it was commonly thought that the most powerful mordant was a drunk man's piss: yet another instance in which alcohol *fastens* the blue. But one can, I think, feel similarly bound, without the spirit.

And when Cornell made *Rose Hobart*, he had to snip away 57½ minutes of the original film in order to showcase the object of his desire. Love, too, can sometimes be a *condensery*.

On the other hand, speaking through the voice of the Egyptian god Thamus, Socrates comes down fairly forcefully for *poison*: "This discovery of yours [i.e. writing] will create forgetfulness in the learners' souls, because they will not use their memories; they will trust to the external written characters and not remember of themselves. The specific which you have discovered is an aid not to memory, but to reminiscence, and you give your disciples not truth, but only the semblance of truth."

But what has a soul to do with memory? I admit that here I run out of ideas; I must again consult the Encyclopedia. "Much of our moral life depends on the peculiar ways in which we are embedded in time." This has the aura of truth, but really it takes us no further. For what has morality to do with memory, or with a soul?

Instead of a roving dialogue unfolding under the shade of a plane tree, this is more like a coarse talk show taking place in a hall of mirrors: no guests, one host.

To do: make a list of people who seem to have found some dignity in their loneliness, and consult it when I feel constitutionally incapable of abiding my own.

"Frequent tears have run the colours from my life" (Elizabeth Barrett Browning).

Does it follow, in spiritual matters, that one's doubt is surrounded by a plateau of certainty? "Whosoever unceasingly strives upward, him can we save," wrote Goethe. But who is to say that faith isn't the abyss, and doubt the surrounding peaks?

For while we may have learned the names for these things, articulation is still a form of accommodation. We stutter to each other in a sort of shorthand, at times carving out shapely analogies. But we cannot be sure that we are talking about the same things, or that we are employing the same code.

– But now you are talking as if you were drowning, your lungs swollen with expired air. Why not just give up the dive? In which case you could start swimming along the surface: a cold spot here, a warm patch there. Same pond.

Remember: the knights pure enough to enter the presence of the Holy Grail never return. It is only those who have been "incompletely transformed" who come back to tell the tale. And some seekers don't come back from the wilderness as shamans, but rather as brain-damaged vegetables whose musculature now resembles gelatin.

Remember this if someone appears in a field of chollas, hands you a loincloth and a tab of pure blotter acid with one hand, and keeps the other out of sight.

We might here note that Andy Warhol was also, for a time, riveted by blue pussy. His blue pussy was a beatific cat, gazing upward from the last page of his 1954 book of watercolors, *25 Cats Name Sam and One Blue Pussy*, looking as if he were happily anticipating "pussy heaven," as Warhol elsewhere termed the feline afterlife.

Perhaps, then, the mistake is to look for a vividness, or a sweetness, *apart* from illusion. In which case we waste much precious time warding off the specter of the *mirage*.

In such moments, death itself may appear a light-hearted occurrence.

Evan Lavender-Smith

> BS: Do you consider *From Old Notebooks* to be a kind of constraint writing? I guess it would have been more of a constraint if you'd only culled things from your notes instead of writing pieces specifically for/relating to *From Old Notebooks*.

Evan Lavender-Smith (ELS): I certainly think that the book shares something important with constraint writing, as I think it does with conceptual writing, although I don't know that it fits neatly into either of these categories. Perhaps it's a kind of faux constraint or conceptual writing. The book's primary constraint – only things written in notebooks are allowed – sort of collapses under the weight of its own self-reflexivity; as you say, the entries become about the book itself, which I think ends up undermining or subjugating the austerity we associate with a more typical constraint-based writing. I suppose there's also a secondary constraint associated with the structure of the book and the ordering of the entries, this zany process whereby I classified entries according to a number (1 through 12, I think) referencing subject/theme, then deleted all of the entries leaving only their reference numbers, then arranged the numbers in something resembling sonata form, then plugged all the entries back into their placeholders. But that's a very secret, Roussel-type constraint, one that perhaps does not do much to create a noticeable intensity of constraint. And also I ended up making many revisions to the order of the entries that broke with the output of my secret formula. So yes, I think something like "sham constraint" writing is probably a more appropriate designation.

> BS: *From Old Notebooks* is very often self-reflective, often feels as if it is struggling to pin itself down. I'm wondering if the form (disjointed notes) allows for that kind of reflection to creep in repeatedly without weighing down the whole book. Does the ability to ask a question and then immediately head off in a totally different direction free you to be self-doubting without wallowing? Does this question make sense? Maybe I should

ask more generally what kinds of content does this form afford that more traditionally structured work might not?

ELS: I am hopeful that the self-reflexivity is less cloying in this book than I find it to be in other highly self-reflexive texts on account of what you mention, the ability of the book to veer off in another direction nearly every time an instance of explicit self-reflexivity occurs. I would say this is also the case with respect to the book's many instances of pathos and sentiment or even bathos and sentimentality: whenever the book broaches sentimentality in an entry, it is followed by another entry about something totally different, which can serve to undercut the sentiment of the previous entry. And this is probably also the case with the book's movement toward and immediately away from entries/fragments dealing with specific literary or philosophical texts/authors with which some readers may be unfamiliar, insofar as one entry might concern Kant's transcendental idealism and the next entry the color of my infant son's poo. The book is quite contrapuntal, in this respect, which is one of the things that original structuring scheme was meant to effect.

As to alternative or unusual kinds of content afforded by the book's form, I'd like to think they are many, but I have always been most excited by what I perceive to be the book's presentation of a kind of form-becoming-content, this process by which the reader is engaged with form as he might otherwise be with character, or with setting, or with plot – part of what's driving the reading experience may be the reader's sense of an evolving form, a form that begins somewhat expositionally, that becomes somewhat conflicted and tense, and that finally achieves a kind of resolution. But, from another perspective, the book's form remains exactly the same from the first to the last page. My reading of the book would posit or project a kind of talk-to/talk-back relationship between form and content; each is strongly influencing our vision of the other, and perhaps, over the course of the book, they become difficult to distinguish.

> BS: In *The Literary Absolute*, Philippe Lacoue-Labarthe and Jean-Luc Nancy write that "each fragment stands for itself and for that from which it has been detached."[4] They go on to explain that the fragment is both "sub-work" (in the obvious sense of being only a small piece of the Work), but also "super-work", as it stands, complete in itself, outside the work and calls up the plural potentiality of the work. What do you make of this idea and how do you understand the relation of the fragment to the Work as a whole?

ELS: I like this idea, but I may have some reservations about generalizing it too far beyond Nancy and Lacoue-Labarthe's intended historical context. In my book, there are perhaps some entries/fragments that possess a sort of

---

4   Lacoue-Labarthe and Nancy, *The Literary Absolute*, 44.

immanent intensity – entries seemingly able to "speak for themselves," so to speak – but there are also very many that do not. I think that the book itself would argue – in fact, I believe it explicitly does so – against this notion that any one of its constituent parts could be removed from the whole and still remain "meaningful" or "true." I imagine the parts of the whole, in this book, not as cogs in relation to some whole mechanics or machine, say, but instead as mechanical movement itself; perhaps the most important thing about any given entry is not what it says so much as the fact that it begins and ends. The book seems to me to be always moving forward in time and space; once a fragment has happened, the book is done with it; there's no turning back, no looking over the shoulder. There's an entry somewhere that goes something like "This book is nothing more than the trash can of my imagination," a potential interpretative model that has become something of a guiding light in my understanding of the book's form: the entries/fragments do certainly accrue, as trash accrues, but we don't necessarily feel compelled to go picking through this heap of trash.

BS: Fragments collected together become a whole that gestures to dozens of other, potential wholes. How, if at all, do you think about your book in relation to the preservation of potentiality?

ELS: Of course I think about this mostly in relation to the fragments/entries concerning specific potential works, the entries that begin "Story about" or "Novel about," etc. As I continue to work to see many of the ideas in the book realized, even today – and as I will likely continue to do for a long time – I remain in a sort of dialogue with the book. So I find myself still writing the book, in some sense, even though the book is already written. One of my favorite things about *From Old Notebooks* is how it opens its own amorphous and evolving prefatory engagement with my future writing. I believe the book references the claim of some critics that *Ulysses* was written in such a way to make it appear as if it were presaged by passages in the New Testament, just as some have claimed that passages in the New Testament were written to create the appearance of having been forecasted by passages in the Old Testament (I believe there is a specific poetic figure denoting this kind of retroactive foreshadowing that I'm now failing to recall). I've always really loved that idea and perhaps still hold out hope that my future writing will serve to indirectly modify *From Old Notebooks* in these types of sly and tricky ways.

Also, in relation to the above-mentioned trash-can model as one of many such potential models for the book's form, there's a way in which the book regularly returns to a reading of itself, always trying to understand how it is working and always coming up with new strategies for its own analysis. So it seems to me, with respect to the preservation of potentiality, that the book is also intent on preserving its own "infinite hermeneutics" (or at least an illusion thereof).

BS: Can you talk a little about the way traditional prose standbys like character and narrative develop out of distinct and disconnected fragments? I feel like this definitely happens in *From Old Notebooks* as well as other texts that use a similar approach.

ELS: I think it's important to address the burden placed on the reader vis-à-vis development when considering narratological staples like character and plot in relation to highly fragmented narratives. In my own reading experience of books in which neat narrative progression is supplanted by a fragmentary or elliptical progression, the reader oftentimes must begin committing to processes of projection and transference in order to eke out that amount of development she would require of narrative. I especially like this possibility for two reasons. The first is that in the absence of stable or "full" development, we may feel inclined, as readers, to fill in the blanks with manifestations of our own, consciousness-specific desire for coherence, which can create a sort of personalized Möbius strip out of reading and writing, artistic creation and reception becoming tangled, distinctions and distances between these categories becoming blurred. The second, which may follow from the first for the more theoretically inclined reader, is that this process may serve to expose our own prejudices about what narrative is supposed to do or achieve, thereby leading us to an anxious readerly condition in which we are forced to confront the poverty of our own understanding regarding the first principles of narrative art. These two effects: 1, tangling the reading/writing experience; and 2, forcing the reader's reconsideration of artistic rule – are, to my thinking, among the most powerful effects available to writing.

BS: To what extent does how you label your texts matter? What is the difference between *notes, fragments, thoughts,* and *aphorisms*? Basically, is taxonomy important? Supplementary question: In *From Old Notebooks*, there is a passage: "Why am I so averse to classifying From Old Notebooks as poetry – because poetry doesn't sell." If you want, this might be a good place to talk about genre classifications as well.

ELS: This answer will surely seem coy or naïve to some people, but the fact is that my own tedious and protracted grappling with the strictures and arbitrariness of generic classification has finally given way to a vision of an imaginative writing largely unfettered by those academic or commercial or cultural pressures which have served to delimit the typological boundaries of art and language. That seems to be a goal for me, anyway, to work to maintain a position of restless and relentless searching in relation to form, and to resist, as best I can, pressures associated with the commodification or canonization of language and form. Of course that position is itself probably overdetermined by pressures both within and beyond my comprehension – e.g. it is very reactionary; very Modernist, in a sense – and it also strikes me to be of a piece with a rather antiquated and distasteful image of artistic creation and the "author-function," but nonetheless it's what I seem to prefer.

> BS: Are there other texts (of or about fragments) that you'd like to recommend?

ELS: Here are some things I've recently read and enjoyed in which I felt the fragment was the text's dominant or near-dominant mode of engagement with narrative/poetic/philosophical development and progression: *Mean Free Path*, Ben Lerner; *Bluets*, Maggie Nelson; *Varieties of Disturbance*, Lydia Davis; *Notes from a Bottle Found on the Beach at Carmel*, Evan S. Connell; *AVA*, Carole Maso; *Reader's Block*, David Markson; *Deepstep Come Shining*, C.D. Wright; *The Passion According to G.H.*, Clarice Lispector; *The Crab Nebula*, Éric Chevillard; *The Book of Questions*, Edmond Jabès; *Monsieur Teste*, Paul Valéry; *Mourning Diary*, Roland Barthes; *The Arcades Project*, Walter Benjamin; *Philosophical Investigations*, Ludwig Wittgenstein; "Diapsalmata," from *Either/Or*, Søren Kierkegaard

Unfortunately, I haven't read much theory discussing the fragment as a narratological device, although I did enjoy the Nancy and Lacoue-Labarthe book you mention above.

> BS: And finally, is there anything you wish I would have asked? Please ask/answer if so.

No, but I might mention that *From Old Notebooks* has recently been reprinted by Dzanc Books.

From Old Notebooks Excerpts[5]

Excerpt 1:
Short story about a church on the ocean floor. Congregation in scuba gear.

Memoir in which narrator struggles to describe her childhood – offering two or more contrary accounts of the same event – having been raised by divorced parents with unresolved anger toward each other such that discrepancies between parents' accounts of each other's involvement in her childhood have damaged narrator's memory beyond repair.

Academic essay entitled "*Cute Title: Serious Subtitle:* On the Preponderance of Precious Subtitling in Academic Essays."

---

[5] The first excerpt covers the first few pages of the book. The second covers pages 16 and 17. These excerpts show how *From Old Notebooks* develops from a series of ideas for texts to a more varied series of notes that further reveal the character, preoccupations, and desires of the writer.

Novel in chapters, each chapter spanning one year, 1977–2006. In lieu of chapter number, photograph of Tom Cruise's face from that year.

Story about a garbage man who cannot fathom how anyone might be content living a life not wholly dedicated to being a garbage man.

Excerpt 2:
Something entitled "From Old Notebooks," simply a transcription of entries from these notebooks.

Story involving a couple whose divorce proceedings center upon the allocation of the books contained in the family library.

Living off-campus on the outskirts of a city where I knew no one, in a studio apartment the size of a large walk-in closet, I would occupy myself in the evenings with and obsessive study of the shadows of my hands against the wall as I faux-conducted piano concertos; and later, after having taken three Ambien, intimate conversations with bits of magma crawling across the carpet that had detached from the glowing wires on my electric space heater. That same year, in a fit of manic loneliness, I invited a raccoon into my apartment with a trail of cracker crumbs.
   Do not let Jackson and Sofia live off-campus as undergraduates.

Cached auto-complete entry options that appear when I type the letter *e* into the search field in the toolbar of my internet browser:
   evan lavender-smith
   "evan lavender-smith"
   "evan lavender smith"
   evan + "lavender-smith"
   evan + "lavender smith"
   evan + lavender + smith

The letter *f*:
   fear of death

Contemporary authors who construct a thick barrier between themselves and their readers such that *authorial vulnerability* is revealed negatively, i.e., via the construction of the barrier.

If Team USA had a mascot, it would be God.

Character who refers to Wellbutrin as his muse.

"I hope to one day storm out on Terry Gross during an interview because I am that kind of eccentric famous author."

Notes that were cut from *From Old Notebooks*

Short story about literary executors sifting through the Gmail account of a recently deceased author.

It would better suit me to drive a hybrid hearse.

First line of a story: "The MFA in creative writing was the degree Shontiqua had her sights set on."

Story/mock-essay: conflation of the obnoxious languages of USA patriotism and MFA workshops.

The flag at half-mast because the market's way down today.

Awakened from dream … saw figure in arrangement of stars … closed eyes … dream changed ….

The smile is perhaps the human equivalent to the dog's wagging tail, with an important caveat: the human can fake a smile.
    Can a man fake an erection?

To *do* philosophy, *Back then I was* doing *some philosophy* – what a ridiculous usage. It is thanks to the proud philosopher who, attempting to justify his existence, humbles himself to a position of activity.

The greatest act of fraud on the part of philosophy is that it attempts to exist *outside of time,* the word of the philosopher presented to us as the Word. This is what Derrida means to criticize when he praises Nietzsche's pluralism, or Levi-Strauss's mythopoetics: Philosophy cannot pretend to be above or beyond the form of the book.

The question of being *flashes through us,* mind and body.
    The *corporealization* of the question of being.

Whereof one cannot speak, thereof one must – write?

The proliferation of MFA programs in creative writing has given rise to the whirlpool of conservatism which is contemporary American literature.

Surely it's no coincidence that I began *From Old Notebooks* shortly after I stopped seeing my therapist.

Somewhere I read Edmund Wilson refer to Beckett's late style as *terminal*. I understand why he would say so, but I would prefer to reserve that term for David Markson's late style.

Random House settles out of court to pay $2.35 million in genre-damages made by James Frey against his readers. What if the publisher of *From Old Notebooks* markets the book as a novel, and it later comes to light that the book was in fact a *memoir*...?

That the problem of death has been *outmoded* is the grand illusion of philosophy after Heidegger. The modern philosopher says, "Death is not my problem. *Being* is my problem." The modern philosopher might call death an *adolescent problem,* and being an *adult problem.* But what he fails to recognize is that the concept of being is merely an abstraction of the concept of death. (He forgets that being is *incidental* to non-being, and that the latter *is only conceivable by way of analogy to death.*) The modern philosopher wants to pretend that death is irrelevant to his project, but it is the impetus for his project.

Surely the reason I lash out against it is that I am *jealous* of poetry. Surely contemporary poetry does not deserve my *wrath*.

Someone could read the book with an almanac in hand and point to certain entries which suggest the concurrence of public events (e.g., terror, war, football), thereby assigning dates to those entries.
    As if.

Do people auction their personal diaries on eBay? I might consider auctioning these notebooks if the book is ever published, in keeping with the spirit of the book, that is, the spirit of facile self-disclosure.

The poem is dead. Long live the poem!

The *ending* of *From Old Notebooks* might contain the *beginning* of the next book – a sequel entitled *Work-In-Progress. From Old Notebooks* might blur into *Work-In-Progress*. The point of physical distinction between the two books would be arbitrary.

Work-In-Progress would be written in the same form as *From Old Notebooks*, but it would be also written in an entirely different form, as the (conception of the) form of the book "*From Old Notebooks + Work-In-Progress*" is an *evolving* (conception of) form, a (conception of) form that is always becoming another (conception of) form.

No matter how much I want to force *From Old Notebooks* to become something called *Work-In-Progress*, I won't be able to: any contrived becoming of that sort would represent a violence on the form of the book. I'm going to have to take a leap at some point, though, a leap out of the book, like a leap from a burning building.

"The Voidhood of the Void; or, An Archaeology of Nothing."

Rather than enact the high drama of self-reflexivity, the new writing will accept self-reflexivity as *status quo* – metafiction's birthday is passed, no need to keep celebrating – in the tradition of the documentary film, the reality TV show, and the internet blog. Such a writing must, by definition, be genreless, or make the question of genre irrelevant: hence, the *post-generic*.

Perhaps my next novel will be a one-page poem.

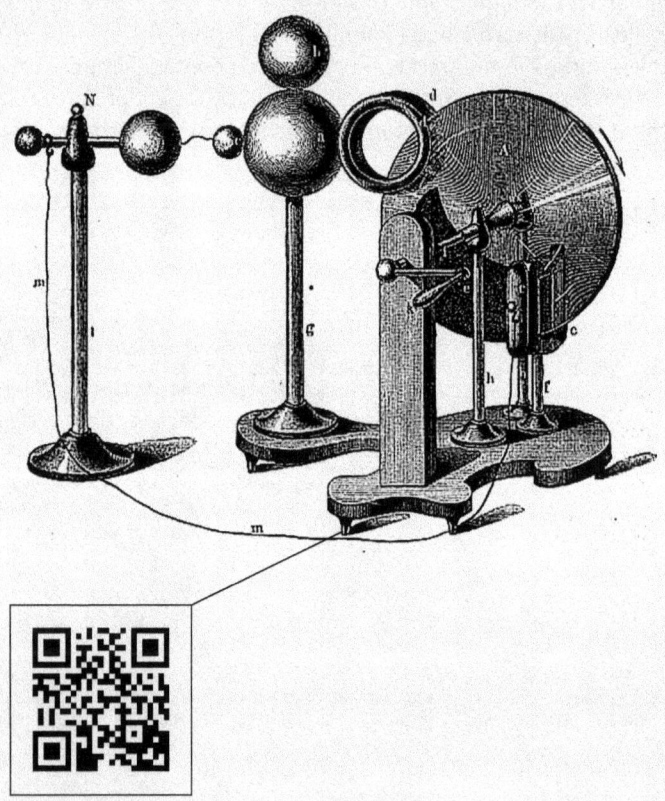

Mad Speculation and Absolute Inhumanism: Lovecraft, Ligotti, and the Weirding of Philosophy

Ben Woodard

Introduction

I want to propose, as a trajectory into the philosophically weird, an absurd theoretical claim and pursue it, or perhaps more accurately, construct it as I point to it, collecting the ground work behind me like the Perpetual Train from China Miéville's *Iron Council* which puts down track as it moves reclaiming it along the way. The strange trajectory is the following: Kant's critical philosophy and much of continental philosophy which has followed, has been a defense against horror and madness. Kant's prohibition on speculative metaphysics such as dogmatic metaphysics and transcendental realism, on thinking beyond the imposition of transcendental and moral constraints, has been challenged by numerous figures proceeding him. One of the more interesting critiques of Kant comes from the mad black Deleuzianism of Nick Land stating, "Kant's critical philosophy is the most elaborate fit of panic in the history of the Earth." And while Alain Badiou would certainly be opposed to the libidinal investments of Land's Deleuzo-Guattarian thought, he is likewise critical of Kant's normative thought-bureaucracies:

> Kant is the one author for whom I cannot feel any kinship. Everything in him exasperates me, above all his legalism – always asking *Quid Juris?* Or "Haven't you crossed the limit?" – combined, as in today's United States, with a religiosity that is all the more dismal in that it is both omnipresent and vague. The critical machinery he set up has enduringly poisoned philosophy, while giving great succour to the academy, which loves nothing more than to rap the knuckles of the overambitious […]. That is how I understand the truth of Monique David-Menard's reflections on the properly psychotic origins of Kantianism (*La Folie dans la raison pure* [Paris: Vrin, 1990]). I am persuaded that the whole of the critical enterprise is set up to to shield against the tempting symptom

represented by the seer Swedenborg, or against 'diseases of the head', as Kant puts it.[1]

An entire nexus of the limits of reason and philosophy are set up here, namely that the critical philosophy not only defends thought from madness, philosophy from madness, and philosophy from itself, but that philosophy following the advent of the critical enterprise philosophy becomes auto-vampiric; feeding on itself to support the academy. Following Francois Laruelle's non-philosophical indictment of philosophy, we could go one step further and say that philosophy operates on the material of what is philosophizable and not the material of the external world.[2]

Beyond this, the Kantian scheme of nestling human thinking between our limited empirical powers and transcendental guarantees of categorical coherence, forms of thinking which stretch beyond either appear illegitimate, thereby liquefying both pre-critical metaphysics and the ravings of the mad in the same critical acid. In rejecting the Kantian apparatus we are left with two entities – an unsure relation of thought to reality where thought is susceptible to internal and external breakdown and a reality with an uncertain sense of stability. These two strands will be pursued, against the sane-seal of post-Kantian philosophy by engaging the work of weird fiction authors H.P. Lovecraft and Thomas Ligotti. The absolute inhumanism of the formers universe will be used to describe a Shoggothic Materialism while the dream worlds of the latter will articulate the mad speculation of a Ventriloquil Idealism. But first we must address the relation of philosophy to madness as well as philosophy to weird fiction.

"There is nothing that the madness of men invents which is not either nature made manifest or nature restored."
– Michel Foucault[3]

"The moment I doubt whether an event that I recall actually took place, I bring the suspicion of madness upon myself: unless I am uncertain as to whether it was not a mere dream."
– Arthur Schopenhauer[4]

---

1   Alain Badiou, *Being and Event 2: Logics of Worlds*, trans. Alberto Toscano (New York: Continuum, 2009), 535–6.
2   One of the central tenets of François Laruelle's non-philosophy is that philosophy has traditionally operated on material already presupposed as thinkable instead of trying to think the real in itself. Philosophy, according to Laruelle, remains fixated on transcendental synthesis which shatters immanence into an empirical datum and an a priori factum which are then fused by a third thing such as the ego. For a critical account of Laruelle's non-philosophy see Ray Brassier's *Nihil Unbound*.
3   Michel Foucault, *Madness and Civilization*, trans. Richard Howard (New York: Vintage, 1988), 283.
4   Arthur Schopenhauer, *The World as Will and Idea*, trans. R.B. Haldane & J. Kemp., vol. 3 (London: Kegan Paul, Trench, Trubner & Co. 1906),168.

Philosophy and Madness

Madness is commonly thought of as moving through several well known cultural-historical shifts from madness as a demonic or otherwise theological force, to rationalization, to medicalization psychiatric and otherwise. Foucault's *Madness and Civilization* is well known for orientating madness as a form of exclusionary social control which operated by demarcating madness from reason. Yet Foucault points to the possibility of madness as the necessity of nature at least prior to the crushing weight of the church.[5]

Kant's philosophy as a response to madness is grounded by his humanizing of madness itself. As Adrian Johnston points out in the early pages of *Time Driven* pre-Kantian madness meant humans were seized by demonic or angelic forces whereas Kantian madness became one of being too human. Madness becomes internalized, the external demonic forces become flaws of the individual mind. Foucault argues that, while madness is de-demonized it is also dehumanized during the Renaissance, as madmen become creatures neither diabolic nor totally human[6] reduced to the zero degree of humanity.[7] It is immediately clear why for Kant, speculative metaphysics must be curbed – with the problem of internal madness and without the external safeguards of transcendental conditions, there is nothing to formally separate the speculative capacities for metaphysical diagnosis from the mad ramblings of the insane mind – both equally fall outside the realm of practicality and quotidian experience.

David-Menard's work is particularly useful in diagnosing the relation of thought and madness in Kant's texts. David-Menard argues that in Kant's relatively unknown "An Essay on the Maladies of the Mind" as well as his later discussion of the Seer of Swedenborg, that Kant formulates madness primarily in terms of sensory upheaval or other hallucinatory theaters.[8] She writes: "madness is an organization of thought. It is made possible by the ambiguity (and hence the possible subversion) of the normal relation between the imaginary and the perceived, whether this pertains to the order of sensation or to the relations between our ideas."[9] Kant's fascination with the Seer forces Kant between the pincers of "esthetic reconciliation" – namely melancholic withdrawal – and "a philosophical invention" – namely the critical project.

Deleuze and Guattari's schizoanalysis is a combination and reversal of Kant's split, where an esthetic over engagement with the world entails prolific conceptual invention. Their embrace of madness, however, is of course itself conceptual despite all their rhizomatic maneuvers. Though they move with the energy of madness, Deleuze and Guattari save the capacity of thought from the fangs of insanity by imbuing materiality itself with the ca-

---

5 Foucault, *Madness and Civilization*, 23.
6 Ibid., 70.
7 Ibid., 74.
8 Dominique David-Menard, "Kant's 'An Essay on the Maladies of the Mind' and 'Observations on the Beautiful and the Sublime,'" trans. Allison Ross, *Hypatia* 15.4 (2000): 82–98, at 85.
9 Ibid., 86.

pacity for thought. Or, as Ray Brassier puts it, "Deleuze insists, it is necessary to absolutize the immanence of this world in such a way as to dissolve the transcendent disjunction between things as we know them and as they are in themselves."[10] That is, whereas Kant relied on the faculty of judgment to divide representation from objectivity[11] Deleuze attempts to flatten the whole economy beneath the juggernaut of ontological univocity.

Speculation, as a particularly useful form of madness, might fall close to Deleuze and Guattari's shaping of philosophy into a concept producing machine but is different in that it is potentially self destructive – less reliant on the stability of its own concepts and more adherent to exposing a particular horrifying swath of reality. Speculative madness is always a potential disaster in that it acknowledges little more than its own speculative power with the hope that the gibbering of at least a handful of hysterical brains will be useful. Pre-critical metaphysics amounts to madness, though this may be because the world itself is mad while new attempts at speculative metaphysics, at post-Kantian pre-critical metaphysics, are well aware of our own madness. Without the sobriety of the principle of sufficient reason (following Meillassoux) we have a world of neon madness: "we would have to conceive what our life would be if all the movements of the earth, all the noises of the earth, all the smells, the tastes, all the light – of the earth and elsewhere, came to us in a moment, in an instant – like an atrocious screaming tumult of things."[12] Speculative thought may be participatory in the screaming tumult of the world or, worse yet, may produce its spectral double. Against theology or reason or simply commonsense, the speculative becomes heretical. Speculation, as the cognitive extension of the horrific sublime should be met with melancholic detachment. Whereas Kant's theoretical invention, or productivity of thought, is self-sabotaging, since the advent of the critical project is a productivity of thought which then delimits the engine of thought at large either in dogmatic gestures or non-systematizable empirical wondrousness.

The former is celebrated by the fiction of Thomas Ligotti whereas the latter is espoused by the tales of H.P. Lovecraft.

"Supernatural horror, in all its eerie constructions, enables a reader to taste treats inconsistent with his personal welfare."
– Thomas Ligotti[13]

"I choose weird stories because they suit my inclination best

---

10 Ray Brassier, "The Expression of Meaning in Deleuze's Ontological Proposition," *Pli* 19 (2008): 3.
11 Ibid., 2.
12 Quentin Meillassoux, "Subtraction and Contraction: Deleuze, Immanence, and Matter and Memory," *Collapse* 3, ed. Robin Mackay (Falmouth: Urbanomic, 2007), 63–107, at 104.
13 Thomas Ligotti, "Professor Nobody's Little Lectures on Supernatural Horror," in *Songs of a Dead Dreamer* (Michigan: Subterranean Press, 2010), 212.

> *– one of my strongest and most persistent wishes being to achieve, momentarily, the illusion of some strange suspension or violation of the galling limitations of time, space, and natural law which forever imprison us and frustrate our curiosity about the infinite cosmic spaces beyond the radius of our sight and analysis"* – H.P. Lovecraft[14]

Weird Fiction and Philosophy

Lovecraft states that his creation of a story is to suspend natural law yet, at the same time, he indexes the tenuousness of such laws, suggesting the vast possibilities of the cosmic. The tension that Lovecraft sets up between his own fictions and the universe or nature (as we know it) is reproduced within his fictions in the common theme of the unreliable narrator; unreliable precisely because they are either mad or what they have witnessed questions the bounds of material reality. In "The Call of Cthulhu" Lovecraft writes:

> The most merciful thing in the world, I think, is the inability of the human mind to correlate all its contents. We live on a placid island of ignorance in the midst of black seas of infinity, and it was not meant that we should voyage far. The sciences, each straining in its own direction, have hitherto harmed us little; but some day the piecing together of dissociated knowledge will open up such terrifying vistas of reality, and of our frightful position therein, that we shall either go mad from the revelation or flee from the deadly light into the peace and safety of a new dark age.[15]

Despite Lovecraft's invocations of illusion, he is not claiming that his fantastic creations such as the Old Ones are supernatural but, following Joshi, are only ever supernormal.[16] One can immediately see that instead of nullifying realism Lovecraft in fact opens up the real to an unbearable degree. In various letters and non-fictional statements Lovecraft espoused strictly materialist tenets, ones which he borrowed from Hugh Elliot namely the uniformity of law, the denial of teleology and the denial of non-material existence.[17] Lovecraft seeks to explore the possibilities of such a universe by piling horror upon horror until the fragile brain which attempts to grasp it fractures. This may be why philosophy has largely ignored weird fiction – while Deleuze and Guattari mark the turn towards weird fiction and Lovecraft in particular, with the precursors to speculative realism (Nick Land) as well as contemporary related thinkers (especially Reza Negarestani, and Eugene Thacker) have begun to view Lovecraft as making philosophical contributions.

---

14 H.P. Lovecraft, "Notes on Writing Weird Fiction," ed. Donovan K. Loucks, *The H.P. Lovecraft Archive* (Oct. 2009), n.p.
15 Ibid., "Call of Cthulhu," in *H.P. Lovecraft: The Fiction*, ed. S.T. Joshi (New York: Barnes and Noble, 2008), 355–79, at 355.
16 S.T. Joshi, *H.P. Lovecraft: The Decline of the West* (Berkley Heights: Wildside Press, 1990), 89.
17 Ibid., 7.

Lovecraft's own relation to philosophy is largely critical (making critical remarks about Bergson and Freud for example) while celebrating Nietzsche and Schopenhauer (especially the latter in the guise of the former). This relationship of Lovecraft to philosophy and philosophy to Lovecraft is coupled with Lovecraft's habit of mercilessly destroying the philosopher and the figure of the academic more generally in his work, a destruction which is both an epistemological destruction (or sanity breakdown) and an ontological destruction (or unleashing of the corrosive forces of the cosmos).

Thomas Ligotti's weird fiction which he has designated as a kind of "confrontational escapism" might be best described in the following quote from one of his short stories, "The human phenomenon is but the sum of densely coiled layers of illusion each of which winds itself on the supreme insanity. That there are persons of any kind when all there can be is mindless mirrors laughing and screaming as they parade about in an endless dream."[18] Whereas Lovecraft's weirdness draws predominantly from the abyssal depths of the uncharted universe, Ligotti's existential horror focuses on the awful proliferation of meaningless surfaces that is, the banal and every day function of representation. In an interview, Ligotti states:

> We don't even know what the world is like except through our sense organs, which are provably inadequate. It's no less the case with our brains. Our whole lives are motored along by forces we cannot know and perceptions that are faulty. We sometimes hear people say that they're not feeling themselves. Well, who or what do they feel like then?[19]

This is not to say that Ligotti sees nothing beneath the surface but that there is only darkness or blackness behind it, whether that surface is on the cosmological level or the personal. By addressing the implicit and explicit philosophical issues in Ligotti's work we will see that his nightmarish take on reality is a form of malevolent idealism, an idealism which is grounded in a real, albeit dark and obscure materiality.

If Ligotti's horrors ultimately circle around mad perceptions which degrade the subject, it takes aim at the vast majority of the focus of continental philosophy. While Lovecraft's acidic materialism clearly assaults any romantic concept of being from the outside, Ligotti attacks consciousness from the inside:

> Just a little doubt slipped into the mind, a little trickle of suspicion in the bloodstream, and all those eyes of ours, one by one, open up to the world and see its horror […]. Not even the solar brilliance of a summer

---

18 Thomas Ligotti and Current 93, "I Have a Special Plan for This World."
19 Venger Satanis, "Devotees of Decay and Desolation," ed. Darrick Dishaw, *Eldritch Infernal* (2008), n.p.

day will harbor you from horror. For horror eats the light and digests it into darkness.[20]

Clearly, the weird fiction of Lovecraft and Ligotti amount to a anti-anthropocentric onslaught against the ramparts of correlationist continental philosophy.

> "Formless protoplasm able to mock and reflect all forms and organs and processes – viscous agglutinations of bubbling cells – rubbery fifteen-foot spheroids infinitely plastic and ductile – slaves of suggestion, builders of cities – more and more sullen, more and more intelligent, more and more amphibious, more and more imitative – Great God! What madness made even those blasphemous Old Ones willing to use and to carve such things?" – H.P. Lovecraft[21]

> "On the other hand, affirming that the universe resembles nothing and is only formless amounts to saying that the universe is something like a spider or spit." – Georges Bataille[22]

Shoggothic Materialism or the Formless

The Shoggoths feature most prominently in H.P. Lovecraft's short story "At the Mountains of Madness" where they are described in the following manner:

> It was a terrible, indescribable thing vaster than any subway train – a shapeless congeries of protoplasmic bubbles, faintly self-luminous, and with myriads of temporary eyes forming and un-forming as pustules of greenish light all over the tunnel-filling front that bore down upon us, crushing the frantic penguins and slithering over the glistening floor that it and its kind had swept so evilly free of all litter.[23]

The term is a litmus test for materialism itself as the Shoggoth is an amorphous creature. The Shoggoths were living digging machines bio engineered by the Elder Things, and their protoplasmic bodies being formed into various tools by their hypnotic powers. The Shoggoths eventually became self aware and rose up against their masters in an ultimately failed

---

20 Ligotti, *Songs of a Dead Dreamer*, 208.
21 H.P. L:ovecraft, "At the Mountains of Madness," in *H.P. Lovecraft: The Fiction*, ed. S.T. Joshi (New York: Barnes and Noble, 2008), 723–806, at 797.
22 Georges Bataille, *Visions of Excess: Selected Writings, 1927–1939*, ed. and trans. Allan Stoekl (Minnesota: Minnesota Press, 1985), 31.
23 Lovecraft, "At the Mountains of Madness," 802.

rebellion. After the Elder Ones retreated into the oceans leaving the Shoggoths to roam the frozen wastes of the Antarctic.

The onto-genesis of the Shoggoths and their gross materiality, index the horrifyingly deep time of the earth a concept near and dear to Lovecraft's formulation of horror as well as the fear of intelligences far beyond, and far before, the ascent of humankind on earth and elsewhere. The sickly amorphous nature of the Shoggoths invade materialism at large, where while materiality is unmistakably real, i.e. not discursive, psychological, or otherwise overly subjectivist, it questions the relation of materialism to life. As Eugene Thacker writes:

> The Shoggoths or Elder Things do not even share the same reality with the human beings who encounter them – and yet this encounter takes place, though in a strange no-place that is neither quite that of the phenomenal world of the human subject or the noumenal world of an external reality.[24]

Amorphous yet definitively material beings are a constant in Lovecraft's tales.

In his tale "The Dream-Quest of Unknown Kadatth" Lovecraft describes Azathoth (an Outer god like Nyarlathotep) as, "that shocking final peril which gibbers unmentionably outside the ordered universe," that, "last amorphous blight of nethermost confusion which blashphemes and bubbles at the centre of all infinity," who, "gnaws hungrily in inconceivable, unlighted chambers beyond time."[25] Azathoth's name may have multiple origins but the most striking is the alchemy term *azoth* which is both a cohesive agent and an acidic creation pointing back to the generative and the decayed. The indistinction of generation and degradation materially mirrors the blur between the natural and the unnatural as well as life and non-life.

Lovecraft speaks of the tension between the natural and the unnatural is his short story "The Unnameable." He writes, "if the psychic emanations of human creatures be grotesque distortions, what coherent representation could express or portray so gibbous and infamous a nebulousity as the specter of a malign, chaotic perversion, itself a morbid blasphemy against Nature?"[26] Lovecraft explores exactly the tension outlined at the beginning of this chapter, between life and thought. At the end of his short tale Lovecraft compounds the problem as the unnameable is described as "a gelatin – a slime – yet it had shapes, a thousand shapes of horror beyond all memory."[27] Deleuze suggests that becoming-animal is operative throughout Lovecraft's work, where narrators feel themselves reeling at their becom-

---
24 Eugene Thacker, *Afterlife* (Chicago: University of Chicago Press, 2010), 23.
25 H.P. Lovecraft, "The Dream-Quest of Unknown Kaddath," in *H.P. Lovecraft: The Fiction*, ed. S.T. Joshi (New York: Barnes and Noble, 2008), 409–89, at 410.
26 Ibid., "The Unnameable," in *H.P. Lovecraft: The Fiction*, ed. S.T. Joshi (New York: Barnes and Noble, 2008), 256–61, at 260.
27 Ibid., 261.

ing non-human[28] or of being the anomalous[29] or of becoming atomized.[30] Following Eugene Thacker however, it may be far more accurate to say that Lovecraft's tales exhibit not a becoming-animal but a becoming-creature. Where the monstrous breaks the purportedly fixed laws of nature (or nature as we know it), the creature is far more ontologically ambiguous. The nameless thing is an altogether different horizon for thought.[31]

The creature is either less than animal or more than animal[32] – its becoming is too strange for animal categories and indexes the slow march of thought towards the bizarre. This strangeness is, as aways, some indefinite swirling in the category of immanence and becoming. Bataille begins "The Labyrinth" with the assertion that being, to continue to be, is becoming. More becoming means more being hence the assertion that Bataille's barking dog is more than the sponge.[33] This would mean that the Shoggotth is altogether too much being, too much material in the materialism.

Bataille suggests that there is an immanence between the eater and the eaten, across the species and never within them.[34] That is, despite the chaotic storm of immanence there must remain some capacity to distinguish the gradients of becoming without reliance upon, or at least total dependence upon, the powers of intellection to parse the universe into recognizable bits, properly digestible factoids. That is, if we undo Deleuze's aforementioned valorization of sense which, for his variation of materialism, performed the work of the transcendental, but refuse to reinstate Kant's transcendental disjunction between thing and appearance, then it must be a quality of becoming-as-being itself which can account for the discernible nature of things by sense. In an interview with Peter Gratton, Jane Bennett formulates the problem thus:

> What is this strange systematicity proper to a world of Becoming? What, for example, initiates this congealing that will undo itself? Is it possible to identify phases within this formativity, plateaus of differentiation? If so, do the phases/plateaus follow a temporal sequence? Or, does the process of formation inside Becoming require us to theorize a non-chronological kind of time? I think that your student's question: "How can we account for something like iterable structures in an assemblage theory?" is exactly the right question.[35]

---

28 Gilles Deleuze and Felix Guattari, *A Thousand Plateaus: Capitalism and Schizophrenia* 2, trans. Brian Massumi (Minneapolis: University of Minnesota Press, 1987), 240.
29 Ibid., 244–5.
30 Ibid., 248.
31 Thaker, *Afterlife*, 23.
32 Ibid., 97.
33 Bataille, *Visions of Exces*, 171.
34 Ibid., *Theory of Religion,* trans. Robert Hurley (New York: Zone Books, 2006), 17.
35 Peter Gratton, "Vibrant Matters: An Interview with Jane Bennett," *Philosophy in a Time of Error* (April 22, 2010).

Philosophy has erred too far on the side of the subject in the subject-object relation and has furthermore, lost the very weirdness of the non-human. Beyond this, the madness of thought need not override.

> "My aim is the opposite of Lovecraft's. He had an appreciation for natural scenery on earth and wanted to reach beyond the visible in the universe. I have no appreciation for natural scenery and want the objective universe to be a reflection of a character." – Thomas Ligotti[36]

> "Unless life is a dream, nothing makes sense. For as a reality, it is a rank failure [...]. Horror is more real than we are."
> – Thomas Ligotti[37]

Ventriloquial Idealism or the Externality of Thought

Thomas Ligotti's tales are rife with mannequins, puppets, and other brainless entities which of replace the valorized subject of philosophy – that of the free thinking human being. His tales such as "The Dream of the Manikin" aim to destroy the rootedness of consciousness. James Trafford has connected the anti-egoism of Ligotti to Thomas Metzinger – where the self is at best an illusion and we plead desperately for someone else to acknowledge that we are real. Trafford has stated it thus, "Life is played out as an inescapable puppet show, an endless dream in which the puppets are generally unaware that they are trapped within a mesmeric dance of whose mechanisms they know nothing and over which they have no control."[38]

An absolute materialism, for Ligotti, implies an alienation of the idea which leads to a ventriloquil idealism. As Ligotti notes in an interview, "the fiasco and nightmare of existence, the particular fiasco and nightmare of human existence, the sense that people are puppets of powers they cannot comprehend, etc."[39] And then further elaborates that, "[a]ssuming that anything has to exist, my perfect world would be one in which everyone has experienced the annulment of his or her ego. That is, our consciousness of ourselves as unique individuals would entirely disappear."[40] The externality of the idea leads to the unfortunate consequence of consciousness eating at itself through horror which, for Ligotti, is more real than reality and goes

---

36 Venger Satanis, "Devotees of Decay and Desolation," ed. Darrick Dishaw (Eldritch Infernal, 2008), n.p.
37 Ibid., "Professor Nobody's Little Lectures on Supernatural Horror," in *Songs of a Dead Dreamer* (Michigan: Subterranean Press, 2010), 211.
38 James Trafford, "The Shadow of a Puppet Dance: Metzinger, Ligotti and the Illusion of Selfhood," in *Collapse* 4, ed. Robin Mackay (Falmouth: Urbanomic, 2008), 185–206, at 202.
39 Matt Cardin, "'...it's all a Matter of Personal Pathology': an Interview with Thomas Ligotti," *The Teeming Brain* (2006), n.p.
40 Neddal Ayad, "Literature Is Entertainment or it Is Nothing: An Interview with Thomas Ligotti," *Fantastic Metropolis* (2004), n.p.

beyond horror-as-affect. Beyond this, taking together with the unreality of life and the ventriloquizing of subjectivity, Ligotti's thought becomes an idealism in which thought itself is alien and ultimately horrifying. The role of human thought and the relation of non-relation of horror to thought is not completely clear in Ligotti's *The Conspiracy Against the Human Race*.

Ligotti argues in his *The Conspiracy Against the Human Race,* that the advent of thought is a mistake of nature[41] and that horror is being in the sense that horror results from knowing too much.[42] Yet, at the same time, Ligotti seems to suggest that thought separates us from nature[43] whereas, for Lovecraft, thought is far less privileged – mind is just another manifestation of the vital principal, it is just another materialization of energy.[44]

In his brilliant "Prospects for Post-Copernican Dogmatism" Iain Grant rallies against the negative definition of dogmatism and the transcendental, and suggests that negatively defining both over-focuses on conditions of access and subjectivism at the expense of the real or nature.[45] With Schelling, who is Grant's champion against the subjectivist bastions of both Fichte and Kant, Ligotti's idealism could be taken as a transcendental realism following from an ontological realism.[46] Yet the transcendental status of Ligotti's thought (and arguably Schelling's in the period of his positive philosophy) move towards a treatment of the transcendental which may threaten to leave beyond its realist ground. Ligotti states:

> Belief in the supernatural is only superstition. That said, a sense of the supernatural, as Conrad evidenced in *Heart of Darkness*, must be admitted if one's inclination is to go to the limits of horror. It is the sense of *what should not be* – the sense of being ravaged by the impossible. Phenomenally speaking, the super-natural may be regarded as the metaphysical counterpart of insanity, a transcendental correlative of a mind that has been driven mad.[47]

Again, Ligotti equates madness with thought, qualifying both as supernatural while remaining less emphatic about the metaphysical dimensions of horror.

The question becomes one of how exactly the hallucinatory realm of the ideal relates to the black churning matter of Lovecraft's chaos of elementary particles. In his tale "I Have a Special Plan for This World" Ligotti formulates thus:

---

41 Thomas Ligotti, *The Conspiracy Against the Human Race*, (New York: Hippocampus Press, 2010), 23.
42 Ibid., 109.
43 Ibid., 221.
44 H.P. Lovecraft, "The Materialist Today," in *Collected Essays 5: Philosophy; Autobiography & Miscellany*, ed. S.T. Joshi (New York: Hippocampus Press, 2006), 75.
45 Iain Hamilton Grant, "Prospects for Post-Copernican Dogmatism: The Antinomies of Transcendental Naturalism," in *Collapse* 5, ed. Robin Mackay (Fallmouth: Urbanomic, 2009), 413–14.
46 Ibid., 415.
47 Ligotti, *The Conspiracy Against the Human Race*, 211.

A: There is no grand scheme of things.
B: If there were a grand scheme of things, the fact – the fact – that we are not equipped to perceive it, either by natural or supernatural means, is a nightmarish obscenity.
C: The very notion of a grand scheme of things is a nightmarish obscenity.[48]

Here Ligotti is not discounting metaphysics but implying that if it does exist the fact that we are phenomenologically ill-equipped to perceive that it is nightmarish. For Ligotti, nightmare and horror occur within the circuit of consciousness whereas for Lovecraft the relation between reality and mind is less productive on the side of mind.

It is (hopefully) easier to ascertain how the Kantian philosophy is a defense against the diseases of the head as Kant armors his critical enterprise from too much of the world and too much of the mind. The weird fiction of both Lovecraft and Ligotti demonstrates that there is too much of both feeding into one another in a way that corrodes the Kantian schema throughly, breaking it down into a dead but still ontologically potentiated nigredo.

The haunting, terrifying fact of Ligotti's idealism is that the transcendental motion which brought thought to matter, while throughly material and naturalized, brings with it the horror that thought cannot be undone without ending the material that bears it either locally or completely. Thought comes from an elsewhere and an elsewhen being-in-thought. The unthinkable outside thought (the thing in itself) is as maddening as the unthought engine of thought itself within thought (the mind or the self) which doesn't exist except for the mind, the rotting décor of the brain.

Hyperstitional Transcendental Paranoia or Self-Expelled Thought

Weird fiction has been given some direct treatment in philosophy in the mad black Deleuzianism of Nick Land. Nick Land along with others in the 1990s created the Cyber Culture Research Unit as well as the research group Hyperstition. The now defunct hyperstitional website, an outgrowth of the Cyber Culture Research Unit, defined hyperstition in the following fourfold:

1. Element of effective culture that makes itself real.
2. Fictional quantity functional as a time-traveling device.
3. Coincidence intensifier.
4. Call to the Old Ones.

The distinctively Lovecraftian character of hyperstition is hard to miss as is its Deleuzo-Guattarian roots. In the opening pages of *A Thousand Plateaus*

---

48 Ligotti, "I Have a Special Plan for This World," 14.

Deleuze and Guattari write, "We have been criticized for over-quoting literary authors. But when one writes, the only question is which other machine the literary machine can be plugged into."[49] The indisinction of literature and philosophy mirrors the mess of being and knowing as post-correlationist philosophy, where philosophy tries to make itself real where literature, especially the weird, aims itself at the brain-circuit of horror.

The texts of both Lovecraft and Ligotti work through horror as epistemological plasticity (too much/not enough knowledge) meeting with proximity (too much space in Lovecraft and not enough in Ligotti) as well as the deep time of Lovecraft and the glacially slow time of paranoia in Ligotti. Against Deleuze, and following Brassier, we cannot allow the time of consciousness, the Bergsonian time of the duree, to override natural time, but instead acknowledge that it is an unfortunate fact of existence as a thinking being. Horror-time, the time of consciousness, with all its punctuated moments and drawn out terrors, cannot compare to the deep time of non-existence both in the unreachable past and the unknown future.

The crystalline cogs of Kant's account of experience as the leading light for the possibility of metaphysics must be throughly obliterated. His gloss of experience in *Prolegomena to Any Future Metaphysics* could not be more sterile:

> Experience consists of intuitions, which belong to the sensibility, and of judgments, which are entirely a work of the understanding. But the judgments which the understanding makes entirely out of sensuous intuitions are far from being judgments of experience. For in the one case the judgment connects only the perceptions as they are given in sensuous intuition [...]. Experience consists in the synthetic connection of appearances (perceptions) in consciousness, so far as this connection is necessary.[50]

Here it is difficult to dismiss the queasiness that Kant's legalism induces upon sight for both Badiou and David-Menard. Kant's thought becomes, as Foucault says when reflecting on Sade's text in relation to nature, "the savage abolition of itself."[51] For Badiou, Kant's philosophy simply closes off too much of the outside, freezing the world of thought in an all too limited formalism. Critical philosophy is simply the systematized quarantine on future thinking, on thinking which would threaten the formalism which artificially grants thought (and philosophy) its own coherency in the face of madness. Even the becoming-mad of Deleuze, while escaping the rumbling ground, makes grounds for itself, mad grounds but grounds which are thinkable in

---
49 Deleuze and Guattari. *A Thousand Plateaus*, 4.
50 Immanuel Kant, *Prolegomena to Any Future Metaphysics*, 2nd ed., trans. James W. Ellington (New York: Hackett Publishing Company 2001), 43–4.
51 Foucault, *Madness and Civilization*, 285.

their affect.⁵² The field of effects allows for Deleuze's esthetic and radical empiricism, in which effects and/or occasions make up the material of the world to be thought as a chaosmosis of simulacra.

Given a critique of an empiricism of esthetics, of the image, it may be difficult to justify an attack on Kantian formalism with the madness of literature, which does not aim to make itself real but which we may attempt to make real (but such mental effort of course only reinscribes the unreality of fiction). That is, how do Lovecraft's and Ligotti's materials, as materials for philosophy to work on, differ from either the operative formalisms of Kant or the implicitly formalized images of Deleuzian empiricism? It is simply that such texts do not aim to make themselves real, and make claims to the real which are more alien to us than familiar, which is why their horror is immediately more trustworthy. This is the madness which Blanchot discusses in *The Infinite Conversation* through Cervantes and his knight – the madness of book-life, of the perverse unity of literature and life,⁵³ a discussion which culminates in the discussion of one of the weird's masters, that of Kafka.

The text is the knowing of madness, since madness, in its moment of becoming-more-mad, cannot be frozen in place but by the solidifications of externalizing production. This is why Foucault ends his famous study with works of art. Furthermore extilligence, the ability to export the products of our maligned brains, is the companion of the attempts to export, or discover the possibility of intelligences outside of our heads, in order for philosophy to survive the solar catastrophe.⁵⁴ To borrow again from Deleuze, writing is inseparable from becoming.⁵⁵

The mistake is to believe that madness is reabsorbed by extilligence, by great works, or that it could be exorcised by the expelling of thought into the inorganic or differently organic. Going out of our heads does not guarantee we will no longer mean we cannot still go out of our minds. This is simply because of the outside, of matter, or force, or energy, or thing-in-itself, or Schopenhauerian Will. In Lovecraft's "The Music of Erich Zahn" an "impoverished student of metaphysics"⁵⁶ becomes intrigued by strange viol music coming from above his room. After meeting the musician the student discovers that each night he plays frantic music at a window in order to keep some horridness at bay, some "impenetrable darkness with chaos and pandemonium."⁵⁷ The esthetic defenses provided by the well trained brain can bear the hex of matter for so long, the specter of unalterability within it

---

52 Gilles Deleuze, *The Logic of Sense*, trans. Mark Lester and Charles Stivale, ed. Constantin V. Boundas (New York: Columbia Press, 1990), 7.

53 Maurice Blanchot, *The Infinite Conversation*, trans. Susan Hanson (Minneapolis: Minnesota, 1993), 388–9.

54 Jean-François Lyotard, *The Inhuman: Reflections on Time*, trans. Geoffrey Bennington and Rachel Bowlby (Stanford: Stanford University Press, 1991), 122.

55 Gilles Deleuze, *Essays Critical and Clinical*, trans. Daniel W. Smith and Michael A. Greco (London: Verso, 1998), 1.

56 H.P. Lovecraft, "The Music of Eric Zann," in *H.P. Lovecraft: The Fiction*, ed. S.T. Joshi (New York: Barnes and Noble, 2008), 174–80, at 174.

57 Ibid., 179.

which too many minds obliterate, collapsing everything before the thought of thought as thinkable or at least noetically mutable on our own terms.

Transcendental paranoia is the concurrent nightmare and promise of Paul Humphrey's work, of being literally out of our minds. It is the gothic counterpart of thinking non-conceptually but also of thinking never belonging to any instance of purportedly solid being. As Bataille stated, "At the boundary of that which escapes cohesion, he who reflects within cohesion realizes there is no longer any room for him."[58] Thought is immaterial only to the degree that it is inhuman, it is a power (a process rooted in an object itself the side effect of forces and processes) that tries, always with failure, to ascertain its own genesis.

Philosophy, if it can truly return to the great outdoors, if it can leave behind the dead loop of the human skull, must recognize not only the non-priority of human thought, but that thought never belongs to the brain that thinks it, thought comes from somewhere else. To return to the train image from the beginning "a locomotive rolling on the surface of the earth is the image of continuous metamorphosis"[59] this is the problem of thought, and of thinking thought, of being no longer able to isolate thought, with only a thought-formed structure.

---

58 Bataille, *Theory of Religion*, 10.
59 Bataille, *Visions of Excess*, 7.

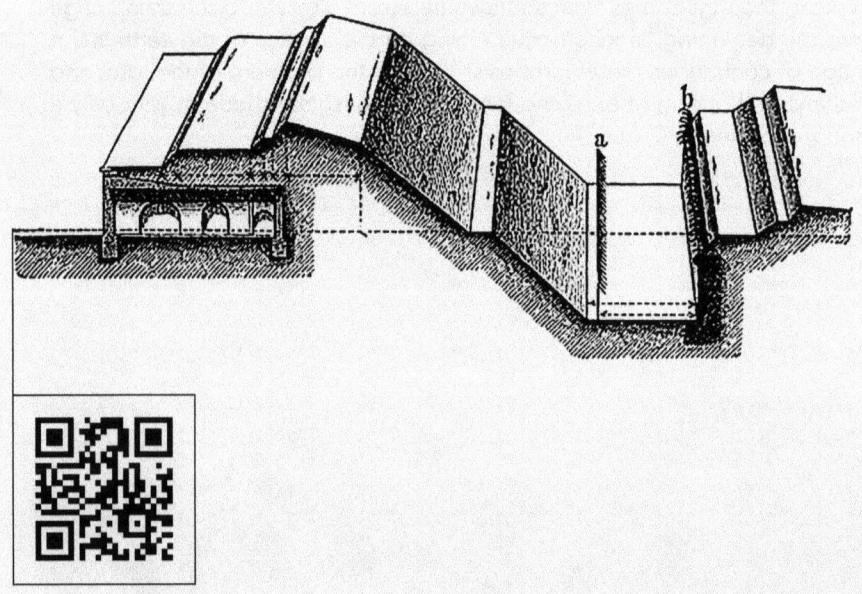

Covering Giorgio Agamben's *Nudities*[1]

Gregory Kirk Murray

> "Here I accoutred myself in my new habiliments; and, having employed the same precautions as before, retired from my lodging at a time least exposed to observation. It is unnecessary to describe the particulars of my new equipage; suffice it to say, that one of my cares was to discolour my complexion, and give it the dun and sallow hue which is in most instances characteristic of the tribe to which I assumed to belong; and that when my metamorphosis was finished, I could not, upon the strictest examination, conceive that any one could have traced out the person of Caleb Williams in this new disguise."
> – William Godwin[2]

A. The Protective Overcoat

The most pervasive, resilient, robust, sneaky, and significant concept in all of Giorgio Agamben's essays is that of separation. This is not the same as alienation. Separation is more nostalgic, for Agamben valorizes an ancient world in which human society and its beings were not subject to such separation. He implies that these separations are damaging to human beings, crippling them at the very level of their identities.

$4.99

1.

"The aim here is not to tap into an original state prior to the separation but to comprehend and neutralize the apparatus that produced this separation." (66)

---

1 Giorgio Agamben, *Nudities*, trans. David Kishik and Stefan Pedatella (Stanford: Stanford University Press, 2011). Subsequent references between parentheses.
2 William Godwin, *Caleb Williams* (New York: Penguin, 1988), 163–4.

B. The Handsome Gloves

Giorgio Agamben's *Nudities*, like *Profanations* before it, employs a wide range of subjects in order to establish separation as a metaphor, in much the same way that interdisciplinary scholars have adopted Michel Foucault's concepts in order to rethink societies and texts. The longest essay from *Profanations*, entitled "In Praise of Profanation," laments humankind's inability to profane as the result of what Walter Benjamin has called "the capitalist religion." Likewise, "Nudity" adopts a pessimistic stance on the Christian theological tradition's perverse asphyxiation of the unclothed body.

$2.50

C. The Hoop Earrings

Religion separates humans from things by procuring for itself items as "sacred," thus taking them out of common use. In this state, human beings are unable to play with them, unable to change their use-value. They become off-limits, museified.

$1,499.00

D. The Uncomfortable Shoes

Biometrics polices identity, replacing meaningful metrics of identity. It is a deplorable situation that leaves human beings in danger of, and indeed already victims of, mass persecution.

$111.75

2.

"The contemporary is he who firmly holds his gaze on his own time so as to perceive not its light but rather its darkness." (13)

3.

"We can therefore only experience nudity as a denudation and a baring, never as a form and a stable possession." (65)

4.

"Just as genius and talent originally distinct and even opposite – are nevertheless united in the work of the poet, so the work of creation and the work of salvation, inasmuch as they represent the two powers of a single God, remain in some way secretly conjoined." (6)

E. The Prince Albert

One could characterize Giorgio Agamben's desire to catalogue a history of ignorance as a recognition that human beings are separated from knowledge by language. Where then is the prophet, and how shall we be saved?

$49.50 + tip

F. The Corset

Franz Kafka's character of Joseph K. has put himself on trial, as in Roman trials when the Kalumniator was marked with the letter K. The torture he undergoes is meant to elicit a confession of the truth. It is possible that Giorgio Agamben perceives his role as a philosopher to be confined to self-trial, and that with every passage he flays the unclothed page with prophetic intent.

$27.00

G. The Derby

Giorgio Agamben himself tries to bridge various separations through exploratory play. He is not a performative writer semantically, but his exploratory style is rooted in the play spirit. His strategy of numbering points is almost comical, yet it is not misleading. It is play, after all, not ruse. He denudes with pecks, like carrion on a tattered corpse.

$11.00

5.

"In our culture, the face–body relationship is marked by a fundamental asymmetry, in that our faces remain for the most part naked, while our bodies are normally covered." (88)

6.

"Every man initiates a slanderous trial against himself." (21)

7.

"The glorious body is not some other body, more agile and beautiful, more luminous and spiritual; it is the body itself, at the moment when inoperativity removes the spell from it and opens it up to a new possible common use." (103)

H. The Trousers

Although Giorgio Agamben is elsewhere concerned with the profanation of religion's apparatuses, in essay nine he would like to consider what is consumed during days of inoperativity, how religion governs these, and nine he would like to consider what is consumed during how to account for our binges and purges. Inoperativity is inextricably bound to feasting, to the festival.

$24.50

I. The Stylish Belt

The only essay in *Nudities* to contain photographs is the essay entitled, "Nudity." All of these photographs project human bodies.

$.01

8.

"As Kleist understood so well, the relationship with a zone of non-knowledge is a dance." (114)

9.

"The deactivation of this apparatus retroactively operates, therefore, as much on nature as on grace, as much on nudity as on clothing, liberating them from their theological signature." (90)

10.

"At any rate, whether festive inoperativity precedes religion or results from the profanation of its apparatuses, what is essential here is a dimension of praxis in which simple, quotidian human activities are neither negated nor abolished but suspended and rendered inoperative in order to be exhibited, as such, in a festive manner." (112)

11.

"This is just how much [of] the land [the] surveyor is allowed to catch a glimpse." (36)

www.ingramcontent.com/pod-product-compliance
Lightning Source LLC
Chambersburg PA
CBHW071742150426
43191CB00010B/1658